Outrageous PC F/X

Tools and Techniques for Graphic Effects

David D. Busch

MIS: PRESS

A Subsidiary of
Henry Holt and Co., Inc.

Copyright © 1995   MIS:Press, Inc.
a subsidiary of Henry Holt and Company
115 West 18th Street
New York, New York 10011

First Edition—1995

Printed in the United States of America.

Busch, David D.
    Outrageous PC F/X: tools and techniques for graphic effects/David D. Busch.
        p.   cm.
    Includes index.
    ISBN 1–55828–394–3
    1. Computer graphics. 2. Microcomputers.   I. Title.
    T385.B868 1995
    006.6--dc20   94-37069
                                                             CIP

10   9   8   7   6   5   4   3   2   1

MIS:Press books are available at special discounts for bulk purchases for sales promotions, premiums, fund-raising, or educational use. Special editions or book excerpts can also be created to specification.

For details contact: Special Sales Director
                        MIS:Press
                        a subsidiary of Henry Holt and Company, Inc.
                        115 West 18th Street
                        New York, New York 10011

Editor-in-Chief, Paul Farrell
Development Editor, Laura Lewin
Copy Editor, Sara Black
Technical Editor, Rich Santalesa
Production Editor, Eileen Mullin
Associate Production Editor, Cari Geffner

Table of Contents

PART IV: COLOR CORRECTION 175

PART VI: ANIMATIONS   269

Preface

Morphing! Fractal textures! Undetectable composites! Extruded, spherized, edge-enhanced images! 3-D rendering! You don't need to be a special effects technician to perform graphics magic today. All you need is an image-capable PC, and tools like Adobe Photoshop, PhotoMorph, or Kai's Power Tools.

While this book deals with specific tricks you can do with images, it really doesn't matter whether you use Photoshop, PhotoStyler, Fractal Design Painter, Corel Draw, Fauve Matisse, Canvas, or some other program. Instead, PC F/X focuses on eye-catching ways any full-featured package can be used to transform ordinary images into triumphant prize-winners for desktop publications, presentations, and other digital applications. *Outrageous PC F/X* will tell you everything you need to know to choose the right software tools, get them working with your PC, and then apply special F/X to your own work.

Outrageous PC F/X is aimed squarely at computer users who are neither dummies nor idiots. You want to know how to do some specific things—the sexy stuff—but don't know where to turn. This book leads you through an exciting series of the most-daunting special F/X tasks—step-by-step—so you can combine images, do sophisticated photo-retouching or make color separations without first spending hours doing boring, basic tutorials.

As a bonus, the included CD-ROM disc is filled with megabytes of textures and filters you can use with your own software, royalty-free scanned images you can freely incorporate into your work, some hard-to-find utilities and applications and working versions of some of the top programs on the market, such as Adobe Photoshop, Aldus PhotoStyler, Pixar Typestry, and Visual Reality.

Introduction

Most computer books promise a lot, but deliver just a little. I'm going to flip things upside-down and promise you just a few things, and then deliver a whole lot more than you expected to get.

First, the promises

Let's get the promises out of the way first:

Promise #1:

No boring tutorials, no exciting tutorials, no tutorials at all. I'm not a tutor, and you're not a tutoree. I don't plan to teach you how to use your computer, nor will I offer instruction on using the basic features of your software. If you don't know how to navigate Windows, you shouldn't be reading this book—just yet.

Nor do I want to waste your time and mine explaining how to install or load software. If you weren't willing to crack the shrink-wrap around the manuals, why would I think you'd be eager to have me rehash the same material here?

If the software was designed properly, you should have no trouble using its basic features. What you're really looking for is information on how to do things that seem hard, but aren't all difficult once you know what to do.

Promise #2:

No wading through tons of background information to get to the good part. I just finished reading a fairly good computer book that packed 300 pages of solid information between its covers. Unfortunately, it was an 800-page book! I've got my first IBM PC in 1982—did I really need a chapter detailing the history of the computer back to 1981? Or do you, who may have gotten your first PC two months ago, really care about ancient history? An original 64K IBM PC has about as much in common with—and relevance to—a 486- or Pentium-based system as a go-kart does to a Lamborghini owner.

So, forget about mindless background filler. I've already deleted 500 pages of useless material from this book, and left only the good parts. That's not to say that I'm not going to provide background information where it can be helpful. You don't need to know the history of the automobile to drive a car, but it's nice to know that your favorite four-wheel-drive vehicle has a tendency to roll over during hairpin turns.

Likewise, you don't need to know exactly how a color television works to view color images on your display monitor, but a little background in how RGB or CMYK color is produced can help you understand why your printed output doesn't (and can't) look exactly like it did on the screen. With a little knowledge under your belt, you can take the steps you need to calibrate your system so that what you see is more like what you get.

Most of the background I do provide in this book will be tucked away in separate chapters, there for you to read when you need (or want) it. If you really do want to become a technoid in slow, easy steps, the information is there in simple-to-digest pieces. But, if all you want to do is ravage your images in new and interesting ways, you can do that, too, without sitting though History of PC and Computing in General 101.

Promise #3:

No tips and techniques that should work—but don't. One of the most interesting parts of many how-to computer books are the step-by-step instructions that don't work when you try them. Perhaps the all-knowing author didn't really do the exercise himself, since, with his complete understanding of the software, he knows that this is the way it should work. Or, maybe, a few steps were left out of the recipe. Everybody knows that you add oregano here, so why mention it?

Two-thirds—or more—of the time spent preparing this book were devoted to actually doing the stuff I'm showing you how to do. That doesn't count the months, or years, spent using many of these techniques in my actual work.

I've put many of the working files which illustrate the various steps in these examples on the CD-ROM, so you can load them into your own computer and pick up for yourself at any particular point in the procedure.

If you find yourself saying "Hmmm...how did he do that?" you can try the same thing yourself, using the same files I used!

Promise #4:

No dead-serious approach to something that should be a lot of fun. Certainly, many of you will be using the techniques described in this book in your actual work. I understand that the stakes may be high, and a lot riding on your ability to do a good job. I won't kid with you over anything that will make a difference in the final quality of your work.

But that's no reason not to have fun, is it? I'm willing to bet that you're working with graphics images on your PC because you enjoy it— even if you happen to be paid for what you do. So, this book, devoid of the royal "we" or phrases like, "the author has...", should not force you to suspend your good time just to learn a few things. I want you to have as much fun reading as I did writing.

That's enough promises for now. This is starting to look too much like the boring background material that I said you would not have to wade through.

PART I
Getting Started

This first section will familiarize you with this book's concept: quick instructions on how to do some sophisticated things with tools like PhotoMorph, Kai's Power Tools, Typestry, Photoshop, PhotoStyler, Fractal Design Painter, Fauve Mattisse, and Canvas. You'll learn about the equipment, software, and preparation you need to perform the techniques outlined in later chapters.

Just What You Need to Create Outrageous Graphics

Just about every book you've ever read starts out with Chapter 1, and this one is no exception. I'll use this chapter and the two that follow to tell you exactly what we'll be doing for the next 400 or so pages. We'll look at what sorts of capabilities you'll be adding to your graphics repertoire—if you pay attention—and what software and hardware tools you'll need to accomplish this magic.

Granted, there's less how-to in this first part of the book, if you define *how-to* as specific image-editing techniques. There's plenty of how-to, though, in terms of information you'll need to put together a solid PC F/X workstation. If you want a solid foundation to work from for the rest of the book, these three chapters will be just what you need. You'll find that it's hardly background material.

But, if you're chomping at the bit to get started transforming images, you can skip ahead to one of the other chapters. My success depends on how well I deliver to you the information you're looking for—not how many chapters I trick you into reading.

What Are You Going to Learn?

If you already have a fast PC, enough RAM, and the right tools, within a few minutes of working at your computer with this book at your side you'll be able to:

- Morph two photos into one. Combine father and son to get a glimpse of what the old chip off the block may look like when he's older. What do you get when you cross a tiger and a hippo? Morphing can show you.

- Use add-ons like Kai's Power Tools or Aldus Gallery Effects to transform images into something new.

- Create 3-D type with shadows, cut-outs, and perspective. Add a metallic sheen or a neon glow. You can get these type F/X with tools like Pixar Typestry or do many of these things with CorelDRAW or Photoshop—if you know how.

- Combine two or more photos seamlessly. It's hard to find exactly the right shot you need, but if you have three pictures with all the elements, you can move buildings, drop fluffy white clouds into an overcast sky, or quickly delete or add individuals to create a composite photo that looks like original camera artwork.

- Change 2-D images into full, 3-D views using rendering software, bring CAD drawings to life, or add perspective to simple line drawings.

- Make prize photos out of images that aren't even good enough for the shoebox. Most photos have defects: spots, holes, blurry areas, etc. Yet, graphic editors make it easy to use cloning tools and filters to retouch, sharpen, blur, and otherwise modify what's on an image.

- Adjust the color to add new life to your photos. You may not know color correction or gamma correction from brightness-contrast controls and may think a histogram is a cold remedy. Even so, excellent pictures may be hiding in some awful images. All they may need are some corrections that can be applied with a sophisticated image-editing program like Photoshop. You can bring off-color or dull originals to blazing life, ready for use in presentations, output to a color digital printer, or transfer to a professional color prepress system. Photoshop 3.0, for example, offers a new, visually oriented mode that lets you choose the best color balance, rather than dial it in manually.

- Make color separations. You can split a color image into CMYK (cyan, magenta, yellow, black) channels and direct them individually to high-resolution output devices as color separations. Most software packages include essential routines to calibrate the program to the monitor, printing stocks, and inks you'll be using. You can compensate for dot gain (spreading) on the press and remove equal quantities of color (which produce a neutral black), replacing them with cheaper black ink. You may also create *traps* (which printers prefer to call *spreads* and *chokes*) to overlap colors that abut one another.

- Create impressive images from scratch. Even the best photo may need some sort of object created with painting and drawing tools. You don't have to be an artist to turn out professional-quality work. Image-editing software today has some unusual filters, including Wind, which produces trailing streaks, and Lens Flare, which brings to the PC the image defects that lens designers hoped multicoating would eliminate.

You can be doing any of these things within minutes if you're already equipped with the hardware or software that you need. If you don't have an outfit, though, you can still be a cowboy. I'll show you exactly what you need to get to do the job.

Most of you will probably need to add a few inexpensive components: perhaps a little more RAM or a better image editor. Others (especially those of you with more ambitious goals) may need to plan an extensive overhaul of their hardware and software inventory. *Chapters 2 and 3* will tell you everything you need to know to plan and assemble your arsenal, hopefully without spending any more than necessary. I'll tell you how much RAM is enough, what add-on boards will really do you the most good, and how to select the software that will do the best job for you.

Who Are You, Anyway?

The official Computer Author Licensing Bureau (It couldn't be legal for just anyone to put their name on the cover of a book, could it?) has some stiff requirements before they'll issue a permit to write a book. An author must file an Intended Audience form that spells out in no uncertain language exactly who a book is written for. That's for your protection.

The form I filled out for *Outrageous PC F/X* raised a few eyebrows down at the Bureau. My audience, I said, was a large group of PC owners: the impatient, the harried, and those who must use image-editing programs but don't want to make a career of them. These are people who never read manuals—unless they have to—but instead call Tech Support and ask, "just tell me how to do this one thing."

The Bureau-crats wanted to know how I was going to convince people like this to read my book. I told them that *Outrageous PC F/X* will tell those folks exactly what they are looking for—just how to do this one thing. Even the most reticent PC users may find that, after they've cut corners and done some quick-and-dirty projects with this book, they have become experts in spite of themselves.

Who Am I?

I know you—but you don't know me. Why should you pay attention to anything I have to say? In a previous life, I was a commercial photographer who wrote several thousand articles on photographic topics for magazines like *Petersen's PhotoGraphic, Professional Photographer,* and *The Rangefinder.* I operated a studio and served as a photo-posing instructor for a Barbizon-affiliated modeling agency in Rochester, N.Y., a town where the competition is particularly stiff because every Rochester Institute of

Technology student and present or former employee of a certain photographic company moonlights as a photographer.

In 1977 I was seduced by the dark side of technology and transformed myself from a photographer of the glamorous into a computer nerd. The hours were longer, the pay worse, and the models I worked with had names like TRS-80 and Apple, instead of Stephanie or Kathy. Obviously, my career-planning acumen is on a par with that of, say, Dexys Midnight Runners. In my current incarnation, I've written roughly 44 books, winning top category awards in The Computer Press Awards the first two years they were given, and served as a contributing editor and/or columnist for eight different computer magazines.

Despite my defection from the ranks of the photography world, imaging has remained my passion. I used one of the very first scanners available for desktop computers (a ThunderScan device that replaced the ribbon on a dot-matrix printer with a crude sensor). Three of my books have dealt solely with scanning topics for the PC, and I've covered and used every package from Photoshop to CorelDRAW and Canvas in transforming images created by myself and others for books, newsletters, presentations, and other digital media.

About the CD-ROM

I compiled the CD-ROM included with this book as an integral part of the book itself. As you read and work, you'll use the files on it continually, and they will significantly enhance your understanding and enjoyment of *Outrageous PC F/X*. I know that concept may take some time to sink in, because most CD-ROMs bundled with books today are just collections of demos and shareware, included at almost no cost to inflate your perception of the book's value.

I'm doing something quite unusual with my CD-ROM. I've used it to, in effect, let you work side by side with me on most of the projects in this book. If you don't have a CD-ROM drive you can still benefit from all the techniques described—but consider getting one soon. You'll never regret it.

My CD-ROM differs from most of the book discs you'll see in the following ways:

- The actual beginning, intermediate, and final files for most exercises are included on the CD-ROM, so that you can load them into your own image editor and try out the functions for yourself, using the exact files I did. The files are located in directories on the CD-ROM labeled with the chapter numbers.

- The demo programs included on the disc are not there as a free advertisement for the software vendor. Other books include such demos so that you can play with the programs and decide if you want to buy them. For this book, the demo programs can be used to try out the effects I describe, even if you don't own the full software package. I'm sure you'll purchase some of the software demonstrated through my CD-ROM, but that wasn't my primary motive for including the test-drive packages.

- Many files used to produce the figures in this book are also included on the CD-ROM. I used the eight-page, full-color printed insert to illustrate many concepts, and the gray-scale images elsewhere in *Outrageous PC F/X* provide clear explanations of others. I would have liked to produce the book with full color on every page, but you wouldn't have spent $75 for this book. The CD-ROM let me do the next best thing: include additional full-color illustrations as files you can load and view. These are color versions of the black-and-white illustrations in the book, so that those of you who don't own a CD-ROM drive aren't missing anything except the color.

- I included a gallery of additional color and black-and-white artwork you can use to practice your F/X skills. These are low-resolution (if you consider 300 dpi low resolution) images, many with slight imperfections, similar to what you might produce yourself. You'll find portraits, scenics, still lifes, and other subjects. Because many readers might not have access to a color scanner, I incorporated these pictures as fodder for F/X enhancements.

The shareware you find on other discs are included here, but I didn't dump every program I could find on my CD-ROM. I included only the programs I thought offered capabilities you might not have or that aren't available from commercial programs. You'll find Photoshop-compatible plug-ins, image file converters, and a trove of other useful utilities and applications.

I knew going into this project that it would be difficult to make my CD-ROM stand out. This one, I think, deserves to be included with *Outrageous PC F/X*. A section at the end of the book tells you how to use the programs and files on the CD-ROM.

How to Use This Book

Computer books often have a section that tells you how to use the book, usually with such incredible insights as a suggestion to read the book from front to back and then to review any portions you don't understand until the information finally sinks in. There's also usually a suggestion to skim over the boring parts that don't interest you.

I'm not quite so stringent in my requirements. I don't care if you choose to read all the odd-numbered pages first or to spend two weeks memorizing the Index. If this book requires an instruction manual to use, then I haven't done my job. I hope there won't be any parts in this book that don't interest you or that require yellow highlighting. I'd rather my books become dog-eared from constant reference and pass-along readership than from all-night cram sessions.

With that in mind, let's get to work.

The Next Step

This chapter gave you fair warning about what I intend to accomplish in this book: show you some cool PC F/X techniques you can use to transform your images from mundane photos not worth filing away in the shoebox to triumphant prizewinners. I listed some of the capabilities you can hope to gain from the chapters that follow and then tried to establish a firm groundwork of trust and respect by recounting a carefully framed outline of my previous accomplishments.

Now, it's time to review your hardware and software arsenal, to see if you're armed and ready to do battle in the imaging wars.

Arming Yourself for Imaging Battle

The computer industry is engaged in a war today, and you and I are in the best possible position: our hard-earned dollars are the booty the combatants are fighting over. Every software and hardware vendor engaged in the conflict is fighting for your approval in the way that benefits us the most: by providing more and more power at lower prices.

To wit: I paid $3495 for my first IBM PC in 1982, one that was equipped with 64K of RAM, no hard disk, and a monochrome monitor incapable of displaying graphics in any form. Only a dozen years later that same sum bought me a 486DX2-66 with 340M hard disk, tape drive, 16M of RAM, a video card and monitor capable of displaying 16. 7 million individual colors, and lots of other add-ons, like a 14.4K bps modem. I haven't purchased a new PC recently, but today I would have a hard time spending that much on a PC, even if I wanted to throw in a quad-speed CD-ROM drive. Pentium systems are available for less than $1500 now, and the cost spiral shows no signs of abating.

Software vendors are offering $895 packages for upgrade prices in the $100–179 range, if you can prove you own a copy of a previous or competing version—say, by faxing a mail-order retailer the front page of a manual. It's usually not very hard at all to qualify for prices that are lower than a Death Valley borax mine.

Because of this major warfare, you can build an image-capable PC for $2000–3000 today that makes an $8000 386-based PC workstation of a few years ago look sick. However, you may not even need to spend that much. In this chapter, I'll tell you exactly what you must have to do computer F/X. I'll explain what compromises you must be willing to make if you don't have an unlimited budget, and which you must not make.

Make no mistake, image editing is among the most demanding types of work you can lay on a PC. Before you start down this road, you'll want to know about the mines that have been planted along the way. Even if you're a bit-chomper, you'll want to at least review the information presented here.

As I promised in *Chapter 1*, I'm not going to drag you down with lengthy explanations and background on terms that have only peripheral relevance to the topic at hand. I'll save the explanations for important subjects. If you encounter a new term, check the comprehensive glossary in the back of this book. If that doesn't help, and you're really curious, check with the user across the hall with the computer that screams "Good Morning, Viet Nam!" on startup. I'll tell you how and why more RAM, a faster microprocessor, a processor cache, or a faster/bigger hard disk can help you—but I won't be explaining how any of these things work.

Building the Perfect Beast

Until very recently, high-powered PC-based graphics workstation were as scarce as cheap hotel rooms at COMDEX. The most amazing thing about Windows is that it brings graphics to a computer architecture seemingly designed to make working with images difficult, if not impossible. Yet, thanks to the miracles of technology, we can comfortably manipulate 2M images with an underlying operating system built to recognize no more than 640K of RAM. We've vanquished the 32M limitation on hard disk volumes, worked around crippling limitations on video displays, and discovered new ways to connect high-speed peripherals. To build a Windows-based graphics-capable powerhouse today, all you need is a wallet that's fatter than a retired Sumo wrestler, and enough applications to justify an expenditure of $12,000 or more.

Those applications will generally be high-end vector- or raster-oriented graphics programs: drawing programs like Aldus FreeHand, CorelDRAW, or MicroGraphix Designer, and photoimage editors like Adobe Photoshop, Aldus PhotoStyler, Fauve Matisse, or Fractal Design Painter.

The outline-oriented drawing programs let you work with *objects*, which you create, twist, extrude, fill, and manipulate to produce professional illustrations, business graphics, and designs, such as packaging. Raster-oriented software focuses on *bitmaps*, for applications ranging from photographic image retouching/editing, painting, image database and archiving, and light-duty document image processing. In the future, you'll see more programs that are adept at handling both types of images in separate layers, like Photoshop 3.0 and Deneba's Canvas.

The common denominator shared by all graphics-oriented applications is that they tax your resources harder than a federal deficit-reduction plan. Though the Windows graphical user interface (GUI) provides a nifty graphics device interface (GDI) that all Windows applications can use, serious graphics applications call for serious hardware support. That's why building the perfect graphics beast is such a challenge.

Avoiding No-Brainers

Don't let Igor choose the brains of your graphics monster. The main system unit: the motherboard, with CPU, bus, RAM, and support circuitry form the foundation on which you build your beast, and limitations here can have a telling effect on overall performance. Let's look at each piece one at a time.

Von Neumann's Machine

Manipulating megabytes of bits or calculating swarms of vectors in real time calls for the fastest microprocessor available. Currently the two hottest chips this side of the Pentium are the Intel 486DX4-75 and 486DX4-100. These are "clock-tripled" 486-25 and -33 microprocessors that operate at 75 and 100 MHz internally but communicate with the outside world at 25 and 33 MHz.

The choice is up to you. The 486DX4-100 is often measurably faster than the 75-MHz version when lots of internal number-crunching is involved. If you're planning a local bus system, remember that the DX chip deals with these peripherals at its speed of 25 MHz, while the DX2 chip works at its "real" 33-MHz clock rate. Cyrix and AMD also have 486-compatible chips with their own mix of on-board cache and operating speeds.

If cost is no object, and you really must remain on the bleeding edge of technology, insist on a Pentium system operating at 90 or 100 MHz—or a system that can be upgraded to either of these chips. (During the life of this book, Pentium chips with speeds of 150 MHz or more are planned, so keep reading the journals for the latest news!) Graphics software always benefits when you crank up the microprocessor.

If you're buying a new PC specifically for image processing, you can choose your system based on its microprocessor and expandability options along these lines:

Good: Your real minimum requirements should be any system with a 25 to 33-Mhz 486 microprocessor.

Better: Upgrade to a 50- to 100-MHz 486 microprocessor. These are faster systems with the speed needed for image processing and the ability to be upgraded.

Best: If you can afford it, you won't regret springing for a 90- to 100-MHz Pentium system. Or, you can even look into an IBM PowerPC-based computer when they become available late in 1994.

Cache Crop

Though all true (Intel) 486 microprocessors have an 8–16K on-board instruction cache, most systems in this performance range have an external, secondary (or Level 2) cache, of 64–256K. Graphics software often includes instructions that are carried out on successive portions of an image through many iterations, so it's a plus to have instructions ready and waiting in the cache. Don't confuse a cache dedicated to handling processor instructions with disk caches like SmartDrive, which are something completely different.

While the difference between a medium-sized external cache and a huge one might be a hit rate of 97% bumped up to 99%, the added cost isn't a lot, and even a single percentage point can translate into a lot of wasted clock cycles. My recommendations for additional cache follow:

Good: 64K, if you have a 486-equipped machine. You're probably running fast enough that an additional 10% speed gain isn't essential.

Better: 128K of cache RAM will improve performance at very little cost.

Best: 256K of cache.

Bussame Mucho

If you're upgrading a lowly industry standard architecture (ISA)-bus machine, don't despair. It's very likely that it isn't the ISA bus that drags your machine down. None of the alternatives—VESA Local (VL) bus, PCI local bus, EISA, or Micro Channel Architecture (MCA)—are necessarily superior in all possible configurations.

Local bus is new, it's hot, it's fast, and it doesn't necessarily offer better performance than the very best of traditional ISA bus peripherals. More recently, Intel's PCI bus has taken over as the local bus of choice, so VL-bus systems could be yesterday's news long before yesterday arrives. Almost all currently produced PCs have one or the other, bundled with fast local bus video cards and hard disk interfaces, at no extra cost to you.

Meanwhile, EISA (extended industry standard architecture) is old, often overlooked, and only marginally faster than ISA. MCA is technically elegant but rarely exploited to its full potential.

Here's the verdict: If you're upgrading an existing ISA system, don't scrap your current motherboard unless you need compatibility with a faster microprocessor or more sockets for RAM. If you're starting from scratch, go for a PCI or VL-bus system: You won't pay a premium for the bus or the cards it uses, and, like chicken soup, it can't hurt. In fact, the latest local bus video and disk cards do give you measurably faster performance, and every little bit helps.

Cram Your RAM

Memory is the cheapest performance enhancer you can pump into a graphics beast. Applications run many times faster when an entire multi-megabyte image, plus the duplicate used to "undo" aborted operations, can be kept in RAM, rather than on your hard disk. With memory going for $25 a megabyte, you're foolish to equip a graphics workstation with anything less than 32M of RAM. If you can't pop for the full complement, please, please, please get at least 16M. You'll struggle along, wait forever while portions of your image are swapped to disk, and may be limited in the size of images you can handle—but anything less will bog you down in a mire of crashes and frustration. A PC with 8M of RAM may be okay for Word for Windows, but should not be used for image editing.

Allocate 2 to 4M to SmartDrive or another disk cache (unless you're using Windows for Workgroups 3.11, which uses its own 32-bit Fastdisk access scheme instead), and possibly another 2M or more to a RAM disk if you're working with a graphics program that insists on creating temporary files. Direct those temporary files to the RAM disk. That solution will not only speed up your application, but you also won't have to hunt and erase scratch files if your system crashes. Reboot, and you have a clean RAM disk.

Leave the rest of your RAM as extended memory, unless you have a perverse need to run DOS applications outside of Windows that require expanded memory (EMS). Windows' own memory management routines can create EMS for DOS programs.

Windows always uses available RAM before it touches a temporary or permanent swapfile, so cramming your system with 32M of RAM will be the best $800 you've ever spent.

My memory recommendations for your PC graphics workstation follow:

Good: 16M of RAM. You can do a lot of useful work with 16M of RAM, particularly if you don't try to load eight or nine programs at once. There's enough memory to load a major application like Photoshop and to work with a large 8-bit or moderately sized 24-bit image. However, you must realize that with only 16M of memory, you won't be able to load two or three 24-bit images and move back and forth between them. Your PC will almost certainly have to swap all or parts of one image to the disk before you can work on the next one. My recommendations follow:

Better: 24M of RAM. With a little breathing room RAM-wise, you can work with larger images, perhaps have another application or two running, and even have a little extra memory to devote to a RAM disk.

Best: 32M and up of RAM. In this range you'll usually have enough RAM to work with, even if you do have several memory-hungry applications open at one time. If you regularly manipulate large color images or have several images open at one time, it's smart to load up beyond 32M, particularly in a Pentium machine. I've spoken with many image-processing professionals who have workstations that break the 100M barrier—and they've never regretted the expenditure. We're talking $6000 just for RAM, here. So don't be shy about spending $600 for another 16M.

Slip Your Disk

Your graphics powerhouse is only as fast as its narrowest bottleneck, so you should pay special attention to the biggest potential roadblock: your mass storage subsystems. Memory operations are measured in terms of nanoseconds, while hard disk speeds are calculated in millisecond increments. The order of magnitude is roughly the same as saying, "I'll get back to you in a second," and then not responding for 31.7 years!

You definitely want the fastest, most expandable hard disk possible, and today that means a FAST SCSI-2 hard disk linked to a bus-mastering adapter.

SCSI is a system-level interface that conveys information in logical terms. As a result, multiple devices can use the same connection in parallel fashion, although more intelligence is required to decode requests from the computer. You can daisy-chain up to seven hard drives, scanners, CD-ROM drives, and removable cartridge devices on a single SCSI bus.

That's easier now that the SCSI-2 specification has finally been standardized, along with an advanced SCSI programming interface (ASPI). Today, you can use any ASPI-compliant SCSI controller and universal driver software, such as CorelSCSI, with just about any SCSI device.

The hard disk doesn't have to be the only intelligent device in the SCSI chain. A bus-mastering host adapter like the Buslogic BT-542B has its own 16-bit microprocessor to coordinate command decoding and data flow at transfer rates of up to 10M/second. It seizes control of the operations that normally flow through the bus to the hard disk to improve efficiency. This card is so fast you won't need a caching controller.

You gain free slots, too. The Buslogic card, for example, supports up to two floppy disks, and because CorelSCSI recognizes so many different types of devices, a single host adapter can service multiple hard disks, a CD-ROM drive, Bernoulli drives, and other peripherals that normally require separate cards.

In choosing a hard disk, don't settle for less than 600M, and go for 1G if you can. Today's graphics applications are huge (a full CorelDRAW 5.0 install tops 50M), and a modest suite of three or four key programs can easily eat up most of a 200M drive. Add 200 fonts, 20M of clip art, Windows, and some utility programs, and the average user barely has enough room for images.

A 600M drive gives you room to breathe. I like to set aside a 125M or larger volume as a "scratch" disk to hold images for a single session. Another 100–200M should be available for current files. Older files can be offloaded to removable storage. Don't waste time hunting for current images because there is no room for them on your hard disk.

My recommendations follow:

Good: 500M. Unless you're working with only a few images at time, don't even try to get by with less hard disk storage. Disks this size are selling for $300 now, so the expenditure won't break you. Disk compression products won't help much, because most imaging applications already use efficient compression routines when they save files, such as LZW (Lempel-Ziv Welch, after the mathematicians who developed the algorithms) applied to TIFF files, or the even more efficient (but lossy, or image-degrading) JPEG (Joint Photographic Experts Group) compression.

Better: 1G. That's a lot of hard disk space, and much more than any PC user who is not working with still images, video, or digital audio would ever need. But if you're playing in the image-processing big leagues, you need a big bat. These drives are selling for around $700 at present and so won't even necessarily break your pocketbook.

Best: 1.7G and up. Or, if your needs are really large, consider a large drive, plus an open-ended storage system, like a SyDOS or Bernoulli drive or optical disk, described later.

Secondary Considerations

Even the largest hard disk drive can fill faster than Yankee Stadium on Bat Day. Your graphics powerhouse needs open-ended storage that is relatively cheap, reliable, and provides near-online access speeds. That requirement eliminates tape backup as a secondary storage medium. You don't want to search a serial medium like tape for end to end when you need a crucial file right now. You might want a tape subsystem to provide low-cost backup of your main hard disk(s) and essential files. However, for extending your online storage, you need something more disklike.

Removable Bernoulli cartridges or SyDOS hard disk cartridges are the traditional choice. Bernoulli media, available in 5.25-inch cartridges up to 150M in capacity, provide nearly crashproof storage, because the type of events that cause hard disk crashes tend to force the giant floppy disk inside a Bernoulli cartridge away from the head. SyDOS carts are true hard disks, but they are robust enough to allow transport to service bureaus. Indeed, nearly all service bureaus can accept graphic files for output on SyDOS cartridges, while a smaller number can work with Bernoulli media. That alone might be enough to sway your decision. At roughly $1 a megabyte or a little less, both Bernoulli and SyDOS cartridges are neither cheap nor outrageously expensive.

Floptical disks, which provide 20M of storage on a disk that looks a lot like a traditional 3.5-inch floppy disk, can be useful for storing a few bitmapped images or a decent-sized collection of vector-oriented artwork. Their capacity is a little skimpy for serious graphics work, but they are much better than 1.44 to 2.88M floppy disks. However, it appears that this type of media, which never really caught on, may have had its brief moment in the sun and be ready to ride off into the sunset. Invest in new floptical hardware only if you can get it really cheap.

In the future, look for more graphic workstations to incorporate some sort of optical disk media. Write once, read many (WORM) drives are excellent for archiving files that will undergo no further changes. The media is inexpensive and tamperproof, and can hold as much as 10G of information (for 14-inch optical disks).

Rewritable optical disks store 128–600M or more and are clearly the mass storage option of the future. When drive prices plummet to the $300 level, the rugged, reliable media will drop to match as the market for this product grows.

My recommendations follow:

Good (but outdated): Floptical disks let you back up a 200M hard drive onto just 10 disks and are less expensive than DAT drives.

Better: Bernoulli or SyQuest drives cost between $199 and $500, and cartridges hold 44–270M of information at less than $1 per megabyte. Access speeds approach that of hard disks.

Best: Optical disks are the unrivaled low-cost leader among ran-
          dom-access secondary storage devices, at least in terms of
          media. Lower-cost read/write drives will make this option the
          one to beat in the next few years.

ROM at the Top

Even though CD-ROM writers are still pricey, you should put a CD-ROM
drive at the top of your must-have peripherals list. The free 22,000 clip-art
images you get with the CorelDRAW 5.0 CD-ROM suddenly become
expensive when you transfer some of them to 200M of magnetic media.
CD-ROM makes a compact, easily accessible storage medium for clip-art
libraries, fonts, reference material, and other data that you purchase.

You'll want to equip your graphics monster with one of the new
triple- and quadruple-fast units with sub-300-ms access times and a 450-
or 600-kilobits/sec transfer rate. Large graphics files can be loaded two
to four times faster with one of these babies. Kodak Photo CD files,
which provide virtual photographic resolution from photofinisher-
scanned negatives, slides, or prints, average around 6M apiece, so the
time saving can be significant. If you plan to use Photo CD discs, you'll
want to purchase a CD-ROM XA compatible drive, which can handle
multisession discs (those that have had images added to them after the
initial processing).

My recommendations follow:

Good: An older single-speed (150-kilobits/sec transfer rate) CD-
          ROM can be purchased for $100 or less, because many
          retailers and end-users consider them outmoded. Still, they
          make a good buy if dollars are tight. A few seconds' wait to
          load data can pay off with cash in your pocket. I would
          rather have one of these than no CD-ROM at all and would
          certainly invest the money saved in, say, another 4M of RAM
          if that was the only way to get additional memory.

Better: A double- or triple-speed drive with Photo CD capability can slice minutes off the time you wait for images to load, but it still costs just $250–500.

Best: Look for a quadruple-speed drive (Plextor's new unit has a street price of under $500) or a quad-speed multi-CD changer (these are expensive!) if you plan to make heavy use of CD-ROM storage. That's not a far-fetched scenario. Many professionals are finding it extremely cost-efficient to have 35mm or larger images scanned at photofinishers or professional labs onto Photo CDs. Thousands of megabytes of image information can be preserved in a stack of Photo CD discs you can hold in the palm of your hand.

I Can See Clearly Now

A really fast CPU and hard disk can make conventional video seem incredibly slow. At resolutions of 1024 × 768 (the minimum for graphics applications) up to 1280 × 1024, and 65,535 or 16.7 million colors, your system has an awful lot of data to supply to your video screen. Nothing is more frustrating than moving a graphic from one part of your workspace to another and then sitting for 30 seconds while the screen redraws.

Any graphics workstation worthy of the name should have a 16- or 24-bit color card that includes a graphics accelerator optimized for Windows. Instead of forcing the CPU to do all the graphics work, which is what happens with simple frame-buffer video cards, the accelerator draws lines and circles, fills rectangles, and moves graphics internally, using its own intelligence. That capability requires a special accelerator chip, such as the new S3, Number Nine, ATI, and Matrox 64-bit chip sets, others from vendors like Chips & Technologies, Tseng Labs, Weitek, and Western Digital. In the real world, the speed of a graphics card is likely to depend on the vendor's implementation and the available drivers, so you can't choose a video card based on type of accelerator alone.

The current champs include cards like SuperMatch's Thunder/24 for Windows (which requires a separate VGA card) and products from Matrox, Number Nine, and other vendors. All are wicked-fast and offer up to 16.7 million colors and have built-in pan-and-zoom features. You can slide your view around a large virtual screen as you move your pointing device out of the current active area and zoom in on a specific portion of the screen at the press of a hotkey. These features are invaluable when you are editing a large image or want to view details close up.

You'll need a monitor to view all those colors. While you can get by with a 17-incher at 1024 × 768 for some types of work, serious graphics applications call for a 20-inch monitor that supports 1280 × 1024 resolution and a high enough vertical refresh rate (70 Hz or higher) to eliminate flickering. Monitors are one component you can choose without getting swamped in technical data; if the screen image looks good to you, it will likely do the job. At this size, a dot pitch of 0.28 to 0.30 mm is fine.

My recommendations follow:

Good: 16-bit color and a 14-inch monitor.

Better: Low-cost accelerated 24-bit color at resolutions of 1024 × 768 or lower on a 17-inch color monitor.

Best: High-end accelerated 24-bit color with hardware pan and zoom to let you work with a spacious virtual screen, displayed on a 20- or 21-inch color screen.

Pointing Device

Can you sign your name with a bar of soap? No? Can you sign your name with a pen? If so, you probably would be more comfortable doing graphics work with a pen-based graphics tablet, rather than a clunky old mouse. Pressure-sensitive tablets with cordless pens are especially cool. Used with applications that support pressure-sensitive pads, such as Fractal Painter and Aldus FreeHand, they enable you to draw thicker lines by just pressing harder. Tablets and pens are a much more natural way of working with graphics; if you can draw, you can use one faster and more accurately than you can sketch with a mouse.

Trackballs and alternate mice are also available as choices if you prefer them.

My recommendations follow:

Good: Stock PC mouse, fine-tuned for your monitor size and working habits.

Better: An upscale mouse or trackball that you find more comfortable or efficient.

Best: A pressure-sensitive drawing tablet (e.g., a model from Wacom) and a desktop big enough to use it.

Color Scanner

Without a color scanner, your only graphics input source will be stuff you create with your own sweaty little hands and existing artwork you obtain from outside sources. A scanner frees you to grab images from photographs, textures from fabric swatches, and artwork from public domain books and publications—practically anything you can see or capture with a camera.

Even though hand-held scanners have come a long way, they are still inconvenient to use and have only limited applications in a production environment. Serious graphics applications call for a 24-bit flatbed color scanner, preferably with 400 dpi or better resolution. Single-pass scanners like the HP ScanJet IIcx are faster and potentially more accurate than models that capture an image with three separate red, green, and blue scans. Don't fall for claims of 600- to 800-dpi resolution without reading the fine print; many of these models use interpolation to approximate the claimed resolution. They may not produce any more usable information than true 400-dpi models. You may gain larger files, but little else.

Color Printer

If the output of your F/X efforts will be used in desktop presentations or used to create color separations that will be printed on an offset press, you may not need a color printer. But, then again, you may. Color output is useful for proofing, filing as a permanent record of a presentation, or making overhead transparencies.

Color printers have come down sharply in cost, and you can now get good output from inkjet models costing less than $1000. A complete discussion of your output options appears in *Chapter 19*. For now, my recommendations are simple:

Good: Inkjet printers with resolutions of 300 to 360 dpi give you reasonable quality at less than $1000 to more than $3000 (for true Adobe PostScript Level 2 output). Canon has introduced a line of inexpensive 600-dpi color inkjet printers. Epson's new Stylus Color inkjet gives you stunning quality and 720-dpi resolution for near-photographic quality.

Better: Thermal wax printers in the $1500 to $4000 price range offer an appealing glossy finish that you don't get with inkjet devices as well as the potential for more accurate color.

Best: Dye-sublimation printers cost $7000–$25,000 but give true photographic quality and as many as 16.7 million colors without dithering.

The Next Step

PC users are fortunate. Victor Frankenstein had to build his beast from old parts his assistant Igor dug up. Your graphics powerhouse is as close as your local computer store or mail order vendor. When you consider what professionals who must create or work with graphics are paid these days, outfitting a serious user with the PC graphics workstation needed to work faster, better, and more efficiently may be the bargain of the decade. Any frustrated user will tell you that graphic violence belongs on television, not the workplace.

This chapter provided some information on hardware considerations for arming yourself for the image-editing wars. The next chapter explores the other side of the coin—your software ammunition.

CHAPTER
THREE

Your Software Suite

If you think working with slow, outmoded hardware is tough, try using the wrong software! Easy tasks become difficult, and difficult tasks approach impossibility. You don't have to spend a fortune on software to work F/X magic, but cutting corners to save a few dollars is false economy, too. It doesn't take too many sessions of laboriously trying to select a tough area in a scanned photo to make you wish you had purchased a software package with a better magic wand.

This chapter provides recommendations for the categories of software you should consider purchasing to equip yourself for the image-processing wars. I include a major look at the leading contender in the image processing wars today, Adobe Photoshop, and shorter reviews of several of the other programs that we'll work with later in this book.

Here is a summary of the major software categories you'll need to consider.

● *Operating System.* This category isn't news: You need Windows, or something very much like it. That means Windows NT or OS/2 (particularly the OS/2 for Windows version). Most of your software requires Windows and an operating system that supports it. If you're using regular Windows or Windows for Workgroups, you should have DOS 5 or DOS 6 for maximum compatibility.

● *Image Editor.* Serious F/X require a serious image-editing program. You'll want one with flexible selection capabilities, a full range of filters, and tools for working with individual color layers using RGB or CMYK color models. If you're doing color separating, it's nice to have that capability built right into the image editor.

● *Add-On Filters.* Filters are what PC F/X are all about. They let you perform some magic on a specific selected area of an image or on the image as a whole. You can sharpen, blur, distort, add textures, or manipulate your image in other ways with filters. While most image editors have a good complement built-in, few F/X junkies will be satisfied with the stock effects. Add-on filters like Kai's Power Tools or Aldus Gallery Effects give you many more new image-processing functions to choose from and work with any image editor that can use Photoshop-compatible plug-ins. These include Fractal Design Painter, Canvas, Aldus PhotoStyler, Picture Publisher, and other programs.

● *Color Separation and Calibration Software.* Depending on what image editor you use, you may also require stand-alone color-separating software to create the individual images for cyan, magenta, yellow, and black films and perhaps to create traps and other effects. Calibration software may be a good idea to make sure your monitor, scanner, and color printer proofing device are all in synch with the offset press used to produce your finished piece.

● *Vector-Oriented Software.* If you want to work with both bitmaps and line art, you may need a stand-alone package that can handle vector-oriented files, such as CorelDRAW, or Aldus FreeHand. Some PC programs, such as Canvas, can handle both. Tools like Adobe Streamline or CorelTRACE can convert bitmaps into editable sets of lines by automatically tracing around the edges of your raster images.

● *Rendering Software.* These packages take your outlines and convert them into realistically modeled 3-D images by coloring, shading, and texturing the surfaces.

● *Type Manipulation Software.* Special packages, such as Pixar Typestry, are available to create stunning 3-D type effects for you, which may be saved as full-color files. These files may be used alone or dropped into images you're working on with your image editor. Some packages also can create animations from a series of progressive frames.

● *Animation Software.* Full-fledged animation packages are complex, high-ticket items that suck their users into time-consuming (but rewarding) careers of their own. Most of the emphasis in this book will be on still effects, but I recognize that many readers will be interested in taking individual images and animating them.

● *Morphing Software.* Programs like PhotoMorph are a combination tool and especially dynamic still photo filter. Like the scenes in Michael Jackson's "Black or White" video, these packages can create smooth transitions from one image to another, transforming a person into a cat or a man into a woman. You can choose one of the intermediate images to work with or animate the series.

A Look at Some Key Packages

This chapter will provide a quick look at some key packages that I used to create the F/X in this book. I'll describe Adobe Photoshop in some detail, because it is both the most popular image-editing software for the PC (it's become a virtual standard since it originally migrated from the Macintosh), and because many of its features are shared by the other software we'll use. Once you understand why a broad range of selection tools (like those in Photoshop) are good to have, you'll know why PhotoStyler or Fractal Design Painter are cool, too.

However, this book is not intended to be a Photoshop book, as there are plenty of them on the market already. Starting in the next chapter, we'll look at a broad range of F/X that you should be able to apply with any of the featured editing programs.

Adobe Photoshop: Up Close

In recent months, the high end of 24-bit image editing got higher—and the price dropped. A $2000 486 equipped with a true color video card and a program like Adobe Photoshop can now do heavy-duty retouching and manipulation that demanded an $8000 PC two years ago—or a $50,000–$100,000 graphics powerhouse two years before *that*.

The original Photoshop was probably the best reason to pay a premium price for a PC. Now, with Photoshop 3.0, we have an even more powerful program, with layers and better control of color. But, what would move you to pay $895 for an image-editing program in the first place? Consider the following features:

- *Color correction of 24-bit (16.7-million-color) images.* You can bring off-color or dull originals to blazing life, ready for use in presentations, output to a color digital printer, or transfer to a professional color prepress system. Photoshop offers a new, visually oriented mode that lets you choose the best color balance, rather than dial it in manually.

- *Color separation.* You can split a color image into CMYK channels and direct them individually to high-resolution output devices as color separations. Photoshop includes essential routines to calibrate the program to the monitor, printing stocks, and inks you'll be using. You can compensate for dot gain (spreading) on the press and remove equal quantities of color (which produce a neutral black), replacing them with cheaper black ink. You may also create traps to overlap colors that abut one another.

- *Image manipulation.* Photoshop offers a dazzling array of selection, and painting tools, a full complement of filters, and special effects. You can retouch images, extract and drop in components, and transform portions to create new or composite images. Up to 16 channels, or layers, per image can be used for masks or as holding areas for components you merge with the main image.

● *Image creation.* Both object-based and pixel-oriented drawing n. tools can be used to create objects, which you may extrude, fill with gradients, use to cast shadows, or combine with editable text. Photoshop has some unusual filters, including Wind, which produces trailing streaks, and Lens Flare, which brings to the PC the image defects that lens designers hoped multicoating would eliminate.

Photoshop, or any other sophisticated 24-bit image editor, has a lot more power than the neophyte needs or can handle. If you know what gray component replacement or undercolor removal are, these programs can provide them. Unless you're a seasoned graphics veteran, you'll probably have to grow into Photoshop's full feature set.

But, all the high-end editors have this stuff. What does Photoshop bring to the party? Photoshop shines in the depth of its options and the ease with which you can apply them. Adobe's long experience in this arena seems to have taught them that image-editing power involves a lot more than assembling a humongous collection of nested menus and populating a few hundred dialog boxes with slider controls. A few quick examples will show what I mean.

Baby, You Know What I Like

Any image editor will allow you to correct a badly balanced or poorly exposed color photo. All you need to do is learn the ins and outs of gamma correction, the intricacies of at least one or two different methods for modeling color space, and, let's see, when you want to remove some red from an image, you add cyan...or is it vice versa? Most of us take a long time to gain the expertise to use such tools effectively, so color correction ends up as a trial-and-error exercise: We jiggle sliders until the Preview looks better than the Original view.

Adobe figures that even if you think a histogram is a cold remedy, you'll know what you like when you see it, so it gives you the option of picking out the color balance and density you want from a line-up. Photoshop's Variations mode caters to your needs like a commercial photo lab caters to a Madison Avenue art director.

In that mode the program arrays a selection of thumbnail versions of your original image, each skewed in one color direction or another: More Yellow, More Red, More Magenta, etc. You can compare the 12 miniature views simultaneously and decide which looks best. If you like, you can start with a "coarser" setting, so that each variation is drastically different from the others. Then, you can select finer increments plus stir lighter or darker versions into the pot.

You'll be surprised at how dramatically you can improve an image without any more fine-tuning than a Grateful Dead sound check. Yet, if you need even more color correction precision, Photoshop doesn't dump you back in the pool with the technosharks. Instead, it gives you the equivalent of an automated densitometer to tune your image to the aimpoints you determine during installation and calibration of your monitor and output device.

That's a lot easier than it sounds. When you install Photoshop, you're invited to load a few sample files and make some adjustments that tell the program how your particular equipment renders color. Later, when you need to correct a color image precisely, you can use the Adjust Levels dialog box to specify white and black points (to adjust the brightness values of the midtones without losing detail in the highlights and shadows) and then change the mix of colors with a few simple controls. You don't need ten years' experience operating a million-dollar laser scanner to use Photoshop.

On the downside, you may edit in RGB or CMYK modes, but Adobe substitutes its LAB mode for the alternative HSB/HSL (hue, saturation, brightness/luminosity) modes, so you can't choose to edit in a mode with a pure saturation axis. That's a technical quibble to be sure, but image-editing mavens may be upset at this oversight.

Photoshop 3.0 has a nifty new selective color correction feature that lets you specify the precise amount of ink applied to a particular color channel in absolute or relative amounts. You can also replace colors to swap all or part of one color with another hue.

It's no longer necessary to convert from RGB to CMYK mode to see how an image will look using the other color model (you would lose some colors if you converted back to RGB with Photoshop 2.5.1). Instead, you may preview CMYK images and receive a gamut warning that highlights any areas that can't be reproduced within the CMYK color model.

Masked Ball

The Quick Mask feature is another example of a complicated procedure made easy. Think of a *mask* as a transparent overlay with areas of density that hold back or protect portions of an image. Masks can be deposited in their own layers, or channels, and then called up when necessary to isolate, say, an object that you want to copy or retouch separately. Creating, modifying, saving, and recalling multiple masks can be a time-consuming procedure with some image editors.

With Photoshop you can turn any selected area into a mask by clicking on the Quick Mask icon. You may then edit the new mask in its own channel, use it immediately, or save it (apply a descriptive name, if you like) for later application. Each time you load that image, the extra layers you've created appear in a Channels window along with the Red, Green, and Blue (or other color) channels.

Camera Sans Obscura

The term *digital darkroom* has become a cliché because simple analogies can save a ton of explanation. Still, Photoshop does so many things like a real photographic darkroom that photojournalists see it as the best thing to hit the field since the zoom lens.

Most photographers, especially those with commercial studios, will know about masking. There is even a technique called "in-camera masking" that works a lot like Photoshop's Quick Mask feature. Selecting the best exposure or color balance from an array of near-duplicates, or from a test strip is a time-honored darkroom procedure.

However, the analogies run much deeper than that. Darkroom workers commonly lighten certain areas of an image by waving a *dodging tool* (often a piece of cardboard taped to a length of clothes-hanger wire) between the enlarger and printing easel during the exposure. Other areas may be darkened, or "burned in" during a subsequent, additional exposure, made through the space between two cupped hands, also kept in motion to "feather" the effects.

Photoshop's lighten/darken icons resemble a dodging frisket and a cupped hand and are intuitively usable by anyone with photographic experience—and almost everyone else, too. You move a copy of a selection to a buffer by "taking a snapshot" and mask out areas of an image with an overlay that looks for all the world like a sheet of Rubylith film etched with an X-acto knife.

Layers Palette

The new Layers Palette in Version 3.0 makes it easier than ever before to composite multiple images, and to draw, apply effects, or use filters in individual layers without affecting other portions of the image. That feature makes it easy to try various types of F/X quickly and to save different effects to different files.

Options Galore

Adobe hasn't let Photoshop become constrained by the darkroom paradigm. You'll never mistake one of its painting tools for a spotting brush. A simple brush can assume any of ten default sizes, from 1 to 100 pixels in diameter, plus any custom shape or size you care to design. Dial in your choice of opacity, from 0 to 100%; then decide whether you want the brush to apply a hard or feathered edge. Next, you can choose the effect the brush has on your image: It can lay down an even layer of tone or only modify pixels that are either lighter or darker than the foreground color.

Alternatively, a brush can change only the hue or saturation of the pixels it passes over or change the saturation without modifying other values. If that isn't enough, brushes can assume a dissolve mode that adds random noise and color or acts like a bleach to mute hues. Other painting/drawing tools, like the airbrush and pencil, have similar flexibility. Figure 3.1 shows Photoshop's tool palette.

Figure 3.1   *Adobe Photoshop has a wide range of powerful tools.*

The biggest advantage Photoshop has over a real darkroom is in the strength of its selection tools. Fancy filters and tricky special effects are of little use if you can't control exactly where they are applied.

Photoshop has the Rectangular, Circle, Freehand (Lasso), and Magic Wand selection tools you would expect to find in a 24-bit image editor. They can be used in combination to extract a precise area from an image without tedious manual tracing. Don't worry about maintaining a steady hand with the Lasso. You can draw roughly in Freehand mode and then adjust the borders of a selection to clean up areas where you rushed or a got a little sloppy. Add portions of a selection a little at a time or subtract parts that were selected in error.

If you hold down the **Shift** key, any new area selected is added to the current selection, even if you switch selection tools. Selections can grow, or extend to include adjacent pixels that fall within a tonal tolerance range you specify or set to include similar pixels anywhere in the image.

New Lighting Effects and Filters

Photoshop 3.0 adds a new Lighting Effects filter that lets you create multiple light sources, with various positions, intensities, and colors, and then add their effects to your image. There's a new Dust and Scratches plug-in to remove or reduce the appearance of dust and scratches on images that have been scanned from photographs. You can also create your own filters with the new Filter Factory plug-in.

Photoshop Puts Out

Because the images you modify with Photoshop may be created by or destined for other applications, the file formats it handles are important. In addition to its proprietary Photoshop (PSD) format, the Adobe flagship can import and export PICT, Windows bitmaps (BMP), PCX, TIFF, TARGA, CompuServe GIF, and Scitex formats—for starters. You'll want to use Photoshop format while you're working on an image, to keep all the channel information and masks in a single file, and then to export to TIFF or Scitex or something else, depending on your final application.

You certainly have other options. Photoshop imports and exports Pixar PXR files, as well as EPS, along with non-PC formats like Amiga IFF, PCPaint, or PixelPaint (but not the PICT format supported by Photoshop/Mac). Kodak Photo CD files can be imported, but not written, and Photoshop also supports the relatively new JPEG format.

The latter can produce smaller versions of large files by quantizing blocks of pixels, discarding some information, and storing the image in a special compressed format. The quality lost varies by the type of image; my 2.5M test image squeezed down to just 50K at the maximum compression ratio, but gradients (such as sky) had a blocky, mosaic appearance that wasn't acceptable. Luckily, you can choose which compression/quality level you want. The JPEG format can be useful for archiving evaluation copies of images stored at full resolution offline (on removable media).

Other Image Editors

There are dozens of image editors for the PC, some priced as low as $100–149. I'll concentrate on the high-end products which are comparable to Photoshop, because you don't want to scrimp when you're planning to work with heavy-duty F/X, do you? Actually, you don't need to pay much more for any of the programs in this chapter. I recently saw the latest version of Photoshop advertised for $179 as an upgrade from another program.

Canvas 3.5

Can't decide between draw and paint programs? Canvas is arguably the best of a breed of programs that don't require you to choose. They let you work with both bitmapped and object-oriented images in the same file. Given the $399 price—about half that of some programs with fewer features—the choice may be fairly easy.

With Canvas you gain the best of both worlds. Outline drawings, which don't lose resolution as you resize them for printing, can be created. You can add bitmapped painting enhancements to these drawings and then print out the combined image. Of course, the bitmapped component of the image will change as you size or scale the drawing, so you should add these details last.

Canvas' text handling has been improved to the point that it now includes a 100,000-word spelling dictionary (how many image programs can boast that?). You can now use tool managers to customize each of the tools you use and then select from among them with a ToolPicker that can load, save, and delete sets of customized tools as they are needed.

What else is different about Canvas from Deneba Software? Most drawing programs allow you to import and work with bitmapped images. However, the goal in most cases is to trace the bit map to convert it to an object-oriented drawing. While Canvas does have autotrace features, you really don't have to convert your scanned images to use them. It combines raster and vector images in separate layers. With an unlimited number of layers available, you can easily combine both types of images.

As a drawing program, Canvas has few equals. It supports full Bézier curves, cutting and joining of polygons, skewing, perspective, and distortion. You can use autodimensioning to resize images as you move them from document to document.

Its painting features are similarly powerful. Canvas will create and edit bit maps at resolutions up to 2540 dpi, so you won't lose any quality when working with scanned images.

Because Canvas has an unlimited number of layers available, you can stack them to produce the color images you want. Canvas is supplied with a Canvas Separator utility. You can create CMYK separations from any Canvas illustration. The utility will print directly to PostScript typesetters and output film compatible with four-color process printing. Precise adjustments are available to control line screen frequency percentage enlargement/reduction and screen angles.

Other color models are supported, including RGB, HSL, and HSV. Canvas can import and export color TIFF, MacPaint, PICT and PICT2 files. Canvas has added EPS export to allow creating images for Corel Ventura, PageMaker, and Xpress without loss of precision. Four EPS formats are available: regular, Adobe Illustrator 1.1, PICT EPS, and Clipboard EPS. The latter two formats allow using EPS images within applications that don't normally support PostScript files.

The latest version has some important new features, such as Envelope (which can stretch, bend, and warp outline-oriented objects, including text) and Fractals (which produce stunning color effects). Figure 3.2 shows Canvas' fractal effects in action.

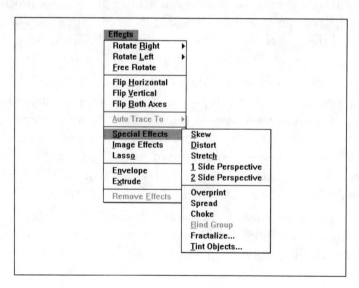

Figure 3.2 *Fractal effects are easy with Canvas.*

Fractal Design Painter/Painter/X2

This is the program that pioneered what are called *natural effects*. That is, you can use Painter's tools to simulate the styles of artists using their brushes. Its /X2 (an announced upgrade to /X3 wasn't received by the time this book was finished) extension adds the ability to work with individual layers as floating bit maps, so you can make changes that can be moved, edited, or undone at any time.

Natural tools give you modifiable parameters that are less computer-like and more like the ones artists actually use. For example, Painter lets you specify the number of hairs in your brush, the amount of jitter in your hand, and add in some random size variation for good measure. Presets can mimic the brushstrokes of artists like Van Gogh, Seurat, or Monet. You can add tiled patterns or textures.

The *liquid media* features let you simulate marbling effects and water-color with nine new liquid brushes. One unique feature is the ability to record and play back an entire painting session, stroke by stroke. Teachers can use this capability as an instructional tool.

Of course, the standard features you need in an image editor are also there: bitmapped design tools, text capabilities, and photo-imaging filters and effects, along with the ability to make color separations and photo-composites.

Painter/X2 lets you apply visual effects to any separate layer of the image, with independent masking controls. Each layer can be saved in a portfolio, where it is identified by a thumbnail image for later retrieval and use.

All these features come at a small price: Active files must be stored in Painter's RIFF file format, which keeps track of the individual floating layers. (This is the same format used by ColorStudio, created by one of the founders of Fractal Design.) You can always export to another format when it comes time to use them with another application. In practice this limitation is no different from using the proprietary formats offered by Photoshop and some other image editors.

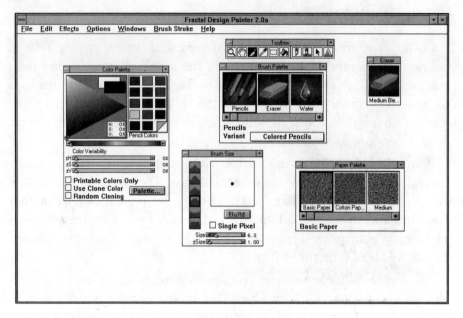

Figure 3.3   *Fractal Design Painter offers unusual natural media tools.*

Aldus PhotoStyler: Up Close

What a strange life PhotoStyler has led. Originally developed by Ulead Systems (which today sells an entirely different image editor as part of its Image Pals package), PhotoStyler 1.0 was reportedly so much like Adobe Photoshop that Adobe threatened to sue Ulead. Acquired by Aldus, and released in a Version 1.1 format that didn't really rival Photoshop in features or appearance, PhotoStyler nevertheless gained a following.

Then, in the strangest turn yet, Aldus was acquired—seemingly—by Adobe, placing two rival image-editing programs under the same ownership. At this writing the merger is far from a done deal, and nobody knows what the final fate of PhotoStyler will be, particularly with a muscular new Photoshop 3.0 looming over its head. I had to debate whether to even include PhotoStyler in this book—will it remain a contender, or is it a dead duck?

If not yet dead, PhotoStyler's latest Version 2.0 is a worthy contender against its stablemate. It has improved masking tools, greater control over the shape and use of brushes, and better color controls. By "better" I mean that PhotoStyler now supports 17 different color-matching systems, including Pantone, Trumatch, Munsell, and the Kodak Precision Color Management System. You won't need most of these unless you already know what they are, but it's nice to know this flexibility is available.

PhotoStyler has also been made easier to use, with real-time preview of filter effects. However, it doesn't have the object layers added to Photoshop 3.0 or the vector drawing/selection tools Photoshop has had since its Version 2.5.

This program supports pressure-sensitive tablets, although you can control either stroke width or opacity, but not both at the same time. You can create custom brush shapes and save them for reuse, but, unfortunately, only the size of the brush, not its opacity, feathering, or other characteristics are saved.

PhotoStyler offers 44 image-processing filters. When the control window for each filter pops up, you can adjust the parameters used to produce the effects and preview your settings in a thumbnail image. There is one triumphant feature: Because you can work with virtual images, you can apply these effects to files that are too large to load into memory all at once.

Picture Publisher: Up Close

UP CLOSE

I've used Picture Publisher for many years, dating back to a weird version that had a special mode you had to use in order to view gray-scale images in anything other than dithered mode. More recently, it's been acquired by Micrografx, and in its Version 4.0 incarnation has been consistently voted as one of the easier-to-use image editors on the market. At $595, it's also several hundred dollars less expensive than most of its competitors (if suggested retail prices mean anything at all these days).

The ease-of-use features include an image browser that makes it easier to find files and a set of thumbnails that let you see different effects filters (46 are available overall) in action so that you can choose the one you want (this is sort of a pre-preview). Picture Publisher was also the first PC program on the market to let you open only a selected portion of an image (rather than the entire file) so that you could work using this FastBits mode on small chunks of a larger image.

It also had object layers long before Adobe Photoshop and has painting tools with a flexibility to rival Fractal Design Painter. You get the same brushes, pens, and airbrushes that other programs provide, augmented with natural media such as crayon, chalk, watercolor, and oil. All these can be extensively modified.

Like Photoshop, you can paint masks onto the image using a brush, but Picture Publisher adds a novel Bézier curve editing feature to its Edit Mask mode. You can specify whether feathering takes place inside or outside the mask and store masks in a separate alpha channel (Photoshop offers 16 separate channels).

Pixar Typestry: Up Close

UP CLOSE

After you've seen the stunning type effects brewed by Pixar Typestry's 3-D rendering alchemy, ordinary logos and lettering will seem as flat and lifeless as an AM radio in a speeding convertible. Add this $299 application to your toolkit, and your desktop presentations, computer-generated transparencies, publications, and advertising will never look the same again.

Typestry supplies the tools to chisel text out of marble or wood, extrude fonts, mold them in plastic, and rotate them on any axis to produce three-dimensional perspectives. Choose the angles and colors of complex light sources, cast shadows, or define walls and floors. Successive keyframes can be modified slightly to produce animated effects you can play back with an included movie module.

The only real limitation of Typestry is that it works only with Type 1 and TrueType fonts; if you want to manipulate any other shapes, you must first convert them to font format with a utility like Altsys' Fontographer. Forget about pasting images from the Clipboard.

Grab That Slab

Start with text typed in any installed font, excluding only a few odd-ball Type 1 fonts that Typestry is unable to interpret. You can choose type of bevel edge and bevel thickness. Any of dozens of different textures—Pixar calls them looks—can be selected from a palette. These range from warm plastic to burnished metal, wood, brick, ceramic tile, and "dragon skin." Any texture you create or scan can be converted into a look using an extra-cost add-on called Glimpse, available from Pixar. However, the built-in textures give you more variations than a Bach fugue.

Now the fun begins. Imagine your lettering engraved on a rectangular slab. Grab the slab at any point and rotate on that axis to create perspective images from any viewpoint. Choose between normal, fish-eye, and telephoto (compressed) camera lenses. Define a wall and floor as an environment for your lettering and give them textures of their own.

There's also a highly touted "cookie cutter" mode that lets you take slices out of your lettering in various shapes, or build up characters from diamonds, cylinders, or plane chunks. I wasn't as enamored of this capability as the folks at Pixar, but it is an impressive effect.

Multiple light sources can be placed in front of, behind, or next to the lettering and attenuated with colors or variously shaped window gels. Cast shadows, add motion blurs, or make your image seem to move through space, leaving a blur in its trail. A floating toolbar and menus let you add or subtract effects quickly. You can't see what each change looks like in the basic wireframe mode, though; you must first render your image.

Slow Down

If you've never worked with 3-D rendering programs before, you'll probably be shocked at how slow the process is. If you have, you'll be impressed with how fast Typestry works. On a 486DX2-66 a reasonably complex picture took roughly four minutes to transform from basic wireframe image to full 3-D splendor with photorealistic shading at the highest quality setting. The program makes heavy use of an available math co-processor, so expect the same job to take six to eight times longer on machine without one.

Those long waits are necessary only to produce your final image. Typestry offers a quick-and-dirty preview mode (and an intermediate "reasonable" setting) that you can use to check overall appearance, shadows, and perspective, which typically rendered an image in a minute or two. You may also process only a small cropped portion of an image, and see your results in a few seconds. Once you get used to previewing in low resolution or using sections of your image, the lack of instant rendering won't bother you much.

When you're satisfied with your results, you can save the image to disk in BMP, TIFF, RenderMan RIB, or TIGA formats. The first three formats support the normal RGB channels used for conventional true color, 24-bit color images. Even if you have only a 256-color display, your renderings are created and saved in full 24-bit color.

TIGA (and other formats, as you'll learn) supports a fourth, *alpha channel,* which can be used to control the amount of transparency of an image. You can overlay TIGA images on top of each other and have the bottom lettering show through transparent objects placed on top.

The rendered bit maps can be further modified only by a bit map editor like Adobe Photoshop, but the wireframe version of an image can be saved separately, reloaded, and edited to produce new renderings at any time.

Animation adds a lot of time to the rendering process, but not much complexity. You can position objects in a new keyframe, and Typestry will calculate all the intermediate frames. There's no need to tediously rotate, enlarge, or move individual objects manually. The program generates an Autodesk Animator FLC-format file and includes the Autodesk Animation Player to view it with. Unfortunately, the animations are limited to an unrealistic 256 colors. Even so, this no-cost added capability might whet your appetite for "real" Windows-based animation. Indeed, Typestry itself is an exciting introduction to full-blown 3-D rendering applications. Even as you bring your desktop presentations to life, you'll learn quite a bit about lighting, perspective, and color.

Your car stereo system never sounds quite as good after you've been to a live Bruce Springsteen concert. Once you've transmogrified lettering with Pixar Typestry, you'll never be satisfied with plain, flat text again.

The Next Step

This chapter provided you with a glimpse at what key products in some of the major categories can do. Magazines like *PC Magazine* and *PC World* provide more in-depth reviews of the latest products and frequently feature roundups that compare and contrast many different packages. If you're serious about staying abreast of the F/X state of the art, you should plan to monitor these articles on an ongoing basis.

Now it's time to put some of these programs to work and create some interesting special effects with our images.

PART II

Combining Photos

There are three simple rules for combining photos seamlessly and effectively. Unfortunately, nobody knows what they are. Like the rest of us, you'll have to achieve outrageously interesting results through hard work and practice. This next section should give you a head start on your journey, while demonstrating that twisting photos into new shapes (through morphing) or merging them with photocompositing techniques doesn't have to be as complicated and difficult as others would make you believe.

We'll start out with the morphing, the glamour tool of the 1990s, and work our way into the less mundane aspects of combining images.

CHAPTER FOUR

Morphing!

You don't need to be a Power Ranger or the director of a Michael Jackson video to use morphing to transform your images into something new and interesting. I'll start off the special F/X in this book by introducing you to a brand-new type of image processing that's become the hottest tool this side of a Hoover vacuum cleaner.

You probably don't have morphing software already, so I've included tryout versions of the sensational Elastic Reality on the CD-ROM bundled with this book. Like all the evaluation software I've included, this is a fully functional version with a few enhancements that will encourage you to purchase the full version if you like what you see.

I'll also tell you about PhotoMorph, which has actually been around longer than Elastic Reality; however, a tryout version of this software was not available for the book.

An important thing to note is that morphing is generally regarded as an animation tool: most of the special F/X you've seen have been movies or videos in which one object changes into another: a man into a woman, a Michael Jackson into a jaguar (the animal, not the car), or a pool of liquid metal into an unstoppable Terminator. That doesn't mean that morphing can't be used to create outrageously modified still images, too. I'll show you how in the sections that follow.

What's Morphing?

The term *morphing* is a contraction derived from the term *metamorphosis*, which comes from Greek words that mean to change form. It's a complex process originally developed in 3-D format for motion picture special F/X, and requiring impressive computer power to handle. Now, your friendly neighborhood PC can generate morphed two-dimensional movies or image files in a much lower resolution mode than that used for digital movie F/X. Because the number of pixels being manipulated is so much lower, the horsepower of an IBM PC-compatible is entirely sufficient.

To understand morphing, it's helpful to think about how cartoons are (or were) produced. You already know that cartoons are made by assembling hundreds of thousands of individual images, with slight changes between frames, so that when they are viewed at 24 frames per second, the brain blends the individual images into smooth motion.

One set of celluloid sheets (or cels) is created with the background that shows behind the cartoon characters. In very simple animation (Flintstones variety), this background changes very little within a scene. So adults (and sometimes children) notice that Fred chases Barney past the same Bedrock bowling alley eleven or twelve times in a given chase sequence. In Disney-style animation, the background cels may change much more drastically or even consist of several layers that produce a perspective or 3-D effect when characters move within a scene.

However, for the concept of morphing, we're more interested in how the characters move. Fred picks up a bowling ball, swings back his arm, brings it forward again, and then lets loose to pick up a strike. The frames in which major changes in the action (or background) occur are called *keyframes*. You might consider the point at which Fred starts to swing his arm backward and the farthest point of his backward arc as two separate keyframes. To keep the motion from looking jerky, the animators need to create in-between frames, each with the arm's next position in the stroke. If the backward motion takes 0.25 second, you need 0.25×24 frames, or six different drawings to depict the movement.

This tweening process was once handled by junior animators or contracted to animation factories in Asia. The lead animators actually created only the keyframes, and the skills of less highly paid individuals were sufficient to handle tweening. Today, computers can actually calculate and draw these in-between frames. It's easy work for them, because they are already doing something much more complicated: morphing.

Imaging Fred swinging his arm back again, but by the time he reaches the back of the arc, his bowling ball has turned into a pumpkin. Again, for the transition to look smooth, we need intermediate pictures: In the first cel the bowling ball is very slightly pumpkinlike, while it looks like a full-fledged jack-o-lantern in the last cel. If you supply a properly written computer program with an image of the bowling ball and another of the pumpkin, it can gradually change the pixels of one into those of the other.

To do that, two things must happen: Pixels may have to move from one place to another if, for example, the bowling ball is smaller than the pumpkin. Those representing the perimeter of the ball must migrate outward to the new perimeter of the pumpkin. Morphing may have to stretch, pull, or squeeze portions of an image to make a new image and an old one combine smoothly.

In addition, the texture, color, and appearance of the two images must transform from one to the other, through a process called cross-fading. Think of this process as making the old image (the bowling ball) gradually become more and more transparent until it vanishes, at the same time that a transparent pumpkin slowly coalesces into view. In practice, it's more complicated than this, but you get the idea. At least, you understand enough to let me skip any further background and get started with some morphing!

Let's use Elastic Reality to see first-hand how the process operates.

Creating Dizzy Gillespie Cheeks

Elastic Reality is remarkably easy to use. Figure 4.1 shows a young girl blowing out a birthday cake into Elastic Reality's Edit window. I used the Pen tool (visible in the Tool palette at the far left) to outline two areas on her face. The inner outline roughly corresponds to the original contours of the girl's lower face and cheeks. I skipped the chin, because I don't want to morph it. The goal here will be to create some cheeks worthy of Dizzy Gillespie (the late, great jazz trumpet player).

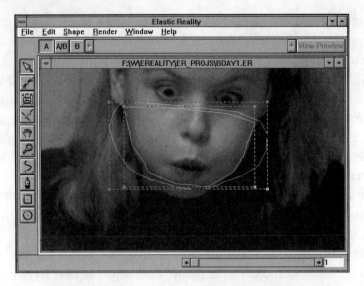

Figure 4.1 *The outline of the cheeks (inner shape) is joined to the new outline (outer shape.)*

The second outline follows the first one closely at the top and bottom but extends outwards at the sides. Elastic Reality uses *Bézier curves* to create its outlines With Bézier curves, you can adjust the position of the lines by dragging control points and change the curvature smoothly by moving control handles. To create this morph, I first linked the two areas, by selecting the inner outline, holding down the **Shift** key, and select the outer outline. Elastic Reality expanded the smaller, inner area to fill the larger, outer area. If I had changed the order of selecting the areas, the outer outline would be shrunk to fit into the inner area (a pinching effect).

Then I used Elastic Reality's **Join** command to cement the relationship I just established. You can preview the effect or go ahead and create the morph, which looks like Figure 4.2. The program has smoothly stretched the original image to fill the specified area, creating exaggerated, ballooned ⁻ks. Unlike the simple distortions that you can create with image edi-ke Photoshop (such as Spherize), morphing generates a smooth undetectable transitions between areas.

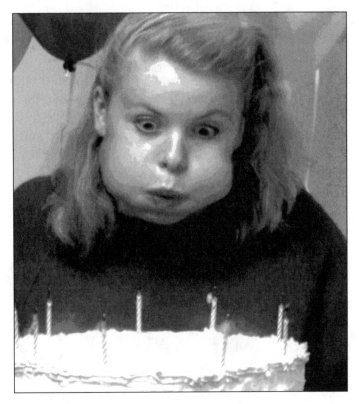

Figure 4.2 *Morphed picture, with ballooning cheeks.*

More Facial Distortions

As you can see, morphing can be useful for distorting images in ways that can't easily be accomplished with image editors. Also note that we didn't need the motion effects you see with video and movie morphing. That's because we don't care about the intermediate images and how the photo metamorphoses from one state to the other. We're only interested in the final effect. This particular mode of morphing, using just one image, is often called *warping* (for obvious reasons).

I'll show you how morphing can be used with another example. We'll take an informal portrait of a young man and distort his face worse than puberty ever did. Again, we'll use Elastic Reality as our tool.

In Figure 4.3 you can see the original photo. Instead of outlining portions of the face freehand with the Pen tool, I used the Box tool to draw a large box around his head and a smaller box that covers just his face. Then, I selected the large box first, followed by the smaller box. The order of selection told Elastic Reality that I wanted to squeeze all the image in the larger box into the area occupied by the smaller one.

Figure 4.3 *Portrait with head and face separately marked with boxes.*

If you were to resize an area with a conventional image editor, you'd be left with a large blank space where the larger box was. A morphing program squeezes the surrounding pixels in, creating that smooth transition again and producing an effect like that shown in Figure 4.4. We can also reverse the process, ballooning the portion contained in the small box outward so it fills the area of the large box. That effect is shown in Figure 4.5.

Figure 4.4   *The image in the outer box has been morphed down to fit in the smaller box.*

Figure 4.5   *Now, the image in the inner box has been morphed to fill the larger box.*

Now, let's create an alien from space. We'll use Elastic Reality to morph several facial features independently of the others. We'll enlarge the eyes to inhuman proportions, while shrinking the nose and mouth. The effect will be quite unsettling. Figure 4.6 shows the "normal" face, zoomed in 2× so that we can work on the features easily.

Figure 4.6 *Zoom in on the face to make it easier to outline eyes, nose, and mouth.*

The first step is to outline the eyes, nose and mouth carefully. I adjusted the Bézier curves to conform to the edges of these features. We don't have to be quite so careful about outlining the new area, as we're trying to produce an unrealistic effect. I did mark the top boundary of the "alien" eyes at the current position, but expanded the lower boundaries down into what would normally be bags under the eyes of a college student after an all-nighter. The outline for the nose and mouth were made a little smaller. You can see the outlines in Figure 4.7.

Steel yourself before looking at the final result, in Figure 4.8. If you thought those Keane paintings of big-eyed children were cute, you never considered anything like this picture. This is morphing as it was intended by those weird folks who make science fiction movies.

Figure 4.7 *Separate outlines have been drawn for existing features and new areas that will be filled by warping.*

Figure 4.8 *Warped photo.*

Morphing Two Images

Every morphing demonstration you've ever seen has shown a man transforming into a woman. I'm not going to do that to you. But, if you have your heart set on such a thing, there's usually a man-woman demo included with just about every morphing package available. You can experiment with this classic transformation all you want. In any case, my emphasis is on still images, and there's not much demand for an intermediate image of a half-man, half-woman. Instead, I'll merge seasons and morph two images of a home, one taken in winter and the other in summer (albeit roughly four years apart). You'll be able to see the tween images in the example pictures, while learning how to morph two images.

It's time to break the news that all the demos you've seen are rigged. Morphing two images works best when certain factors are considered, and you can bet your last RAM chip that the vendors took them into account when choosing images for demo morphing. Your results may vary, from perfectly awful to very good, depending on how much you keep these "secret" factors in mind. Those factors, roughly in the order of importance, follow.

- *Similar size and outline.* Morphing works best when the two objects have roughly the same size and shape. If you wanted to create an amazing man-to-woman morph, you must choose pictures of a man and woman in which their faces are about the same size, and both had short haircuts (or the woman had her hair tied back). It would be difficult to match up the outlines of clothing, so your image would be a head-and-shoulders picture with bare shoulders.

  Certainly, you could morph a larger head into a smaller one, but the shrinking effect would detract from the realism of the transformation. It would seem less like a man turning into a woman, and more like two heads being exchanged through some sort of computer dissolving effect.

- *Similar perspective.* Obviously, you wouldn't morph a profile into a full face shot. But, you wouldn't want to merge two photos in which one person's face was angled just slightly, and the other wasn't. A more subtle consideration is the elevation of the camera.

If one picture was made at the subject's eye-level, you wouldn't want to use a second photo made a little below eye-level (you see more chin, less top of the head) or a little above (more top of the head).

Note that the lens or lens setting used to take a picture can vary the apparent perspective of the image. On a 35mm camera, an 85 to 105mm lens (or zoom setting) usually produces the most flattering results. A longer lens (say, a 200mm optic) tends to flatten and widen a face. Shorter focal lengths (50mm to 24mm) narrow the face and exaggerate features like the nose, which may appear larger because it is closer to the camera.

These distortions are all apparent (caused by the distance rather than the lens itself) rather than real, because if you backed off from your subject and took a picture with a 50mm lens and then enlarged a small portion to coincide with the image you shot with a 200mm lens from the same position, they would look identical.

● *Similar features.* You can morph two humans, especially if the sizes of key features like eyes, nose, mouth, and ears are all of similar size and outline, and are located in roughly the same places. Morphing a cat and a human is also possible, because cats have two eyes, a nose, and a mouth, even if they are not quite the same as ours. Try to morph a human and a lobster, and you'll find your results may be less than satisfactory. The transformation is just too extreme.

● *Similar coloration and texture.* Morph two Caucasian faces, and the transition between the two will be hard to detect. Perform the same operation on a very dark face and a very light face, and you'll definitely notice the change. However, the intermediate shades produced when morphing two differently colored subjects can be interesting by themselves, so don't place too much importance on this factor.

The lesson here is that you may want to choose images carefully and possibly do some work with your pictures in an image-editing program to match sizes, if smooth morphing is important to you.

For the following exercise, I resized one of the pictures to more closely match the other house image, but I ignored several of the other rules. The angle and elevation at which the two pictures were taken is slightly different. However, these photos weren't taken with morphing in mind; I just happened to find them in the same shoebox.

Setting Up Corresponding Shapes

Morphing two images is done using what Elastic Reality terms A and B rolls. The terminology stems from the motion picture editing technique of using parallel rolls of film. Each might be, say, 1000 feet long. Roll A would contain the first scene, starting a fade at the 200-foot mark, followed by black leader after the fade is complete. Roll B would have 200 feet of black leader, then a fade in of the next scene. The process would be reversed with the next fade, to the end of the reels. When editing was finished, the intermediate would be exposed first to the A roll and then to the B roll, producing smooth transitions between scenes.

I've oversimplified the process quite a bit, but you can see how A and B rolls are used to generate morphs. The pixels in the initial image are stretched, squeezed, or otherwise transformed toward those of the second image and then faded out. At the same time, the pixels of the other image are transformed backward toward those of the first, and faded in.

To create a two-image morph, you need to load one image into the A roll window and the second into the B roll window and then outline some key shapes in both pictures. Figure 4.9 shows the shapes drawn in the summer picture using Elastic Reality's Pen tool. I outlined the peak of the house, the roof of the gazebo, one section of the room addition at rear, and two sections of the decks. Then, I selected all the shapes and chose **Edit>Copy**. Switching to the B roll (by clicking on the button in the bar under the window's title bar), I pasted the shapes into the winter image and then moved them individually to their rough locations. Elastic Reality's point-editing tools let me change the outlines so that they more closely approximated their counterparts in the winter image, as shown in Figure 4.10. Finally, I joined matching shapes in the two windows by choosing the A/B view, which superimposed the pair of images on top of each other. Then, I selected first the summer version of a shape, the winter version, and joined that pair. Figure 4.11 shows this dual view.

Figure 4.9 *The summer view of the house with several structures outlined.*

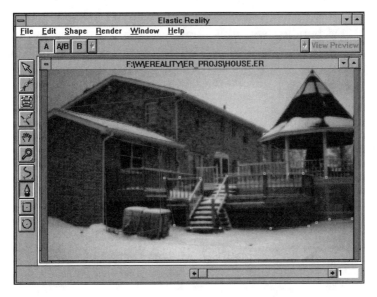

Figure 4.10 *This is the winter view of the house, with the same structures outlined.*

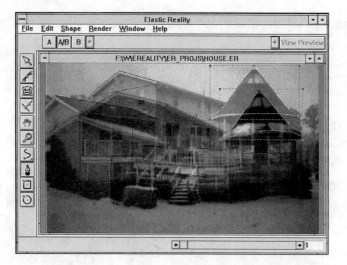

Figure 4.11 *With both images and their shapes visible, join the matching outlines.*

I asked Elastic Reality to create two morphs with ten different intermediate frames. The first morph was output as a movie, which can be viewed to watch the transition between summer and winter. I included that movie on the CD-ROM bundled with this book. For the second morph, I specified output as individual image files. Four of them are shown in Figure 4.12 and in Color insert Figure 1.

Figure 4.12 *Four intermediate views as summer turns to winter.*

A Close-Up Look at PhotoMorph

Morphing has come a long way in a very short time. The original programs that performed this operation used a mesh of lines and control points that were overlaid like a fishnet on images. The next generation of morphing software like PhotoMorph didn't treat an entire object as a unit: They allowed users to define each major shape in the image using short line segments and then match similar shapes in the two images being morphed.

You can see how swarms of points can be matched up in this way in Figure 4.13, which shows PhotoMorph in action.

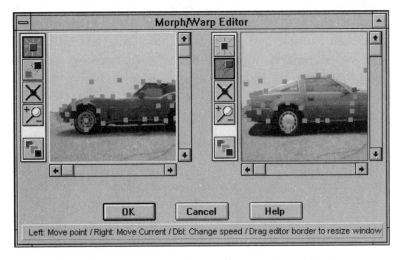

Figure 4.13 *PhotoMorph uses an array of control points to establish the corresponding areas of each image.*

PhotoMorph and an early rival, Digital Morph from HSC, were two of the original morphing programs for Windows. I first saw them demonstrated at Spring COMDEX in 1993 and was quite impressed. Now, PhotoMorph has gone into its second generation, as PhotoMorph 2. The new version has some enhanced features that make it suitable for producing sophisticated Video for Windows AVI files, with morphing, warping, distortions, complex transitions, and realistic superimpositions using a process called *chromakeying* (also known as *blue screening.*)

You've undoubtedly seen this effect on your evening television news- and weathercasts. The weather person stands in front of a blue panel and points at various features of the map, using an off-screen monitor for reference. The camera that records the human is electronically forced to ignore that particular shade of blue, so that the map itself can be superimposed around the weather reporter. It's called chromakeying because the effect is dependent on using specific colors or chromas to provide a self-matting or masking effect. Today, blue screens aren't always blue—you can key images based not on color but brightness—luminance—so that a broad expanse of bright snow can be used to superimpose images.

PhotoMorph 2 also supports alpha channels like those used in Photoshop, PhotoStyler, and other still image editors. There are 12 new dynamic video effects for sharpening, embossing, tracing edges, and adjusting brightness contrast, hue, and saturation. Other special F/X at your command include spherizing, swirling, tearing, twirling, and zooming. Check out PhotoMorph 2 if you're serious about finding new ways to distort your images for effect.

The Next Step

Morphing techniques won't stand still, since software developers, driven by the needs of Hollywood, are highly motivated to find new ways to twist and bend images in mind-boggling ways. Indeed, the trend even today is toward creating complex shapes using Bézier curves, which potentially represent thousands of individual correspondence points. Instead of tediously setting up points yourself, they are generated automatically from the curves and lines you draw. Elastic Reality was the first program for the PC to use this approach, as well as the first to provide professional level features. So, check out this program first if you're looking for the best morphing available on the PC.

I moved this morphing chapter to near the beginning of the book because I wanted to toss you right in and show you some of the amazing transformations you can perform with the right software. You'll enjoy creating some of these on your own with the morphing tryout packages included on the CD-ROM.

Now that you've seen what specialized applications can do, you'll appreciate even more the F/X you can create with the image editor you already own. We'll create dozens of those in the next few chapters, starting with some interesting composites (images made up of multiple images) in Chapter 5.

Compositing!

If you study vendors' ads, you'd think high-end image-editing programs are used primarily to transplant the Eiffel Tower to Sunset Boulevard. Indeed, merging two or more images seamlessly to generate a new one is one of the most powerful special F/X you can produce with your PC. Whether it's rearranging the Pyramids of Egypt, to produce a better photographic composition (as National Geographic controversially did for one of its covers), or sending Michael Jackson out for a date with Lisa Marie Presley (Oops. Stop the presses. Better make that Elvis out on a date with Loni Anderson), combining, or *compositing*, images can create new and interesting images from old ones.

Compositing also has more mundane applications that involve nothing more than blending several photos with no overt intention to deceive. In this chapter, we'll tackle something a little more realistic than moving the Eiffel Tower, but still challenging. The goal is to combine the best features of four or five flawed images to produce a postcard-quality photo that doesn't scream FAKE!—until you look at it very closely.

As you'll see, image-editing software has some powerful features that streamline the complex selection, masking, color-balancing, and drawing tasks involved in this process. Many half-hour jobs—like color correction—can be telescoped to one or two automated steps. We'll touch briefly on some techniques that are explored in more detail in later chapters, so that you can get a taste of what can be done with image editors.

And, to make the assignment interesting, I worked with *outtakes*— photos that were so dark, blurry, or otherwise defective in other ways that they never even made it into the shoebox!

First, let's look at exactly what you need to know to do effective compositing.

Basic Tools

This section will discuss the basic tools you'll use when combining images. Many of them also come into play when you're retouching photos, so the effort you spend in becoming adept at each of these will be time well spent.

Selection Tools

Manipulating portions of one or more images often involves selecting a specific section and cutting, enlarging, or pasting it in another position. The ability to grab one part of a photo accurately can be crucial. Your selection tools include:

- *Rectangular and Oval marquee tools.* These let you select portions of an image that are rectangular, square, oval, or circular. They may be the easiest tools for grabbing things like wheels, human eyes, or walls. Learn how your image editor's shape selectors work.

PHOTOSHOP

In Photoshop you can constrain either of these tools to generate perfect squares or circles by holding down the **Shift** key as you drag with the mouse. Hold down the **Alt** key, and the shape will be drawn from the center outward, rather than from the corner where you start dragging. That feature can be useful if you happen to know, or can estimate, where the center of a selection should start.

- *Lasso tool.* The Lasso lets you draw selections freehand. In Photoshop it's represented by an actual Lasso icon, with the "hot" spot being the end of the "rope." Keep the **Caps Lock** key on to turn the Lasso's cursor into a more useful cross hair.

- *Magic Wand tool.* The Magic Wand of any image editor chooses adjacent pixels that fall within a tolerance range you specify in a dialog box. (Double-click on Photoshop's Magic Wand to bring up the dialog box.) You can use this tool for selecting areas that have similar tones, such as sky or walls.

It's also important to know how to add to or subtract from your selections. Any of the tools described previously can be used to add to the current selection by holding down the **Shift** key while you specify a new portion. Hold down the **Control** key to remove portions that are already selected from the current selection.

Note that areas you add to a selection don't have to be adjacent. You could select a square area in an image, hold down the **Shift** key and select another square area elsewhere. Both would be part of the same selection.

Although the Lasso is probably the most useful tool for adding or subtracting small portions at the edges of selections, don't forget about the Magic Wand. If your selection includes most of what you want, but there is an area of consistent (or similar tones) that you want to add (or subtract), choose the Magic Wand, hold down **Shift** or **Control**, as appropriate, and then click in the other area.

Another key tool is the ability to invert a selection. You may want all of a human figure in your selection but find that it's easier to select the plain background instead. Do that and then invert the selection (in Photoshop use **Select>Inverse**). This capability is also helpful when you want to apply one filter to an area of an image and then apply a second filter to everything except the first area.

Your image editor may have additional selection parameters, such as the ability to create a fuzzy or antialiased border of pixels around your selection so you can cut and paste with a smooth transition instead of a sharp outline. Photoshop also allows you to "grow" a selection to encompass similar pixels adjacent to selected pixels or to "select similar," which expands the selection to include all pixels in an image that fall within the range of the Magic Wand's current tolerance setting. We'll use this capability later in this chapter to select all the sky pixels that show through the vanes of a windmill.

Cutting and Pasting

You also need to learn how your image editor handles cutting and pasting. Generally, you'll be most interested in ways you can modify how an image is pasted into another image. These modes include:

- Paste Into. Use to paste the Clipboard's contents into the selected area only. Portions that don't fit are obscured by the original image. We'll use this mode to paste some mountains into an empty sky area, so that the base of the mountains is obscured below the horizon.

- Past Behind. Use to paste the Clipboard's contents behind the selection.

- Paste/Composite controls. Use to specify the transparency or opacity of the selection being pasted or to control how it blends with underlying tones or colors. These are fairly advanced capabilities, but you can learn to use them as they are needed. We won't use this set of controls for the exercise in this chapter.

Selecting, cutting, and pasting encompass most of what you need to know, so if you're comfortable with these tools, let's get started.

Shoebox Rejects

You can see what we have to work with in Figure 5.1 and Color insert figure 2 in the color section. Ugh! These aren't even good snapshots! About the only thing salvageable from the photo in the upper left-hand corner is the clouds. The stone wall and sappy tourist have to go. The mountain vista at upper right isn't all bad, but it lacks an interesting focal point. All by itself, it isn't much of a photo. In the lower left-hand corner we have a photo of some interesting, craggy cliffs overlooking a dead-flat Mediterranean Sea. Then, in the lower right-hand corner there's that tourist again, this time obscuring several of the original windmills mentioned in Cervantes' classic *Don Quixote*.

Figure 5.1 *These photos are typical vacation snapshots, although they were the worst of the lot. Special F/X can combine them into a great image.*

Can we do anything with this collection of off-color, badly composed rejects from a vacation in Spain? You'll be surprised at how easy it is to fashion a silk purse when you have the right tools. Compositing actually requires some retouching skills (described in *Part III*), and the ability to cut and paste creatively. But, that's about all.

You can work along using your own image editor (I won't use any techniques that aren't widely available in the better programs). You'll need MOUNTAIN.TIF, WATER.TIF, CLOUDS.TIF, WINMIL1.TIF, WINMIL2.TIF, as shown in Figure 5.1, plus another image, CHURCH.TIF. Use your own copy of Photoshop or the tryout version on the CD-ROM bundled with this book, if you want to follow along semi-exactly.

How Green Is the Ocean?

The first step is to extract the ocean/cliffs portion of the file WATER.TIF and prepare it to accept the other elements we'll be adding. You can create a new image to contain all the images you composite or select one that has "room" for the individual pieces and add them to it. That's what I decided to do for this image. To prep WATER.TIF, follow these steps.

1. Use your image editor's Brightness/Contrast controls to add some contrast and snap to the image to make the water and cliffs stand out more sharply. Boost each of those values by around +13% for brightness and +30% for contrast, as shown in Figure 5.2.

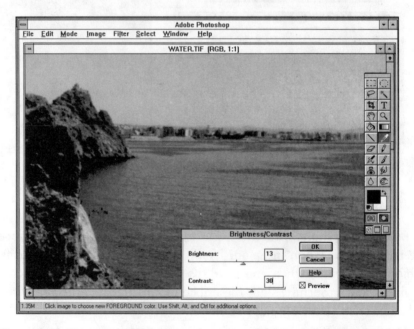

Figure 5.2 *Increase the brightness and contrast of the water and cliffs to add snap.*

2. Use your image editor's Hue/Saturation control to make the water even bluer and more saturated. With Photoshop you can try the values shown in Figure 5.3, but don't hesitate to experiment if you'd like a slightly different color scheme.

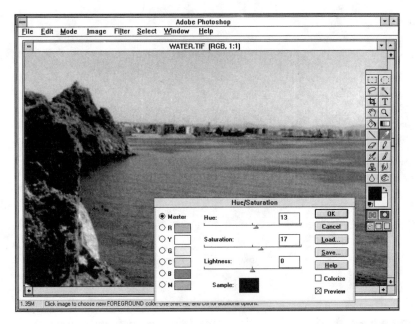

Figure 5.3 *Add a little blue to the overall hue and boost the saturation a little.*

3. Remove the sky portion of the image by selecting it and then
    choosing **Edit>Cut**. The sky is homogeneous enough in tone that
    the Magic Wand does a good job of grabbing most of it. Set your
    Magic Wand to a pixel tolerance of about 32. (In Photoshop
    double-click on the tool to bring up the dialog box.) All pixels
    falling within a color/density similarity of plus or minus 16 shades
    of the average sky tone will be selected. Add to the selection (In
    Photoshop use the Lasso and hold down **Shift** while dragging) to
    round up any loose pixels. I evened up the bottom edge of the
    selection with the Square marquee tool to provide a smooth hori-
    zon. When you've selected the entire sky, fill with white or use
    Edit>Cut to remove it. Figure 5.4 shows our image with the sky
    deleted.

Figure 5.4 *The sky has been selected and deleted, leaving only the water and cliffs.*

Making Mountains out of Foothills

Next, we need to retrieve the cloud and mountain images we want to paste into the water image. Follow these steps to collect the portions we'll be adding.

1. Load CLOUDS.TIF, and select the upper two-thirds of the picture (the part without the tourist and wall) with the Square marquee tool. Choose **Edit>Crop** to cut out everything except the selection, as shown in Figure 5.5.

2. Load MOUNTAIN.TIF. We can use a couple tricks to make this quick work. Select the sky using the Magic Wand (set tolerance for 20) and delete or cut it. Don't bother trying to remove the village below the mountains because the village will fall behind the ocean when we paste this section into the sky area of our main picture. Figure 5.6 shows what your mountains will look like when the sky has been removed.

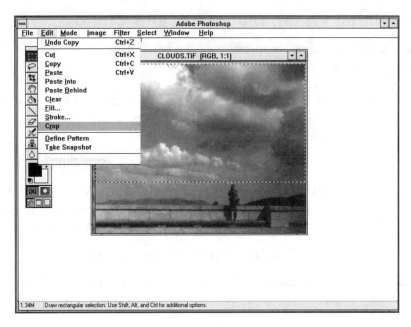

Figure 5.5 *Crop the clouds to exclude the extraneous portion of the image.*

Figure 5.6 *The sky has been removed from behind the mountains.*

Combining Water, Mountain, and Clouds

Compositing the major components of the new image is easy if you follow these steps in the proper order.

1. Use the Magic Wand to select the (empty) sky area in the Mountains image; then invert your selection so that you've chosen the mountains and village.

2. Choose **Edit>Copy** to copy the mountains to the Clipboard.

3. Switch to the water/cliffs image. Set your Magic Wand for antialiasing, if your image editor offers that feature. (In Photoshop double-click on the Magic Wand tool and check **Antialias**.)

4. Use the Magic Wand to select the (empty) sky area.

5. Choose **Edit>Paste Into**. The mountains and village will be pasted into the sky area only, behind the water and cliffs of the main image.

6. With the mountains still selected, move them so that all the village falls under the horizon. Your image should look like Figure 5.7.

Figure 5.7 *Adding mountains makes the scene look like a calm bay.*

7. Switch to the Clouds image and select all of it (in Photoshop use **Select>All**). Then, use **Edit>Copy** to copy the clouds to the Clipboard.

8. Return to the water image (which now has mountains in place) and use the Magic Wand to select the remaining sky area.

9. Choose **Edit>Past Into** once again to paste the clouds behind the mountains. You may need to resize the clouds to fill up the entire area. Use **Image>Effects>Scale** and drag the control handles horizontally to widen the cloud image. Don't worry, your "stretched" clouds will still look normal.

Your image, so far, should look like Figure 5.8.

Figure 5.8 *The scene with mountains and clouds added looks like this.*

Add a Church and a Windmill

Our photo is starting to look interesting, but there's nothing about it that says, "Spain." It wouldn't make much of a postcard as-is. Let's add a typical Spanish cathedral and a windmill to clutter it up a little. Just follow these steps.

1. Load CHURCH.TIF and outline the cathedral using the Lasso tool. Turn on antialiasing (In Photoshop double-click on the Lasso) to avoid jagged edges.

2. Invert your selection and use **Edit>Cut** to remove everything from the picture except the cathedral. Save the file under a new name (I used CHURC2.TIF) in case you need a church image for a later project.

The cathedral is shown in Figure 5.9.

Figure 5.9   *The selected cathedral is ready to copy into the main image.*

3. Switch back to the main image and choose **Paste** to insert the cathedral.

4. With the cathedral still selected, resize the image, if you like, to provide a reasonably scaled, yet impressive image. I put the cathedral right on the shore of the Mediterranean and made it somewhere between huge and massive. Figure 5.10 shows the image with the other components in place.

5. Load WINMIL1.TIF and WINMIL2.TIF. Choose the unobstructed windmill vane and tower from WINMIL2.TIF with the Lasso, and use **Edit>Copy** to copy it to the Clipboard.

6. Switch to WINMIL1.TIF and paste this section over the tourist. We've combined the horizontal view of the first image with the unobstructed windmill in the second image. Everybody's happy, except for the tourist who lost his chance at fame and recognition. Figure 5.11 shows the result.

Figure 5.10 *Now the image starts to look like an interesting scene, with mountains, clouds, and an imposing cathedral.*

Figure 5.11 *Select a portion of one photo, copy it, and paste over the tourist in the second photo.*

Now we can tackle an image editor's nightmare: How do you cut the sky out of each and every one of those little openings in the blades of the wind-mill so the new background can show through? Photoshop makes it easy.

7. Select the sky near the blade with the Magic Wand, using a Color Tolerance of around 20. Broad areas of the sky outside the wind-mill blade will be selected.

8. Choose **Select>Similar**, and Photoshop goes hunting for other simi-larly colored pixels elsewhere in the photo and adds them to the selection. When a section of sky is selected, cut it to isolate the windmill. Because blue pixels in this picture are generally found only in the sky area, you can use this technique to remove the sky neatly, without touching other pixels in the photo. You can see the progress we're making in Figure 5.12.

Figure 5.12 *Select>Similar lets you grab all the pixels in the openings of the windmill's vanes.*

9. Use the Magic Wand to select the white area that surrounds the windmill and then use **Select>Similar** one last time to choose everything in the image except the windmill. Invert your selection to choose the windmill itself and then use **Edit>Copy** to copy it to the Clipboard. The finished windmill selection looks like Figure 5.13.

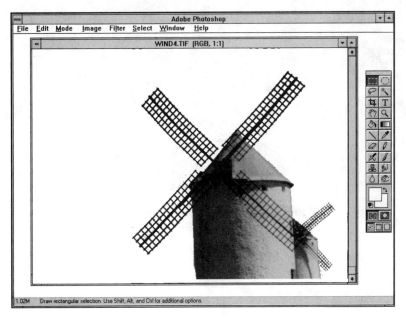

Figure 5.13 *Now the windmill is ready to be pasted into the image.*

10. Switch to the main image and choose **Edit>Paste** to position the windmill in the foreground. Notice how the background shows through the blades when we drop the windmill into the photo in Figure 5.14 and in Color insert Figure 3.

Our postcard is almost finished. However, you might want to use the Blur tool in your image editor to blend in some of the edges, such as around the windmill or the tops of the mountains. You can see how easy it was to combine four images into one that looks realistic—until you examine it very closely.

Figure 5.14 *The picture is finished...or is it?*

The Next Step

We're almost ready to practice some new skills creating special effects with retouching. But first, let's take time out for some background on image editors and their tools, which will help you choose or use your own program more effectively.

CHAPTER

SIX

Your Photocompositing Toolkit

In *Chapter 5*, I took you through a relatively simple compositing task, in which we merged images from several different photographs into one. Some of the techniques, such as retouching with the Clone or Rubber Stamp tool, will be discussed in more detail in later sections of the book. In this chapter, we'll look at some of the other tools in more detail, providing you with a foundation for going on to more complicated merged images.

Introduction to Advanced Selection and Mask Techniques

As you saw in *Chapter 5*, the ability to select a portion of an image is among the most important of all special F/X tools. Unless you can isolate one picture element and work with it separately, everything you do must apply to the image as a whole. While a few filters and other effects do look good when used to process an entire picture (as you'll learn in *Chapter 8*), merging photos, retouching, and other techniques all require exacting selection methods.

By exacting I don't mean that you must somehow select an area precisely, down to the finest pixel. I mean that the boundaries between a processed and an unprocessed area of a photo should not be apparent to the viewer. Consequently, you must give some care to how that portion is selected, manipulated, and then laid down in the final image. Your image-editing software gives you tools to create undetectable transitions between images, through blurring or, in most programs, by actually recalculating the values of the pixels at the boundaries so they combine the characteristics of old and new images smoothly. Let's look at some of the more advanced selection features you can use in your image editor.

Using Bézier Curves

Some high-end programs have Bézier curve selection tools. Don't be alarmed. Bézier curves aren't that difficult to understand; they're simply what mathematicians call cubic polynomials. In other words, they are a way of representing a curve that allows great flexibility in manipulating the curve. Bézier curves are adjusted using endpoints and anchor points. You draw a curve by placing endpoints and then adjusting the anchors, or control points, to modify the shape of the curve. Bézier curves can be used to produce highly accurate—yet smooth—selections in our drawings.

You might want to use one to isolate the curve of a sleek sportscar, if it doesn't happen to rest against a clean background that you can grab with the Magic Wand. Other curved shapes can be outlined using Bézier tools much more quickly than through freehand drawing.

Photoshop has had a Bézier selection tool since Version 2.0. Fractal Design Painter/X2 has a special Line tool in its Frisket (masking) toolkit, but it can't create smooth curves. However, Bézier selection has become such a powerful feature that if your image editor doesn't provide it now, you can expect such an enhancement in the near future. Meanwhile, if you're using Photoshop, or the tryout version of Photoshop included on the disk with this book, you can see for yourself how useful this selection tool can be.

PHOTOSHOP

Photoshop's Bézier curve tool, called the Pen, is often overlooked because Adobe moved it to the Paths palette with Version 2.5 and 3.0. There was a simple reason behind the move from the Tools palette. Using the Pen isn't complicated, but it does require some practice. Giving it a palette of its own allowed Adobe to group several related Pen functions in one place with icons of their own and not unintentionally hide them from the sight of novices. When you're ready to devote a little time to learning how the Pen works, the extra effort to make the Paths palette appear (**Window>Show Paths**) will be worth it (use **Window>Palettes>Show Paths** in Photoshop 3.0).

How Bézier Selections Work

With Photoshop and similar image editors, Bézier selections exist on a separate layer from the rest of your image. You can prove this yourself by choosing any area with a conventional selection tool and then dragging the selection. What happens? The portion of your image inside the selection is moved, leaving a blank spot (in the background color or some other hue, depending on how your preferences are set). Now, mark roughly the same area with a Bézier selection tool, grab one of the points in the shape with the Paths palette's Arrow tool, and move it. Now what happens? Only that portion of the outline, not the image within it, moves.

You can edit Bézier selections to your heart's content, move them, or save them to disk for reuse later. But to make them actually operate on your image you must convert them to conventional selections. In Photoshop that procedure involves nothing more than pressing the **Enter** key when you finish adjusting your selection.

When you create this kind of selection, you're actually creating a path of lines, defined by a series of points. That's where the first difficulty comes in for beginners, because they are accustomed to drawing continuous lines by dragging the cursor. However, as your hand wavers, so does your nice, neat line. No such problem exists when drawing Bézier curves.

Photoshop has five distinct Path tools, as shown in Figure 6.1.

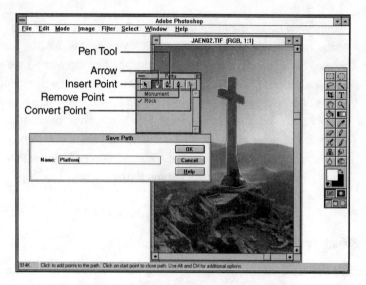

Figure 6.1 *Photoshop Paths palette.*

● *Pen tool.* Draws paths one point at a time. You can select any complex shape by clicking repeatedly along the path that represents the outline of that shape.

● *Arrow tool.* Used to drag the points and control handles on the path to change its shape.

● *Insert Point tool.* Adds new points to an existing path.

● *Remove Point tool.* Deletes a point but does not create a break in the path.

● *Convert Point tool.* Changes an existing point to a corner point (one between two straight segments) or smooth point (one that connects two curved segments in a continuous arc).

N O T E

Because Photoshop can convert a selection to a line using the **Edit>Stroke** command, the Pen tool can be used to draw new lines on your image, too.

Reusing Selections

The ability to reuse selections is an important capability, especially when you must change images, or you wish to perform multiple operations on a particular portion of the image at different times. Most high-end image editors let you save selections and apply either an identifying number or a name you specify to each selection. Indeed, Fractal Design Painter/X2 lets you store selections in one or more libraries that can be accessed and used in any image and load Encapsulated PostScript (EPS) files as selections. Figure 6.2 shows a typical library of friskets.

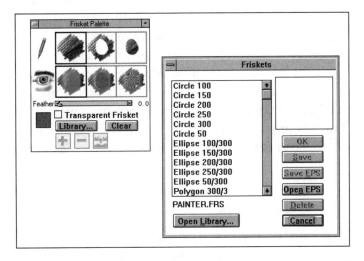

Figure 6.2   *Fractal Design Painter/X2 stores friskets, or masks, in a library.*

The selection information is stored with the image, too, although you may need to use the image editor's proprietary file format to do this. Photoshop can save selections using either Adobe's PSD format or TIFF, but other programs may not be able to load TIFF files that have embedded selection information (called alpha channels).

Selections that have been saved and are available for reuse are usually called *masks* or *friskets*. If they can "float" above other portions of the image and be manipulated without affecting the rest of the image, such selections are said to be layered. Like many tools found in image editors, these terms came from the manual methods used by artists for decades or centuries before the advent of the computer.

Masks or friskets were originally nothing more than sheets of celluloid that were cut out with a sharp knife to isolate a portion of the image. Masks can also be created photographically. If your image editor has an unsharp masking option, it comes from the technique of producing a slightly out-of-focus photographic image of an image (or portion of an image). Some masks are produced on a sheet of red film called Rubylith, which may resemble the mask layer in editors like Photoshop.

Another way to reuse selections is simply to allow multiple "live" selections in a single document. Picture Publisher and Fractal Design Painter/X2 (the version with the optional X2 extensions) can do this. You may operate on each selection independently, so that it's possible to perform an operation on one portion of an image, select another area and work with that, and then return to the other selection. In contrast, Photoshop 2.5 and 3.0 lets you create multiple, unconnected selections in an image, but they are really all part of the same selection. You need to use Photoshop 3.0's layer features to truly have multiple selections in a single image.

Softening Selections

Feathering or antialiasing are ways of avoiding the sharp edges that would appear if we selected with a hard-edged tool like the Lasso. *Antialiasing* recalculates the edges of the selection to reduce the jagged edges, while *feathering* gradually changes the opacity of the pixels at the edge of the selection using a radius you specify, so that the selection fades out. Your image editor may allow you to change a selection to a feathered selection after it has already been created.

Like masks, feathering, too, has its beginnings with manual techniques. Airbrush artists originally feathered friskets by raising it slightly to allow the stream of paint to spray slightly beyond the limits of the mask. In the digital world, feathering is a good tool for pasting a selection into an image seamlessly. Figure 6.3 shows an image selection being feathered.

Figure 6.3 *An image selection can be feathered seamlessly.*

Other Selection Variations

Each new image editor on the market refines the capabilities of its selection tools. Fractal Design Painter/X2 lets you send floating selections to the back, bring them to the front, or move them forward or backward layer by layer. They can be grouped, turning several selections into a single selection, or ungrouped. You may also be able to grow a selection (add adjacent pixels within the current magic wand tolerance value) or add similar pixels (anywhere in the drawing that fall within the tolerance range) with your image editor.

Controlling the Composite

I kept the examples in *Chapter 5* simple, because I wanted to show how sophisticated compositing can be done without first learning much beyond the basic features of your image editor. However, as you begin producing more advanced composites, you'll want to gain greater control over how multiple images are merged.

You are given a variety of tools for this task with your image editor. Fractal Design Painter/X2, for example, lets you fade the last operation you applied. You could select a portion of an image, paste, drop the selection (X2 selections float above the image until you specifically drop them in), and then fade the selection using a slider control and preview thumbnail (as shown in Figure 6.4).

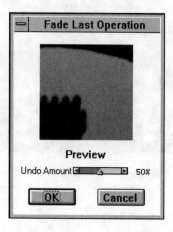

Figure 6.4 *Fractal Design Painter/X2 lets you fade selections seamlessly.*

Most image editors, including Photoshop, have similar tools to modify how selections are pasted into the image. In Photoshop use the Edit>Composite Controls dialog box, shown in Figure 6.5.

The Composite Controls dialog box has six different types of options you can call on.

- *Blend If.* Lets you choose whether a specific range of colors or gray tones should be excluded from the selection or the original portion of the image after the paste operation is completed. Colors that are excluded disappear from the finished composite. The actual amount of tone removed is determined by the two sliders below. This option specifies whether the tone shall be in the red, green, or blue channels alone or be removed from all channels equally (gray).

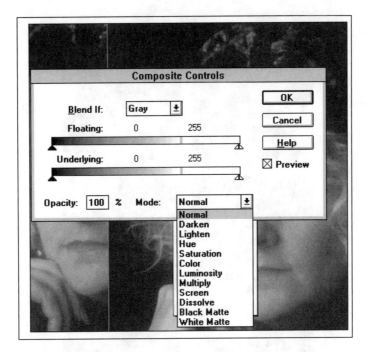

Figure 6.5 *Photoshop's Composite Controls dialog box.*

- *Floating.* Specifies removal of tones from the selection being pasted.

- *Underlying.* Specifies removal of tones from the original image.

- *Preview.* Applies the effects you're specifying to the image immediately. Click on **OK** and they will become permanent (subject to Undo, of course). Click on **Cancel** to negate the effects of the Composite Controls dialog box and remove it from the screen.

- *Opacity.* The amount of translucency of the selection being pasted.

- *Mode.* Provides a drop-down list of 12 overlay modes that govern how Photoshop calculates the merger of the selection and the original image. These modes are the same used for brushes, the Rubber Stamp, and other tools. Figure 6.6 shows an image composited using several of these options.

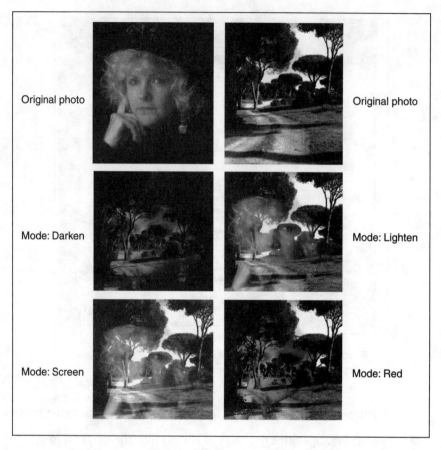

Figure 6.6 *Compositing using different modes produces these effects.*

The mode options include:

- *Normal.* Each pixel is applied just as it was originally, except for other effects (such as Opacity or Blend If) that might have been specified.

- *Darken.* Pixels in the selection are applied only if they are darker than the pixel in the underlying image. When used with color images, the color balance can change.

- *Lighten.* Pixels in the selection are applied only if they are lighter than the corresponding underlying pixel. When used with color images, the color balance can change.

- *Hue.* The hue values of the selection are used with the saturation and luminosity values of the underlying image. We've gotten a bit ahead of ourselves here: Chapter 12 explains the Hue-Saturation-Lightness color model. This option has no visible effect on gray-scale images.

- *Saturation.* Similar to the Hue option, except that Photoshop uses the saturation value of the selection and applies it to the hue and lightness values of the original image.

- *Color.* Uses both hue and saturation values of the selection, retaining the luminosity value of the underlying image.

- *Luminosity.* Applies the luminosity values of the selection to the hue and saturation values of the original image.

- *Multiply.* Mixes the colors of the selection and original image, producing a darker image with the combined values of both. The Photoshop manual compares this effect to superimposing two color transparencies on a light table; I think the analogy is a good one. Visualize two color slides and the areas that overlap: a medium blue and a medium red pixel would produce a darker magenta pixel.

- *Screen.* Subtracts the colors of the selection and original image, producing a lighter image. Again, the Photoshop manual comes up with a good analogy: superimposing two negatives and then printing them onto photographic paper. A medium blue and a medium red pixel would produce a darker magenta pixel—in the combined negatives—and print as a lighter, green tone (the opposite of magenta) when reversed as a photographic print.

- *Dissolve.* Atomizes the pixels in the feathered edges of the selection, producing an interesting edge effect.

- *Black Matte/White Matte.* Feathered selections dropped into a black or white background produce a feathered edge of the opposite color of the background. The Black Matte/White Matte options eliminate this objectionable transition.

The Next Step

In this chapter, you learned that morphing and photocompositing—warping, combining, or merging two or more images—can be done fairly simply realistically, without delving deeply into highly technical imaging techniques. This chapter also introduced you to some of the more advanced tools you can use to produce even better effects now that you've mastered the basics.

Now, it's time to go on and explore another way of modifying photos and creating special F/X: retouching. You'll discover how tools like the Rubber Stamp or Clone tool can remove or change defects in an image as well as ways in which filters can add interesting details. You'll find all that in Part III.

PART III

Photo Retouching

Every picture tells a story, but even the best stories can benefit from a little editing. One of the many differences between very good amateur pictures and most of the professional photographs you see published is that the pro image probably had some retouching done sometime during the production process. Subtle tweaking here and there can make dramatic improvements.

This sections shows you how easy digital retouching can be, and reveals a few simple techniques that you can use to transform sound, but imperfect, images into prize-winners. The emphasis here is on improving the appearance of color or grayscale images with F/X that the photographer forgot to use, or was unable to apply at the time.

Choosing and Using Tools for Retouching

Photography has always been part craft, part science, and part fine art, with a little alchemy and magic mixed in. Many photographers in the mid-1800s were skilled woodworkers and machinists who built their own cameras and then mixed chemicals to sensitize photographic plates. The highly creative images that were exposed during this era are a tribute to the versatility of these early artisan-artists.

Digital imaging cranks up the science component several notches, giving the artist in all of us more powerful brushes and an infinite palette of colors, tools, and effects. Retouching is one area that has seen the most dramatic changes wrought by computerized image-editing software. A necessary evil anytime photographic images are used in desktop publications, presentations, or other work, retouching is usually poorly understood and imperfectly implemented. We'll change all that.

The goal of simple retouching is to remove defects from a photograph. Of course, a defect is often in the eye of the beholder (if not in the bags underneath). A high school senior portrait (male or female) showing less than silky-smooth skin is sometimes viewed as a disaster by those who have just transversed the rocky roads of puberty. On the other hand, removing the character lines from the face of a 60-year-old corporate chief executive would provoke outrage. Emphasizing that steely glint in the eye may be much more important.

In advertising photography, The Product must be presented just so, and if 20 hours of retouching is required to achieve the desired effect, so be it. Because reshooting the entire photo series may be prohibitively expensive (thousands of dollars in location shooting, props, models, stylists may be involved), it may be much cheaper to pour more bucks into retouching an original transparency.

In either case, the defects removed by retouching may, in fact, be minor. In the old days (less than a decade ago), nearly all retouching was done using the photographic media—negative, slide, or print. Skilled retouchers can use special dyes to smooth out the smiling faces of high school seniors right on the color negative film. Extensive work can be performed on medium- to large-format color transparencies (4 × 5- to 8 × 10-inches or larger). Frequently, color or black-and-white prints are almost good enough to use but will have a few white spots caused by dust on the negative. A few minutes with a spotting brush can clean them up nicely.

The retouching you see (or don't see) in those cover photos in supermarket tabloids (you know, the one with the Iowa farmer wrestling a 60-pound grasshopper to the ground) often combine composite photographic techniques like those discussed in the last section of this book with airbrush retouching—in effect, painting on a print.

Any of these techniques can be duplicated—and surpassed—digitally. This chapter will show you what your tool options are and how to apply them to improve your own photographic images.

Retouching a Portrait

The easiest way to show you simple retouching techniques is to actually fix up a photo. You can use the Adobe Photoshop tryout version included on the CD-ROM bundled with this book or work with your own image editor. All the methods I'll be using have equivalents with every image editor on the market.

For this first exercise, we'll work with a portrait, because we're inherently more fussy about portrayals of human beings, particularly faces. An unfortunate shadow on a picture of a tree may be unnoticed or ignored, but a shadow can convert a serious portrait into an unintended rendition of Pinocchio. You'll find that much of the photo retouching you do will involve making people look more like themselves, or more as they would like to look. The original file I used and the final retouched image are included on the CD-ROM in the Chapter 7 folder as CATHYRT1.TIF and CATHYRT2.TIF.

Both pictures are shown in Figure 7.1, so that you can compare them and easily see the changes I made. Not all the defects will survive the halftoning process, so you can view the file used to print this illustration from the CD-ROM, if you like.

What Can Go Wrong?

You never really believe a picture is worth 1000 words until somebody starts critiquing one of your beloved photos. We could easily take 1000 words to describe the minor problems with the original photo—so let's do so. Maybe we can learn something about the common defects you're likely to find in a photoimage. I'll list them in order of frequency and importance.

Dust Spots

The most common defect you'll encounter in an original will be dust spots, especially when the photo was made from a 35mm negative or slide original. Because 35mm film must be enlarged at least four times from its tiny 1×1.5-inch (24×36 mm) size (to 4 x 6 inches or larger), any dust present is enlarged, too. It's difficult to keep a negative or slide 100% spotless, so your prints (and reprints, especially) are likely to have at least a couple of these little devils.

Dust on color or black-and-white negatives will manifest itself as white spots on the print. Dust that resides on a color slide will appear to be black when the transparency is viewed or printed. It's well known that there are two colors of dust—white dust, which settles on dark-colored automobiles, and black dust, which is attracted to white or light-colored automobiles.

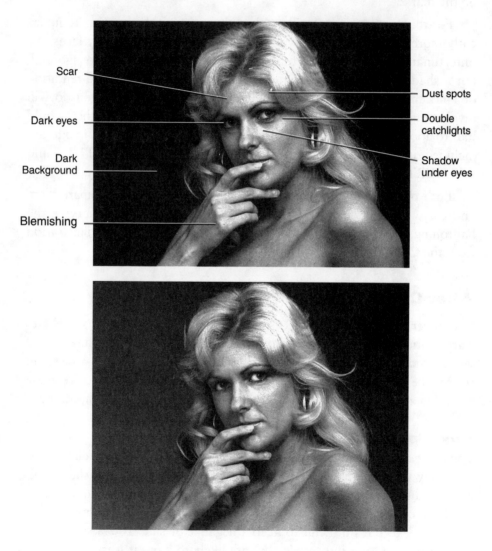

Scar

Dark eyes

Dark
Background

Blemishing

Dust spots

Double
catchlights

Shadow
under eyes

Figure 7.1 *The original image and retouched version.*

Actually, both kinds of dust are the same; the material on negatives is reversed from black to white, just like the rest of the image, when the negative is printed. If you happen to notice black specks on a print made from a negative or white (or, more often, colored) specks on a print made from a transparency, you probably have a defect in one (or more) of the film's emulsion layers, which make up the image.

White or black, these specks are easy to fix. Our sample portrait is peppered with them, including several humongous spots that have germinated on their way to becoming dust bunnies. We'll remove these later.

Scars, Skin Blemishes

A little before most of us are able to sit up unaided, our skin loses its perfect complexion. We're usually able to live with these small defects in real life, but we don't want to be reminded of them in our portraits. Although a few celebrities like Madonna, Cindy Crawford, and Mikhail Gorbachev have converted minor characteristics into trademark features, you'll want the option to remove them if you or the subject deems it desirable.

We'll remove one forehead scar and a few skin blemishes from the portrait. I left a few in the final image to work on if you need more practice.

Technical Stuff

There are several kinds of defects that only photographers know about but that are important nevertheless (that's why they're pros: they know this secret stuff).

For example, whether you're conscious of it or not, you're acutely aware of those little reflections—called *catchlights*—that appear in the eyes of every portrait subject who is looking at the camera. When a catchlight is present, the subject's eyes look lively and alert. If no catchlight is found, the eyes look dead and dull.

If you don't believe me, open up a copy of *Time* or *People Magazine*, find a few photos of famous people you hate, and color in all the catchlights with a marking pen. Notice the difference? With a stroke of a pen you can convert a fiery politician into a sedated serial killer. This is much more subtle and devious than blacking out a few teeth or drawing a mustache (plus it works with males and females alike).

To produce the desired favorable effect, catchlights must be clean and visible, appropriately positioned (not on opposite sides of the pupil, for example), and not oddly shaped. Because they are often reflections of windows, square or roundish catchlights are best. Often, you'll see hexagon-shaped catchlights representing the photographer's umbrellas; that's distracting—unless you're doing a photo story about a model or actor.

Double catchlights, which are reflections from two different light sources, are also a no-no. Our sample picture suffers from these, and the solution will be to simply blacken or remove the extra reflection in each eye.

Another technical defect with our sample photo is a background that is too dark for the final image. The blonde subject in front of a black, seamless background is a bit too contrasty for my taste. In the final image, I substituted a medium gray to dark gray diagonal gradient, which starts in the lower left-hand corner of the image and fades out to almost black in the upper right-hand corner. The effect is very similar to what would have been achieved if I feathered a background light on the seamless backdrop at the original photo session.

If you'll compare the original image with the retouched version, you'll see that softening the background from stark black reduces the apparent contrast of the whole picture, even though I didn't touch the brightness/contrast controls.

Dark Shadows

Our model didn't really have bags under her eyes, but the way the shadows fell made it appear so. In addition, the lighting darkened the white part of the eye (the sclera) so it appears gray rather than white in the original photo.

We can lighten these shadows easily so that the eyes show up better and more attractively in the final version. You can use the same techniques to improve the appearance of subjects who have "sunken" or bloodshot eyes. We'll need to use restraint, however: eyes, nose, and mouth are the features we use most to identify other humans. They must be represented accurately or the portrait won't look "right."

The simple lighten/darken techniques you'll learn in this chapter can be applied to other image-retouching tasks, too.

Starting on our Portrait

If you're working along, copy the CATHYRT01.TIF file from the CD-ROM onto your hard disk (so that you can save your changes) and load it into your image-editing software (Photoshop, Picture Publisher, or whatever). The tryout version of Photoshop will let you follow along exactly, if that's important to you.

We're going to correct the problems identified by the callouts in Figure 7.1, one at a time, starting with the dust spots, blemishes, and facial scar. All of these problems can be quickly removed using your image editor's Rubber Stamp or Clone tool.

What's the Rubber Stamp/Clone Tool?

The Clone tool, usually represented by a Rubber Stamp icon, duplicates part of an image, pixel by pixel, in a location of your choice. The stamp analogy isn't very good, however, because you actually draw with a brush that you can size and control in other ways allowed by your image editor (e.g., transparency of the image laid down or some other behavior).

Cloning can be used to copy portions of an image to another location in the same or a different image. If your desert scene is too sparse for you, a single cactus can be multiplied several times or even copied from a different desert altogether. You may add a window to the side of a building by "painting" one from another building using the Clone tool.

Your cloning brush will have several optional modes, depending on which image editor you use. A key parameter you can set is how the tool applies tones from the point of origin to the destination point. I'll use Photoshop terminology to describe these differences, but your own image editor should have an equivalent of its own.

● *Clone (aligned).* Once you determine the origin point, the Clone tool maintains a fixed spatial relationship between it and the destination portion of the image, no matter how many times you apply the brush. This feature is easier to visualize if you examine Figure 7.2.

Figure 7.2 *Cloned image aligned with the original.*

For the picture in Figure 7.2, I wanted to clone the round window near the top center of this section of the photo into an empty space in the wall below. I set the point of origin at the top upper edge of the original window (in Photoshop press Alt-Click with the Clone tool selected). The first place I clicked with the mouse after that was painted over with the pixels from that point of origin. Any additional brushing applies more pixels copied using a fixed spatial relationship. That is, if I moved the tool over an inch to the right and started painting again, I'd apply pixels copied from an area an inch to the right of the point of origin.

Cloning an aligned image makes it easy to duplicate objects from one portion of an image (or from a different image), because you can use multiple brush-strokes to copy the same object. If you make a mistake, just select Undo and reapply only the most recent strokes.

● *Clone (unaligned).* In this mode, after you set the point of origin, each new click somewhere else in your image starts painting with pixels from that point, until you release the mouse button. Use this option to apply a pattern to an image, rather than to copy an object in multiple strokes.

● *Clone (from saved).* This mode can save your neck when you discover you've cloned too much of an image or have made any other sort of error that needs correction. The point of origin is automatically set to the equivalent pixel position in the last saved copy of the file, so, in effect, you can paint over a changed portion of the image with the original version. Use this option when you have done considerable work on a file since you saved it and only want to cancel out some of the changes you made. The so-called Magic Eraser (in Photoshop hold down the Alt key while using the eraser) can also change portions of an image back to its previous state, albeit not with the flexible brush sizes and effects of the Clone tool.

Some image editors clone portions of an image as they were when you started the process. If you start to copy an area that has been modified by cloning, you'll apply the original pixels, not the changed ones. That feature helps avoid repeating patterns that result when you clone a clone. If your program doesn't operate in this way (Photoshop, for example), create a duplicate of your original image and clone from that to avoid the problem.

If you're simply retouching a photo with no intent to add or subtract anything other than the defects, the Cone tool is useful for copying portions of an image over the parts you want to replace. In the next section, we'll copy skin tones from good portions of our image over dust spots and other artifacts.

Canceling Dust Spots

Let's erase Moby Dust Spot and some of his friends from CATHYRT01.TIF. Just follow these steps.

1. Zoom in to a magnification that will let you work comfortably with a portion of the image. I recommend a 4× zoom ratio.

2. Choose your image editor's Rubber Stamp or Clone tool. Set the tool to copy from a fixed place in the current image. (In Photoshop double-click on the tool and make sure the Clone (aligned) option is set). Choose the smallest brush size and set the opacity (or transparency) of your clone brush to 100%, as shown in Figure 7.3.

Photoshop users will also want to depress the **Caps Lock** key to get rid of the ridiculous Rubber Stamp cursor and replace it with a more useful plain cross hair.

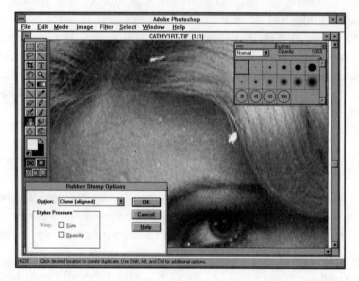

Figure 7.3 *Set the Rubber Stamp to Clone (aligned) and choose a small brush size.*

3. Place the cursor near a portion of the image having similar tones to a dust spot or other area you want to cover up and set that as the area to copy from. (With Photoshop hold down the **Alt** key and click the mouse button.)

4. Now, click on the dust spot area. Work inward from the edges, changing only a pixel or two at a time. Change the point of origin for the cloning from time to time as required to maintain a good match of tones.

5. Repeat Steps 3 and 4 for each spot, blemish, scar, or other area you want to cover up.

6. Remove the extra catchlight in each eye using the same cloning method.

When you're finished, the image should look like the area shown in Figure 7.4.

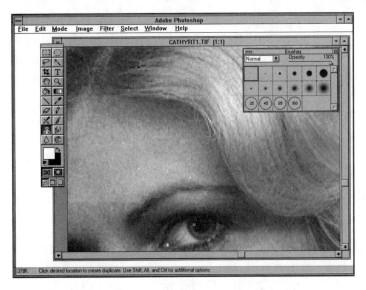

Figure 7.4 *The dust spots, double catchlights in the eye, scar, and other defects have been removed.*

Dodging Shadows

When color or black-and-white prints are made by exposing photosensitive paper under an enlarger, the darkroom worker can modify how the image appears. That's done by giving extra exposure to some areas of the print, and holding back other areas so that they aren't exposed as long.

The image is visible in negative form on the paper as the exposure is made, so that the process is relatively simple. An area, such as a shadow, that would appear too dark on the finished print can be made lighter by inserting an object between the lens and the paper. This casts a shadow, which prevents that portion of the image from being exposed for the full length of time. A portion of the image that has been *dodged* in this way will appear lighter than if the entire image were exposed evenly.

Sometimes, the darkroom worker will use a hand to obscure large areas of the image, but more frequently a dodging tool is used. Often handmade from coat-hanger wire and a piece of cardboard, the dodging tool looks something like an all-day sucker (but can actually take any shape). The tool is waved around over the area being dodged, so that the handle doesn't show up and the edges of the dodging effect are feathered.

The opposite procedure, called *burning*, is also used to give additional exposure only to areas of the image that need it, such as highlights that would appear too light or burned out in the final print. The most common tool for this effect isa pair of hands: a roundish opening between them can be varied in size to burn more or less of the image, as desired.

Our portrait needs some judicious dodging to lighten some shadows under and above the eyes of the subject. We can also use dodging to create larger, lighter catchlights in the eyes and to brighten up the white part of the eye. As you see, dodging is a versatile tool, indeed.

To dodge our picture, just follow these steps.

1. Select your image editor's Dodge or Lighten tool. (In Photoshop it resembles the darkroom worker's all-day sucker and shares a palette button with the Burn tool, represented by a cupped hand icon.) Double-click the Dodge or Burn tool (whichever is active in your palette) and, in the Options dialog box, change to Dodge (if necessary). Figure 7.5 shows Photoshop's version of the dialog box.

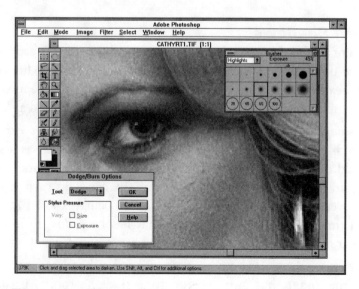

Figure 7.5 *Choose the Dodge tool to lighten an area of an image.*

2. For the first modification, choose the smallest brush size (usually one or two pixels in width) and set Exposure to 50%. The Exposure parameter controls how much the Dodge tool will lighten an area with each application.

3. To dodge the remaining catchlight in each eye; click on the catchlight and, holding down the mouse button, drag to lighten that area of the pupil. Repeat for the other eye.

4. Select a slightly larger brush size (four to six pixels), one with a feathered edge if your image editor offers it. We want to affect a broader portion of the image for the next step to produce a subtler effect. Drop the exposure down to 15%.

5. Use the Dodge tool to lighten the white part of both eyes so that the blood vessels and dark shadows are no longer visible. Try not to remove all the tone and details from those areas. Because the exposure has been reduced, you may have to go over an area two or three times to produce the desired effect.

6. Select an even larger brush size (one about the size of the pupil in our model's eye) and use it to remove the shadows under her eyes and beneath the eyebrows. Don't go overboard: dodge a little at a time using broad strokes. Stop and look at your results and then apply more lightening until the image looks good.

Most image editors let you open a second view of the same image, through a New Window or New File command. Select a 1:1 magnification ratio for one version; then zoom in to 4:1 or larger in the second window. Any F/X you make in the close-up view will be immediately reflected in the full versions. It's an easy way to check your work as you go.

Figure 7.6 shows the finished portion of the image after dodging has been applied.

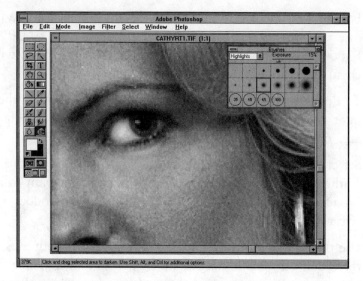

Figure 7.6 *Dodging lightens portions of an image selectively.*

Making the Gradient

The next thing to fix is that atrocious black background. I actually used a cheap black velveteen fabric for this photo, because it really sucks up all the light. This background is truly black. However, it's a little stark and not at all warm. We can replace it with a gradient that almost duplicates the effect you would get if a background light were used at the original photo session. Just follow these steps.

1. Select only the background. Because it's mostly an even black, that won't be much of a problem. Use the Magic Wand tool and change its tolerance to a fairly low number—two or three should suffice. (In Photoshop double-click on the Magic Wand tool to invoke the dialog box you can use to set that option.) Select **Antia**lias to create a soft edge around the subject if your image editor offers that. Click in the right side background to select that entire area and then repeat to select the left side background.

2. The tolerance level we selected probably won't grab the dust spots that appear in the background. Add to the selection to encompass

them as well. (With Photoshop hold down the Shift key and drag around the extra areas with the Lasso tool.)

PHOTOSHOP

Remember that, in Photoshop, you can more easily see what areas are selected by clicking on the QuickMask icon (see Figure 7.7). The nonselected area is shown in a contrasting color (red or another of your choice). You can add to the selected area by erasing portions overlaid with red or subtract from the selection by adding additional red tone with a brush. When you are finished, click on the Normal mode box to change the mask back into a selection.

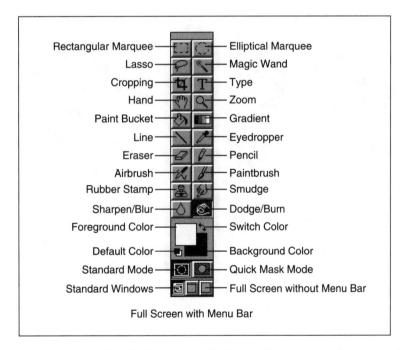

Rectangular Marquee — Elliptical Marquee
Lasso — Magic Wand
Cropping — Type
Hand — Zoom
Paint Bucket — Gradient
Line — Eyedropper
Eraser — Pencil
Airbrush — Paintbrush
Rubber Stamp — Smudge
Sharpen/Blur — Dodge/Burn
Foreground Color — Switch Color
Default Color — Background Color
Standard Mode — Quick Mask Mode
Standard Windows — Full Screen without Menu Bar
Full Screen with Menu Bar

Figure 7.7 *QuickMasks let you see which area of an image has been selected.*

3. Select the Gradient tool. (See Figure 7.7 for the Photoshop version; all other image editors have their own.) Gradients provide a continuous blend of tones from the foreground color to the

background color. This is much the same effect you get when a light is feathered onto a background—brighter in one area and then gradually dropping off to a darker tone.

4. Because we want our gradient to be fairly subtle, choose a medium- to dark-gray foreground color and a background color that is a lighter medium gray.

5. Photoshop users should change the Midpoint Skew value to 80%. That will weight the gradient heavily toward the foreground color. When the midpoint is set at 50%, the foreground and background tones will "meet" halfway through the gradient. Photoshop's Gradient Tool Options dialog box is shown in Figure 7.8.

Figure 7.8 *Gradient tool options let you control how the blend is applied.*

6. Apply the gradient by placing the cursor in the upper left-hand corner of the selected area and dragging down to the lower right-hand corner. Note that a gradient can easily span two or more independent selected areas. The image editor treats them all as if they were one continuous area.

The final results are shown in Figure 7.9. The gradient doesn't show well in the halftone, so you can load the actual finished file CATHYRT02.TIF to view the result.

Figure 7.9 *Finished photo with gradient applied.*

Major Surgery

Many of the photographs you'll need to retouch won't be in as "good" shape as the one we worked on in the first part of this chapter. Frequently, you'll be asked to salvage a real dog of a photo that absolutely must be resurrected from snapshot hell for one reason or another. Perhaps it's the only picture available of someone (or something), or it has some importance for historic reasons.

For example, while still in high school I started my photographic career photographing local bands for sale to the groups themselves and a regional newspaper. A classmate of mine organized a band called The Measles and recruited a Cleveland guitar player named Joe Walsh, who ended up attending Kent State University as I did and who went on to fame with the Eagles and as a solo act. I also photographed a fellow named Jerry Casale, singer in an art-rock band that preceded his spud-boy career with Devo. Eventhough the pictures weren't all that good (see Figure 7.10), they have sentimental value. (I don't know what The Measles' drummer, Buddy, is doing today, but according to my records, he purchased one 8 × 10 and eight wallet-size photos of himself playing with Joe Walsh!)

Figure 7.10 *Thanks to the magic of direct flash, Jerry Casale of Devo (lower right) and Joe Walsh of the Eagles (upper left, at right) were captured early in their musical careers.*

You may find yourself in the same situation, performing major surgery on photos in one of these categories.

- *Photorestorations.* Pictures from 20 to 150 years old may have been damaged by the ravages of time, and you'll need to remove scratches, replace missing sections of the photo, and perhaps reconstruct facial features from the fragments that remain.

- *Photo travesties.* These snapshots have major digressions from the desired content. That is, there's a tree growing from someone's head, an unwanted bystander gawking at the main subject, or other pictorial clutter. Your job will be to remove these elements.

- *Major facial surgery.* Your subject is wearing glasses in the photo, but switched to contacts years ago. An unfortunate accident of lighting accentuated slightly protuberant ears, transforming them from an interesting characteristic to features that would make Dumbo blush. Bad shadows have given someone a double chin. They don't really look like this photo—can you improve it?

I let you work on a fairly decent photograph at the beginning of this chapter. Let's tackle a real disaster next to see what we can do.

Redesigning a Snapshot

We'll work with a basic, unadulterated snapshot, shown in Figure 7.11 and in Color insert Figure 4. It's one of those direct-flash pictures from a point-and-shoot camera and features the traditional two-finger salute behind the head that originated in a high school class painting during Roman times. Our subject-victim is wearing a black nylon jacket that has faded into the murky background. Can we do anything with this shot?

Follow along as I outline the surgical procedures used to improve this picture. The description in this section is not a true step-by-step exercise, because so many different things must be done to the picture. You probably wouldn't want to spend two hours retouching this picture, in any case. Instead, I'll provide an overview, and you can use the techniques described to retouch a photo of your own that has similar problems. If you like, you can also work on the same original I did, stored on the CD-ROM as SNPSHOT1.TIF.

Figure 7.11 *This unaltered picture needs a lot of work.*

Coat of any Colors

Our first task will be to make that jacket a little more distinctive—and visible—with a quick digital bleach and dye job. I followed these steps.

1. Select the jacket using your favorite method with your image editor. I used Photoshop's Quick Mask mode to let me "paint" a mask over everything in the picture that wasn't the jacket. It's easier than constantly selecting and deselecting portions, and the contrasting color of the mask and remaining image make it easy to outline the exact portions you want. When finished, resume Normal mode and

save the selection as a layer. Figure 7.12 shows the photo with the jacket isolated by a mask.

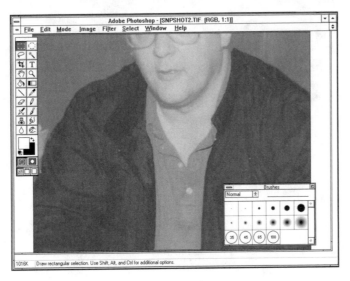

Figure 7.12 *A selection mask isolates the jacket from the rest of the photograph.*

2. Use the Brightness/Contrast controls to increase the brightness of the jacket, so it isn't inky black; then modify contrast so the texture shows.

3. With the jacket still selected, select your image editor's Hue/Saturation control and modify the color. I selected a yellow-green that is compatible with the shirt. Figure 7.13 illustrates the improvements so far.

4. Select the background of the photo (Inverse Selection is a good place to start); then remove the face from the selection as well, leaving just the background.

5. Fill the background with a solid color (I used green again) and modulate it by adding some noise (in Photoshop, use **Filter>Noise>Add Noise**). You'll replace the distracting background with a solid, grainy one that is less obtrusive. Figure 7.14 shows the image with the new background.

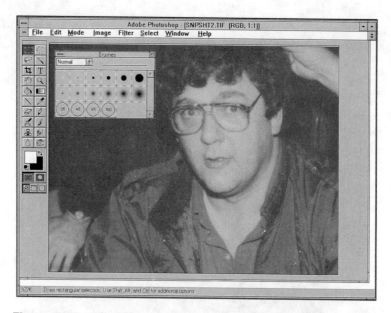

Figure 7.13 *The jacket has been lightened and changed to a green color.*

Figure 7.14 *The old background has been replaced with a green grainy pattern.*

I could have dropped in an entirely new background if, as you learned how to do in *Chapter 5*. However, this chapter is concentrating on retouching, so I just worked with the image I had available.

Some Serious Work

Now, let's try something very tricky—removing our subject's glasses, using nothing more than retouching techniques. There will be no compositing in new images from another photo. We'll retouch the picture using the Clone tool to replace the glasses with surrounding skin tones. Just follow these steps.

1. Using the Clone tool, copy areas of the cheek over the rims of the glasses. Set new origin points constantly to maintain a good match of skin tones. For example, the rims of the glasses at the left side of the photo can be replaced by the cheek edge immediately below. In Figure 7.15 I replaced part of the lower rim of the glasses at the right side with surrounding cheek tones.

Figure 7.15 *Replace the glasses with portions of surrounding skin tones, using the Clone tool.*

2. The portion of the eye on the right side that's obscured by the glasses is more tricky. Clone portions of the other eye, as shown in Figure 7.16, to provide the missing portions.

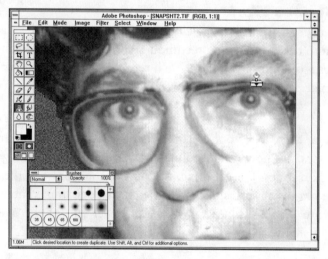

Figure 7.16 *Use portions of the eye on the left to replace missing parts of the eye on the right.*

3. We did a few more subtle things to the photo. Because of the direct flash, the catchlights, as they were, ended up in the pupils of the eye rather than the iris. Often, this produces the undesirable "red eye" effect you often see. Fill in the catch lights with the Burn tool and then used the Dodge tool to create new catchlights at the 11 o'clock position of each iris.

4. Use the Blur tools to smooth rough edges around the eyes where the skin tones don't match exactly and then follow up with some dodging and burning to match skin tones around the face. The semifinal image is shown in Figure 7.17.

5. Clone portions of the desktop to cover up the potato chip bag at the far right and use the Burn tool to darken the edges and corners of the photo. Professional photographers call these burned in corners. Figure 7.18 shows the original photo and the almost-finished picture. You can compare the two in full color in Color insert Figure 4, or in the original file, which is included on the CD-ROM.

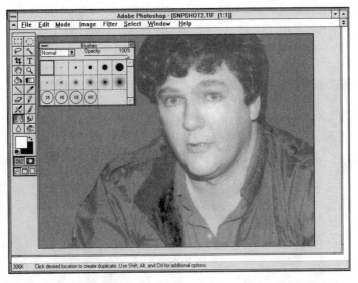

Figure 7.17   *New catchlights in the eyes and some minor adjustments produced this image.*

Figure 7.18   *With cloned desktop and burned corners, the photo is almost finished.*

A New Background

After all that work, I still didn't care for the background, so I decided to replace it with a new one. I loaded the Green Adobe Wall texture file from the Textures folder on the CD-ROM, set the Clone tool for Clone (align), and then painted in the new texture as a replacement background. The final results are shown in Figure 7.19 and Color insert Figure 4.

Figure 7.19 *A new textured background has been cloned into the photograph.*

As you can see, the differences between the first and last version of this photo are significant. You can easily accomplish similar miracles with your own photos, using only the basic retouching tools discussed in this chapter.

The Next Step

This chapter introduced you to using basic image-editing tools for retouching. You can see how the Clone tool can be used in a variety of ways to modify images. This chapter concentrated on human faces because they will be your most common retouching subject. However, you can also use the same techniques to remove objects from scenic photographs or to duplicate windows, street lamps, or even mountains.

Now we'll explore some of the retouching F/X you can achieve using filters, which are plug-in miniprograms that can be used with Photoshop, Canvas, Fractal Design Painter, and other image-editing software.

CHAPTER

EIGHT

Saving Your Bacon with Filters

Outside the computer world, filters are relatively simple. They process things like air, water, motor oil, drip coffee, or smoke, letting the good stuff through while leaving bad things behind for collection or disposal. The only parameters you have to worry about are the size of the openings in the filter (which helps determine what can pass through and what remains behind) and the capacity of the filter before we have to empty it, clean it, or throw it away.

Computer filters operate in a similar, but much more complex way. In a word processor a filter may examine an incoming stream of text and control characters, holding back bits that your application doesn't understand, while substituting equivalent codes that it does. In an image editor a filter may perform a similar process to translate an image file from its native format into one that your program is able to handle.

A third kind of filter—the image-processing filter—is even more powerful, because it functions as a miniapplication of its own. Those filters are found in the Filter, Plug-In, or Special Effects menu of your image editor. Although many programs have special filters that are proprietary to that software, a growing number have conformed to the plug-in standard set by Adobe for its Photoshop product. You'll find Fauve Matisse, PhotoStyler, Fractal Design Painter, Corel PhotoPaint, and others among these.

Using Plug-Ins

Plug-ins are image-processing filters, usually kept in a single folder, that your software examines each time it loads. Any plug-ins found during this process are automatically listed in the appropriate menu of your program and are available for immediate use. Figure 8.1 shows typical plug-in lists for Photoshop, Fauve Matisse, and PhotoStyler. The Photoshop menu has been augmented by Aldus Gallery Effects, Kai's Power Tools, and Pixar 128 third-party filters.

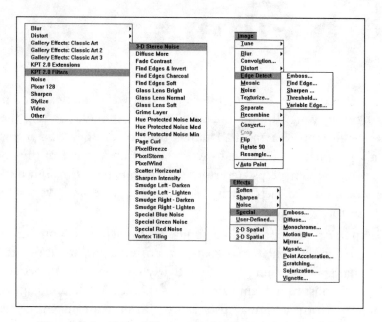

Figure 8.1 *Typical filter menus for Photoshop (upper left), Fauve Matisse (right), and PhotoStyler (lower right).*

If you add a filter to your Plug-Ins folder after you load your image editor, you'll need to exit and reload the program before it can recognize the addition.

Several image editors can share the same set of plug-ins. Most programs have a facility for specifying the folder in which plug-in filters are stored.

T I P

Filters of this type perform some operation on the currently selected portion of your image (or the entire image if you have made no selection). As I noted, the filter is actually a miniprogram that operates on the pixels of the selection in some way. A sharpen filter looks at each pixel in turn, and its tonal relationship with the pixels which surround it, and then increases the contrast so that the image looks sharper. A blurring filter reduces the contrast. You can use the filters available in your image editor in a variety of ways:

- *Blurring filters* reduce or eliminate the effect of artifacts such as dust in your image or concentrate attention on the areas that you don't blur. Throwing a background out of focus with a blur filter makes the subject of a photograph stand out more sharply.

- *Sharpening filters* are a great way to bring fuzzy details into focus. You may find that fine lines that you want to see more clearly will indeed look much better through the extra contrast that sharpening adds. Don't overdo sharpening, or your image will look extra contrasty and grainy.

- *Distortion filters* let you twist and twirl portions of an image to create special effects. You can add waves and whirlpool effects, pinch portions of an image, or wrap the photo around a sphere with the correct filter.

- *Noise/despeckle filters* either add or remove random pixels in your image. You can change a smooth background to one with interesting grain patterns or smooth out a speckled image with one of these filters.

- *Stylizing filters* perform other types of special effects, such as creating 3-D embossed, halftone-dot, or mosaic effects. Most vendors of image editors offer their own special complement of these effects.

Filters are an easy and fun way to experiment with special F/X. They help add a desirable random quality to the sterile perfection often found in computer-generated images. Figure 8.2 shows the results of several different filters on an image.

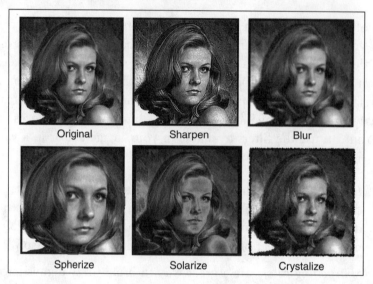

Figure 8.2 *Five different common filter effects available in most image-editing software.*

Applying Filters

We'll work with several different filters in this chapter to create some interesting effects. I'll show you a couple of quick techniques for salvaging defective photos with filter F/X that you can use in your own work. As always, the files I worked with are included on the CD-ROM. You can use the tryout version of Photoshop packaged with this book for some of the effects, but others use special filter arsenals such as Kai's Power Tools or Aldus Gallery Effects. Near the end of the chapter, I'll present a sampling of effects you can achieve with Fauve Matisse, PhotoStyler, Corel PhotoPaint, and other tools.

Any serious F/X worker really needs both Kai's Power Tools and Gallery Effects (assuming you have an image editor that is compatible with

Photoshop plug-ins). If you want to run out now and purchase them before we continue, I'll be happy to wait. There's no hurry.

For the first exercise, you'll need the file **CATHYB04.TIF** from the CD-ROM (located in the Chapter 8 subdirectory) and a texture file called **CLOUDS.TIF** from the Textures subdirectory.

I've included several dozen background textures on the CD-ROM that you are free to use in your own work. They were all developed using Fractal Design Painter and Kai's Power Tools.

T I P

Experimenting with Filters for Backgrounds

Our example photograph is a little too flatly lit for my taste, but the real flaw we'll fix in this exercise is the uninteresting white background. Actually, photos with plain backgrounds like these are especially easy to composite and plop into new backgrounds because it's no problem to select all the background, invert the selection, and then copy the subject. We just can't leave the photo as-is with that stark surrounding.

Neither can we expect the filters we want to apply to perform much pixel magic on an all-white field. The first step is to replace the white seamless paper with something else. The Cloudy Skies texture (**CLOUDS.TIF**) actually closely approximates a kind of background portrait photographers have used for years: splotches of paint applied to a piece of canvas (often applied with the edge of a sponge).

When I had a studio, I made up a bunch of these backgrounds on the flat side of old sheets of fake-wood 4 × 8-foot paneling in various color combinations. Rolls of canvas are more portable, but the paneling was actually cheaper. It took hours to paint one of these. Now we can have the same effect with a few minutes' work and our favorite image editor. You don't even have to go that far, since you can use the textures I've prepared for you.

To put the new background in place, just follow these steps.

1. Load **CATHYB01.TIF** and select the background using your image editor's Magic Wand tool. Save the selection as a mask (if your image editor allows it) so that we can rework the background later. (With Photoshop, use **Select>Save Selection.**)

2. Load **CLOUDS.TIF.** Because we'll blur the image a bit, let's sharpen it up first.

3. Chose your image editor's Sharpen filter and apply it to the entire **CLOUDS.TIF** image. (In Photoshop, use **Filter>Sharpen>Sharpen More.**)

   You might think the background would look better if there were some gradation in the background, and I agree. I left it plain so that you could modify it to suit yourself.

4. Choose your image editor's Gradient tool and select a Radial gradation. Set the transparency of the gradient to about 62%, and use a pure-white-to-black start and end color set.

5. Apply the gradient to the **CLOUDS.TIF** image, starting from the center. Your image will look like Figure 8.3.

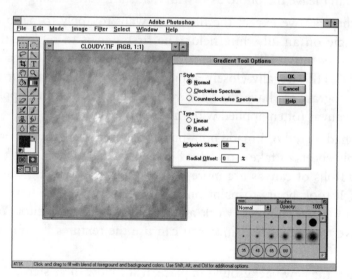

Figure 8.3 *A radial gradation adds a lighting effect to the background.*

6. Select the entire **CLOUDS.TIF** image and copy it to the Clipboard.

7. Switch to **CATHYB04.TIF** and paste the clipboard image into the selection. (With Photoshop, use Edit>Paste Into.)

8. The CLOUDS.TIF background won't be large enough to fill the entire selected area. Resize it while it is still selected to fill the background. (In Photoshop, choose **Image>Effects>Scale**.) Then drag the corners of the background selection to fill up the white space. Your image will look like Figure 8.4.

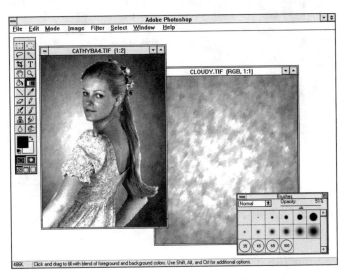

Figure 8.4 *The background has been added to the image.*

Our results aren't too bad, and we got to use the Sharpen filter. But there's a lot more we can do with this image. Let's move on.

Breaking Up Isn't Hard To Do

Here's a quick trick that produces an interesting background. Just follow these steps.

1. Reselect the background you just applied. (Use Photoshop's **Select>Load Selection** choice if you need to.)

2. Use the **Filter>Stylize>Tiles** effect to break up the background into little chunks. I selected a grid of tiles 10 × 10 and had them filled with the (black) background color, but you can experiment with larger or smaller tiles and different fills. Your results might look like those in Figure 8.5.

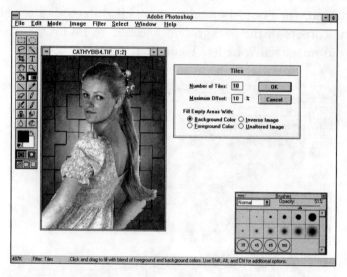

Figure 8.5 *Adding a tile effect to the background produces a new image.*

3. Save your file if you want to keep this effect for reference. All the results are on the CD-ROM so that you can compare your results with mine.

If you have Kai's Power Tools, let's try another effect.

1. Load the previous version again, and select the background.

2. Apply KPT's Pixelwind effect. Your results will look like Figure 8.6.

KPT users should repeat Step 1 to load another copy of the picture and then try out Fractal Explorer. Play with the controls to select an interesting fractal pattern. Click on the OK globe, as shown in Figure 8.7. It's unlikely you will reproduce the exact fractal background I came up with, but your results will be interesting. You can see my version in Figure 8.8.

Fractals are created by mathematical equations that create recurring patterns with infinite detail. In other words, as you zoom in on a fractal design, you'll discover that the basic pattern is repeated in smaller and smaller versions.

T I P

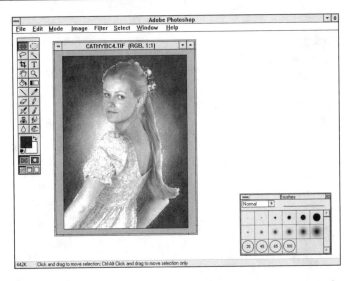

Figure 8.6 *The Pixelwind effect from Kai's Power Tools acts like a pixel "atomizer."*

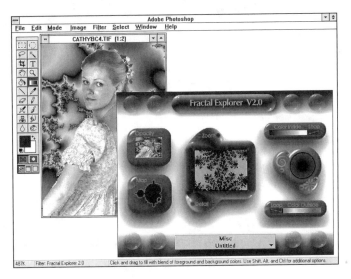

Figure 8.7 *The Fractal Explorer of Kai's Power Tools produces an endless variety of effects.*

Figure 8.8 *The final image with a fractal background.*

Little Lost Kitten

Let's salvage another photo that wasn't good enough for the shoebox. This one's a picture of two kittens resting on a doormat at the corner of a deck. The expression on the face of the kitten in the foreground is interesting, and I don't really mind the "framing" effect of the brick wall at right, but that second kitten in the background has got to go. Our working photo is shown in Figure 8.9.

Figure 8.9 *We have one kitten too many in this photograph. Can we remove it with retouching?*

Can you use what you've learned about retouching so far to make this a better picture? Let's try. Use the KITTEN.TIF image from the CD-ROM and your own image editor or Photoshop. Just follow these steps. I'll move through the first batch of steps quite quickly because we've done all this before.

1. Select the foreground kitten using your favorite method. I did it by clicking on Photoshop's QuickMask icon and painting the parts of the photo I wanted to select.

2. Save the selection (In Photoshop use **Select>Save Selection**).

3. Invert the selection so that the foreground kitten is protected from changes.

4. Use the Clone tool to clone portions of the doormat over the unwanted kitten. Eradicate his head with pieces of the deck in the lower left of the photograph. Your results should look something like Figure 8.10.

Fairly impressive, right? We can do more.

Figure 8.10   *The extra kitten has been removed with the Clone tool and extra deck boards painted in to fill the gap.*

5. With the background area still selected, choose your image editor's Blur filter to throw the background out of focus. Repeat a few times—we really want to blur that background.

When you're finished, the photo will look as if it was made with a wide-open aperture (that is, the iris of the lens—like the iris of your eye, which produces what photographers call a narrow *depth of field* (not *depth of focus*—that's something different). The cat is still sharp, but the background is now very blurry. You can see the results in Figure 8.11, if there is much difference after the printing process. If not, check out the actual figure on the CD-ROM.

Let's do one last effect.

6. If you have Kai's Power Tools, apply the Pixelwind filter to the background. If not, try your image editor's Noise filter. Crank up the noise to a relatively high level. You'll end up with an image like that shown in Figure 8.12.

Figure 8.11 *A blurry background makes the cat stand out more sharply.*

Figure 8.12 *Pixelwind adds a painterly effect to the background.*

Experiment with the filters provided with your own image editor to see what they can do to your images. If you remember to save a copy of a photo before you apply each filter, you can always retreat to your last version, even if you goof and do something that prevents undoing that step.

Choosing Image-Processing Add-Ons

As you can see, you're not limited to the filters included with your image editor. A wide variety of add-ons are available from third-party vendors, thanks to Adobe, which established the Photoshop plug-in standard. Because software developers are able to sell these products to the huge established base of Photoshop users, as well as owners of other products.

In this next section, I'll describe two of the leading filter packages. Most cost just $70–200, so you can easily add both of them to your special F/X arsenal.

Kai's Power Tools

If your image editor supports Photoshop plug-ins and you're not using Kai's Power Tools, you're stuck in the Kindergarten of special F/X. Thanks to the work of Photoshop genius Kai Krause (and a few friends), KPT can turn any compatible image editor into an F/X workshop.

Although this product interfaces with your software as a plug-in, it's more properly thought of as a full-fledged image-processing application in its own right, which just happens to work seamlessly with other software. KPT boasts its own decidedly non-PC interface, which looks something like the dashboard of a Buick Riviera designed by Martians. It takes a while to get used to the Krause way of doing things, but you'll find this new way of approaching graphics does help you think in new and creative ways. The Kai's Power Tools dialog box for one component, Texture Explorer, is shown in Figure 8.13.

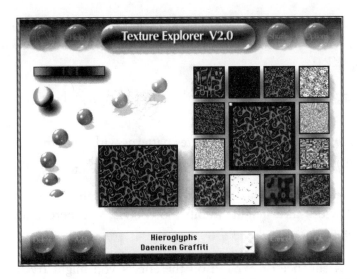

Figure 8.13 *You can generate thousands of abstract textures with Kai's Power Tools' Texture Explorer.*

Each of the odd controls is a door to hundreds of variations and parameters. For example, under the Fabrics drop-down menu at the bottom of the dialog box, you'll find 21 different categories of textures, with names like Fire, Hieroglyphs, Liquids, Minerals, and Woods. Each of those contain from a few to several dozen variations. We're up to 400 or 500 different textures at this point. Guess what? Once you settle on one of these, you'll find additional controls that provide dozens more versions (called mutations in KPT-speak).

Some of Kai's Power Tools' 33 plug-ins are straight filters, called one-step filters. You select a portion of your image and choose that option from the Filters or Effects menu of your image editor. Many KPT filters pop up under the conventional filters classifications, such as Distort or Stylize. Others are available from the special **Filters>KPT 2.0** menu choice. You'll need to experiment with each filter to discover how it works, although KPT does offer previews in many cases.

The one-step filters go way beyond what you'll find in the basic set packaged with your image editor. Four new ones were added to the latest version of KPT:

- *Page curl,* which simulates the effect of a page being peeled back, like the old Kodak logo.

- *Seamless welder,* which creates patterns with smooth transitions.

- *Fade contrast,* which reduces the contrast and intensity of a selection.

- *Selection info,* which provides information about a selection, such as width and height, number of pixels, and percentage of total image area.

Other tools enhance or expand on the effects you might try to get with your standard plug-ins, these include:

- *Smudge Darken/Lighten* (located under the Blur filters), which creates a multilevel blurry blend.

- *Glass Lenses* (found under the Distort filters), which consists of three different filters that create a 3-D effect, as viewed through a glass lens. I'll use this one in Chapter 9 to show you what it does.

- *Stereo Noise* (found under KPT filters), which uses a special dithered noise algorithm to create 3-D pictures from any gray scale image.

- *Pixelstorm/Pixelwind/PixelBreeze* (found under KPT filters), which consists of three filters that atomize your image by dispersing its pixels over a 30- to 200-pixel area of your screen.

The following three filter types are found under the Noise filters listing.

- *Grime Layer* adds a dark, transparent layer of noise (it looks like soot!) over your image.

- *Hue Protected Noises,* which all three color layers of your image, changing the hue randomly. These three filters— in minimum, medium, and maximum grades—don't have that problem.

- *Special Noises,* which works only with one layer of your image: red, green, or blue, respectively, producing interesting and varied F/X.

- *Sharpen Intensity* (found under the Sharpen filters), which produces stronger contrast and brighter colors.

The following filters are found under the Stylize filters listing:

- *Diffuse More,* which is roughly four times as intense as Photoshop's Diffuse filter.

- *Find Edges and Invert,* which combines the two Photoshop filters into one step.

- *Find Edges Charcoal,* which produces faint grayish edges on white.

- *Find Edges Soft,* which is less harsh and intense than Photoshop's own Find Edges filter.

- *Scatter Horizontal,* which scatters your image only on a horizontal plane.

- *Cyclone.* (found under the Video filters listing), which produces an array of color variations.

Instead of the sliders used with other filters, you vary the intensity of KPT effects by pressing a number key from 0 (intense) to 9 (mild) while choosing the command.

The filters provided in KPT fall into several categories. The most complex effects are produced by the miniprograms called Texture Explorer, Gradient Designer, and Fractal Explorers. You can use these miniprograms to experiment with hundreds of different pattern textures, gradient blends, and fractal segments. The Texture Explorer, for example, lets you choose from five different tile sizes or expand a given texture to fill the selection. The Gradient Designer adds controls to choose the angle of gradation, the center point for the blend, and the amount of blur applied to neighboring hues.

Aldus Gallery Effects

The three volumes (so far) in the Aldus Gallery Effects: Classic Art series include dozens of filters that reproduce various painting and drawing methods. These were the first third-party filters I ever used, and they're still among the best.

You can use Gallery Effects as a stand-alone application, a desk accessory, or a Photoshop-compatible plug-in. Even those who don't have an image editor that accepts plug-ins can still apply these effects.

Volume 3 includes filters with names like Conté Crayon, Crosshatch, Cutout, Glass, Halftone Screen, Ink Outlines, Neon Glow, Paint Daub, Plaster, Plastic Wrap, Reticulation, Sponge, Stained Glass, Sumi-é, Torn Edges, and Water Paper. Each offers previews. I'll use several of these filters in the next section.

Like KPT, Gallery Effects is a cross-platform F/X generator, with separate versions for both Macintosh and IBM PC systems. If your organization has both types of computers, the ability to outfit them all with similar tools can be important.

A Filter Effects Gallery

If I've whetted your appetite for filter special effects, I'd like to take you on a whirlwind tour of some of the effects you can achieve with programs you may own that aren't included on the CD-ROM with this book. I'll take one picture and apply many different filters to it, so that you can compare how each filter affects the image. The original photo we'll use is shown in Figure 8.14. It's a straight head-and-shoulders portrait, and the full-color version is available on the CD-ROM in two different versions. The one I used for this exercise was sharpened quite a bit so that the filter effects would be more apparent and cropped. It's stored in the Chapter 8 subdirectory as **CATHYD10.TIF**. The original unmodified, uncropped image is in the CATHY\GLAMOUR subdirectory as **CATHYG16.TIF**.

Figure 8.14 *Unfiltered head-and-shoulders portrait.*

Lighting Effects

Photoshop 3.0 introduced a versatile Lighting Effects filter, which lets you position and modify several "light" sources within your image. You can adjust the intensity and color of the light, specify properties (from glossy to matte, plastic to metallic), and adjust intensity. There's even a provision to add a texture channel. Custom lighting effects that you create yourself can be saved and reused. The Lighting Effects filter in action is shown in Figure 8.15.

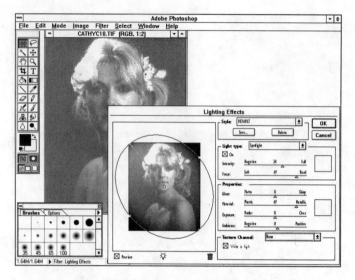

Figure 8.15 *Photoshop 3.0's Lighting Effects filter.*

In this example, I added light from the upper left, which happens to be the same general direction as one of the electronic flash units used to make the original photograph. (You can see the effects of this light in the hot spot in the model's hair.) The Lighting Effects filter just accentuated this effect, and produced a darker shadow effect at the upper-right and lower-left corners. The final version is shown in Figure 8.16.

Difference Clouds

Photoshop 3.0 also includes a new Difference Clouds filter, which creates realistic cloudlike effects with a solarized appearance. Solarization is a photographic effect that was originally produced by exposing partially developed film to light, partially reversing some of the developed image. You can see the Difference Clouds effect, applied only to the background of our test image, in Figure 8.17. The image is more interesting in its original color version, included in the Chapter 8 subdirectory on the CD-ROM, since the colorful clouds add a slightly ominous mood to this portrait. To see another application of this filter that I used it with a figure study, **CATHYF05.TIF**, look in the \CATHY\GLAMOUR\FX subdirectory on the CD-ROM.

Figure 8.16   *Photo with Photoshop 3.0 Lighting Effects applied.*

Figure 8.17   *Photoshop 3.0 Difference Clouds filter applied to the background.*

Gallery Sponge Effect

Aldus Gallery Effects: Classic Art, Volume 3, includes a Sponge filter that can be used to add a painterly texture effect to an image. You'll find similar filters in most image editors that produce brush strokes, dots, spongy smears, or other abstract patterns. You'll find these useful anytime you want to change a photographic image to something that resembles a painting. Filters of this type can salvage an unsharp image, one with scratches or other defects, or even be used to cover up unflattering physical characteristics of the model, such as poor skin.

Figure 8.18 shows what this filter does to our test portrait. I applied it to the subject only, and not the background, but you may prefer to apply a painterly filter to the whole image, or, perhaps, a separate treatment to background and subject.

Figure 8.18 *Aldus Gallery Effects' Sponge filter applied to portrait subject.*

The Gallery Effects suite of filters includes many filters of this type, including Dry Brush, Dark Strokes, Palette Knife, and Plaster.

Wrap it Up

I really like the Plastic Wrap filter in Gallery Effects: Classic Art, Volume 3. You can select just about any object in an image and transform it into a shrink-wrapped, glossy object that shows the original through the transparent covering. It's a great filter for creating plastic-looking objects with realistic reflections and surface texture. Although our test portrait is probably not the best image to use as a demonstration for this filter, you can see exactly what it does in Figure 8.19.

Figure 8.19 *Aldus Gallery Effects' Plastic Wrap filter adds a transparent, glossy surface to any object.*

Tile

U-Lead Systems offers an indispensible set of image utilities in its Image Pals collection. I used the Image Pals Album facility to catalog thumbnail versions of all the images compiled for the CD-ROM bundled with this book and Image Pals Capture for all the screen shots. The latest version of this package also includes an excellent image editor, which should be no surprise, because U-Lead developed PhotoStyler, one of the very top photo manipulation programs on the market.

You may buy Image Pals just for the Album utility, as I did, but don't neglect the image editor, which includes some great features and some surprisingly useful filters. I applied the Shatter filter to our test image. Like the Tile filter found in most image editors, this one breaks up the image into small pieces, separated by "grout" that can be white, black, or some other color. The effect is shown in Figure 8.20.

Figure 8.20 *Tile filter from the Image Pals' editor.*

Warp Factor 10

I give a 10 to the Warp filter included in the Image Pals' editor and also found in a similar filter in Corel PhotoPaint under **Effects>Transformations>Mesh Warp.** While not as flexible as the warping you can do with programs like Elastic Reality, the effect produced by this type of filter is startling but easy to achieve.

The filter's preview window shows a thumbnail version of the image, overlaid with a mesh grid with control points at the intersections of the lines. The grid can be set for fine, medium, or large gradations. You may drag the control points to create a new layout for the image. When the filter is applied, the image within each grid area expands or contracts as required to fit within the web's new shape.

Image Pals' Warping filter is shown in Figure 8.21.

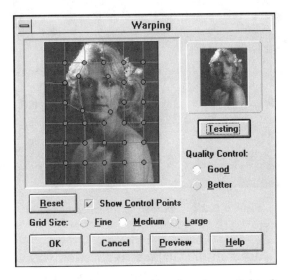

Figure 8.21 *The Warping filter from Image Pals' editor.*

Solarize

PhotoStyler is far from unique in having a good solarization filter, but its implementation is quite versatile. This program's preview window is large, and you can drag the image around within it so that you can preview any filter on the portion of the original you want, with sufficient area shown for you to judge easily how the effect will look. Although solarization has been over-used, it can still be a useful filter, as shown in Figure 8.22.

Figure 8.22 *PhotoStyler's solarization effect.*

As I mentioned earlier in the chapter, solarization was originally applied to photographic film, often unintentionally, when light was allowed to strike partially developed film. Portions of the film that have already been developed (generally, the most heavily exposed parts of the image—the highlights) are affected less than the undeveloped shadows, which are effectively reversed by the process. This mixture of positive and negative in one image produces a uniquely weird image, much beloved for record album covers during the psychedelic 1960s.

Conventional solarization is pretty much a trial-and-error, unpredictable procedure, because, once you expose developed film, there is no way to undo the process and no way to control the exact degree of solarization applied. Electronic solarization, on the other hand, is repeatable, undoable, and adjustable. You can apply a little solarization, or a lot, and keep trying until you get the effect you want. Figure 8.23 shows PhotoStyler's solarization controls in use.

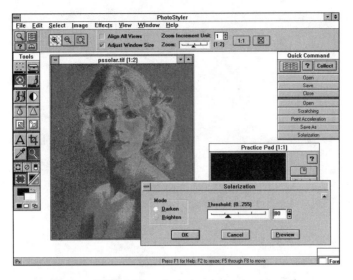

Figure 8.23 *PhotoStyler's solarization controls.*

Vignette

Vignetting helps draw attention to the central subject matter of an image by fading the edges and corners to black, white, or another tone. It's hard to trace vignetting effects back to any one source: painters applied this technique to canvas long before photography was invented. All camera lenses produce a circular image, and a square or rectangular picture is usually cut out of this coverage area. When you use a lens that doesn't have sufficient coverage for a particular size film or plate, which often happened in the early days of photography, another kind of vignetting is produced. The effect can also be generated in the darkroom by exposing a print through a cut-out in a burning tool.

PhotoStyler's Vignette filter lets you choose from dark or light surround, as shown in Figure 8.24. If your image editor doesn't have this filter, you can create the same effect by selecting an oval area of the image, and then feathering the selection over a wide area—say 40 to 50 pixels.

Figure 8.24 *PhotoStyler's Vignette filter.*

Psychedelia

Corel PhotoPaint includes a great Psychedelic filter under its Effects>Special menu, which is a combination solarization, posterization, and colorizing filter rolled into one. The filter produces an effect much like solarization, except that individual color bands are assigned contrasting and complementary hues. At the same time, the number of different tones in the image is curtailed. The result is an image that smacks of the LSD-influenced graphics of the late 1960s.

Corel PhotoPaint itself has an interesting history dating almost that far back, being in one sense a direct descendent of PC Paintbrush, Zsoft's image-editing program that was one of the very first available for IBM PCs. That DOS-based software eventually became available in a Windows version, was adopted by Microsoft in another version as the Paint program furnished free with Windows, and finally maturing as Photo Finish and

Corel PhotoPaint. Corel has incorporated many new features in integrating PhotoPaint with Corel Draw 5, including roll-up dialog boxes and Photoshop filter compatibility.

PhotoPaint's psychedelic filter is only one of a full complement of interesting special F/X available with this program. It is shown in Figure 8.25.

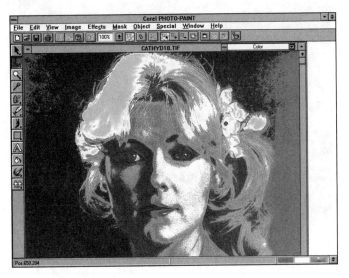

Figure 8.25   *Corel PhotoPaint's Psychedelic filter.*

Good Impressions

PhotoPaint's Impressionist filter under the Effects>Artistic menu (there is also a Pointillism filter in that submenu) is stupefyingly slow but generates an interesting pixelated effect a little like the Pixelwind filter from Kai's Power Tools. A much faster version that's not as flexible is available under the Effects>Mapping menu. This filter is shown in Figure 8.26.

Figure 8.26   *Corel PhotoPaint's Impressionist filter.*

Create Your Own Filter

Most image editors include a user-defined filter facility that can be used to define your own effects. These filters present you with a grid of pixels surrounding a theoretic "subject" pixel in an image. You specify the amount of brightness to be added or subtracted from the pixels surrounding the subject, based on the value of the subject pixel in the center.

In Photoshop 3.0, the concept is taken to its logical conclusion with its new "filter factory." A more traditional approach is found in other programs, including Fauve Matisse, which calls its user-filter capability Convolution. This module is shown in Figure 8.27.

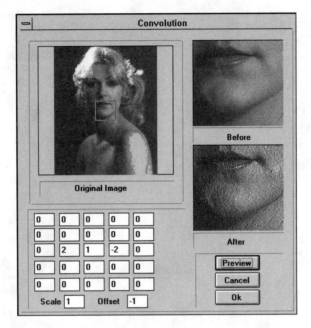

Figure 8.27 *Fauve Matisse's Convolution filter.*

You can experiment with this filter by typing in different values and then applying the filter to a test image. You don't have to figure out in advance what a particular filter will do. If you get something you like, save it to disk and then tell all your friends you meant to do that.

Shattered

Fauve Matisse has a great Shatter filter, which is similar to the Tile module found in other programs. However, it has the added ability to specify the height and width of the "pieces," so that you can produce tall, thin slivers or short, squat slabs, depending on the effect you want to achieve. I elected to use the squarish tiles shown in Figure 8.28. Different colors are added to each tile, lending a distinct 1962 flavor to the image. You may want to check out the original illustration on the CD-ROM to see what I mean.

Figure 8.28   *Fauve Matisse's Shatter filter.*

The Next Step

We've done some fairly major work on the pictures we retouched and filtered in this chapter, even though the photos themselves still represent the originals relatively closely. In *Chapter 9* I'll let out all the stops and use filters to develop some truly outrageous F/X. I'll turn our little kitten into the Cat From Outer Space and work with additional photos to generate special images.

CHAPTER

NINE

Special F/X with Retouching

In this chapter we'll experiment further with special F/X you can create using only retouching techniques, especially with some of the filters introduced in *Chapter 8*. There will be no compositing magic used here: We'll work solely with the image elements already present in a single picture.

I selected four different pictures to work with, all available on the CD-ROM if you'd like to work along. None of them are portraits; we've worked with people pictures extensively in this book, and I want to give you a chance to manipulate some other types of images.

You'll need an image editor, preferably one that accepts Photoshop-compatible filters. We'll transform one of the images using only filters that you are likely to have built into your graphic application. I'll use some of the others to show exactly how third-party tools such as Kai's Power Tools can help you.

Transformations with Basic Filters

First, let's see what the basic filters you have available can do. We'll work with a file called **STEEPLE1.TIF**, which is a photo of a parish church in Ciudad Rodrigo, an historic Spanish city that also boasts a fine cathedral. This photo, which is shown in Figure 9.1, wasn't too bad to begin with: The clouds are profuse and fluffy, and the texture of the walls is interesting. However, the sky could still be improved, and there's an unsightly lightning rod at the left side of the photo. Let's start by fixing those two problems. Just follow these steps.

Figure 9.1   *The unaltered photo of a church in Ciudad Rodrigo, Spain.*

1. Load the **STEEPLE1.TIF** file, and zoom in to isolate the lightning rod.

2. Select the entire sky area of the photo. I found that the Magic Wand with a pixel tolerance of 40 grabbed the lighter and darker areas of the sky in two neat chunks. Just set your tolerance (in Photoshop double-click on the Magic Wand tool) and then click inside the light area of the sky. Hold down the **Shift** key and click in the darker areas to add them to the selection.

3. Save the sky selection as a mask (or frisket) if your image editor lets you do that. We'll use the mask to protect the church area of the image while we work on the lightning rod and then to change the tone of the whole sky.

4. Use the Rubber Stamp or Clone tool to copy portions of the sky over the lightning rod and its connecting wire, as shown in Figure 9.2.

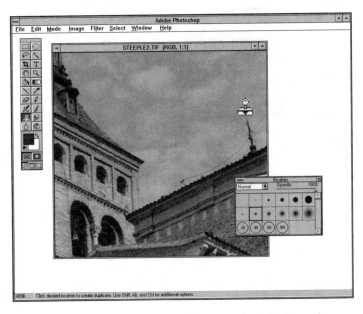

Figure 9.2 *The Clone tool removes the lightning rod.*

5. With the sky still selected, choose the Burn tool. Specify the largest brush possible (I used the 100-pixel setting) and set the exposure low. I used 7%, so that I could darken specific areas of the sky a little at a time.

6. Burn in the lighter portions of the sky at lower left and darken other parts selectively to enhance the appearance of the clouds. I chose to darken two areas to make the sky more interesting. Note that darkening portions of an image using the Burn tool gives you more of a random, artistic effect than simply changing the brightness of the entire sky with the Brightness/Contrast control.

7. Use Brightness/Contrast to darken the entire cloud field. Boost the contrast to make the clouds stand out from the blue sky. I darkened 30% and raised the contrast by 30%, but you can use the settings you prefer.

Your image should now look something like that shown in Figure 9.3.

Figure 9.3 *The sky has been enhanced.*

Applying Some Special F/X

Let's experiment with a few special F/X, using the church and its steeple as our subject. I'll use only the basic Photoshop filters for the next few transformations; your own image editor should have rough equivalents that you can use instead. Just follow these steps.

1. Invert the selection so that the church is selected and the sky is protected from changes.

2. Save the image so that you can go back to it after trying out different F/X.

3. Experiment with each of the filters described below in turn, using a fresh copy of the image each time. I won't repeat the instructions to load the image and select the church each time; remember to do that on your own.

   - *Radial Blur.* This filter produces a blurring effect that progresses outward from a center point. There are two common types of radial blur. One looks as if the image were spun at high speed on a turntable. The other gives the effect of a zoom lens that is zoomed during exposure. I used the Spin mode for this image, as shown in the dialog box in Figure 9.4. Note that you can select the amount of blur (up to 100 percent), and position the center point of the effect just by dragging it with the mouse in the preview box. The final effect is shown in Figure 9.5.

   - *Pinch.* The Pinch filter stuffs portions of your image down an invisible black hole, distorting it with an unusual pinching effect. In this case, the resulting image looks a little like a Japanese pagoda (see Figure 9.6). Portions of the sky are sucked in as well to fill in the missing areas, so you'll need to use the Clone or Rubber Stamp to smooth out the transitions.

Figure 9.4 *A radial blur is an interesting effect for many types of photos.*

Figure 9.5 *The church has been blurred using the Spin effect.*

Figure 9.6 *We've pinched the church. Note how the sky area was pulled in to fill in the missing portions of the image.*

● *Twirl.* I went nuts over the outrageous effect the Twirl picture had on our church picture. I think you might like it, too. This filter twisted the steeple as if it were something out of a Dali painting. All the image in Figure 9.7 needs is a limp pocket watch draped over the roof!

● *Crystallize.* This filter produces an unusual painterly effect. Its effects are a little gross when you specify larger cell sizes (10 or above), but I used a setting of 4 to generate this impressionistic effect that doesn't obscure all the detail in the image. Figure 9.8 shows the image I ended up with. It's unusual, because the sky hasn't been pixelated like the church. If you want other brush-strokes effects, try Facet, which converts the image into a dry-brush masterpiece, or Mosaic, which adds a tiled-wall effect.

Figure 9.7 *Twirl shows what this church might have looked like if painted by Salvador Dali.*

Figure 9.8 *The Crystallize filter adds a painterly effect and doesn't obscure too much detail if you use small cell sizes.*

● *Trace Contours.* I cheated on this one. The original effect gave an interesting stark white image, but it looked a lot better when the colors were inverted. I set Trace Contours to work with the lower (darker) tones only, and set it for a level of 16. I decided this one was a keeper, so you can view the full color version in the color section of this book in Color insert Figure 5. The gray scale version is shown in Figure 9.9.

Figure 9.9 *Trace Contours was used and then the image was reversed to produce this stark effect.*

● *Etching.* This is a custom filter I prepared especially for the readers of this book. It's a relatively simple filter that performs operations on some adjacent areas around each pixel in your image. To use the filter, copy it from the CD-ROM (it's in the Chapter 9 subdirectory) to your image editor's directory and use the **Filter>Other>Custom** choice (in Photoshop) to select the Etching filter. Apply it to your image. The results are shown in Figure 9.10. I've also included another custom filter, Light Emboss, that you can experiment with.

Figure 9.10 *The custom Etching filter, generated especially for this book, produced this effect.*

Some Uncommon Effects

Now, let's go on and use one or two of the effects available with Kai's Power Tools to jazz up a couple more images. If you don't have this add-on, your image editor might offer something similar—or you might consider buying either or both after you view the effects I came up with.

Through A Glass, Lightly

On a recent trip to Niagara Falls, Canada, I sprung for the helicopter tour of the Falls as a way to grab some breathtaking aerial images of one of our continent's natural wonders. The image shown in Figure 9.11 wasn't quite as breathtaking as I'd hoped, so I used a KPT filter to fix it up a little.

Figure 9.11 *Niagara Falls, as viewed through the window of a helicopter.*

If you want to duplicate the effect, load **NIAGARA.TIF** from the CD-ROM into your image editor, install Kai's Power Tools, and then follow these steps.

1. Select KPT Glass Lens Soft (found in the Filters>Distort menu in Photoshop.) You'll end up with an image that looks as if it were being viewed through an oblate glass globe. There's no need to select any special area of the image; the filter operates on the whole picture.

2. Select the globe-area of the image produced by the filter. The easiest way to do that with most image editors is to use the Oval selection tool, constraining it to select from a center point outward (with Photoshop hold down the **Alt** key). It may take you a few tries to find the exact center. (You could always draw two diagonal lines in a separate layer and use their intersection, but you can usually find the center on your own.)

3. Use the Sharpen More (or similar) filter to sharpen up the image in the globe. Don't be afraid to sharpen it drastically or use the filter several times. The image has been blurred quite a bit by the globular effect.

4. Invert the selection and choose your editor's Brightness/Contrast controls to darken the area surrounding the globe. This procedure de-emphasizes the background so that the globe-image shows up more brightly but keeps the globe from floating in an empty space. Your finished results should look like Figure 9.12. You can view a full-color version in Color insert Figure 5.

Figure 9.12   *Niagara Falls, as viewed through a glass globe or fishbowl.*

Kitten on the Keys

Remember our kitten photo from *Chapter 8*? We're not done with it yet. I added some special F/X from Kai's Power Tools to provide additional variations on the original feline theme. I won't give step-by-step instructions for these transformations, because they are pretty straightforward. Select the image, apply the filter, and then look at these F/X.

● *Fractal Fantasy.* For this image, which is shown in Figure 9.13 and Color insert Figure 5, I selected the background and then applied a fractal overlay using Kai's Power Tools' Fractal Explorer. Your results may differ, even if you have KPT, because of the infinite variety of fractal patterns available. Next, I inverted the selection to isolate the kitten and used the Hue/Saturation control to give him green highlights and magenta eyes. The eyes were touched up a little with a brush and the Dodge tool.

Figure 9.13 *Kitten with a fractal background added.*

Trash to Treasure with Painting Filters

I visited Segovia, Spain, about six times in the last 20 years, and each time I come back with a different view at its ancient Roman aqueduct. The one shown in Figure 9.14 is the worst of the lot, rescued from the out-take basket to illustrate how you can salvage bad pictures with heavy retouching. You can use any image editor to accomplish the same results I got.

Figure 9.14 *Roman aqueduct from a bad angle: too many parked cars are shown.*

The featureless sky is bad enough, but the worst fault may be the collection of cars that line the street parallel to this 2000-year-old structure. I decided that some heavy impressionist brush-strokes could obscure the offensive automobiles, while adding a desirably painterly effect to the image. I performed the following surgical steps on this candidate for photographic intensive care.

1. Select the lower right-hand corner of the image, with the sidewalk, parked cars, and building at far right.

2. Use the Fractal Design Painter filter to apply some heavy brush strokes. It really smeared up things, so that the cars are barely noticeable.

3. Select the sky. I couldn't apply any brush strokes yet, because there was no image to stroke.

4. I select a portion of the already processed image immediately above where the building used to be and clone that into the sky. I used Clone (non aligned) so that the strokes would be varied. A moderately-overcast cloudy sky effect was produced.

5. Use the Blur and Smudge tools to smear up the sky randomly, making it a little more skylike, albeit with some rainy-day ominous overtones.

6. Use a rough brush to add strokes to the sky.

7. Invert the selection to capture the aqueduct itself, plus the area already stroked. Then remove the latter area from the new selection, leaving only the aqueduct. (In Photoshop, hold down the **Control** key while selecting with the Lasso or another selection tool to delete portions.)

8. Use one of the smaller brushes to stroke the aqueduct, ending up with the image you see in Figure 9.15 and Color insert Figure 5.

Figure 9.15 *Brush strokes turn this photo into a painting.*

Two Filters, One Image

The last effect I'll show you in this chapter involves a single image, with two mundane filters applied using some slightly unusual techniques. The image illustrates how you shouldn't use filters blindly, but carefully choose how to apply them to a picture.

The original photo showed a model holding a large, bright red flower. I wanted to give the image the look of a painting using a texture-heavy filter but was afraid of losing the detail of the flower petals. The Crystallize filter I planned to apply would have tended to smear everything together. I followed these steps to achieve the final image shown in Figure 9.16 and Color insert Figure 6.

Figure 9.16 *The flower at upper left was outlined with Trace Contours and then inserted into the photo. The whole work was pixelated with the Crystallize filter.*

1. Select the flower alone and apply **Filter>Stylize>Trace Contours** to it.

2. Reverse the colors of the image using **Image>Map>Inverse** to change the outlines of the flower back to a bright red.

3. Deselect everything in the photo and then selected the bridge of the model's nose. Reverse the selection so that everything in the image is selected except for the bridge of her nose. Without this step, the Crystallize filter produces an unpleasant "ridgy" effect on the outline of the nose as it pixellates the picture.

4. Apply the final filter using **Filter>Stylize>Crystallize**. I used a cell size of 6 pixels to achieve the desired effect. The filter was not applied to one area of the nose, but you'd never notice that in the final image.

The Next Step

That's all we'll do with retouching for now. However, I hope you'll continue to experiment with filters and the other tools we've explored in this section to create your own special F/X. Retouching is one way to salvage bad pictures and make good ones even more interesting.

PART IV

Color Correction

Sometimes a horrid-looking image may have nothing more wrong with it than the balance of colors used to represent the image. Other times, the balance may be okay, but you'd like to make the colors look horrid in order to produce a desired special effect in your image.

Color correction doesn't have to be a chore, if you know what you're doing. It can actually be a lot of fun—and your entree to some useful PC F/X.

Color Correction is Abecedarian

I always wanted to write a chapter in which the hardest thing to understand was the title (*Abecedarian* is an actual word. Honest. It means elementary, or as simple as A-B-C) That's the case with color correction—or is it? An image looks too blue, so you take blue away using your dandy image editor. Manipulate a few sliders, and you're done, right? Not necessarily.

But don't panic, yet. It's not my job to take something simple and make it seem hard so you'll be relieved you bought my book. No, I need only to help you avoid the pitfalls that await you, and there are a few along the path to easy color correction. This chapter will map out the chuckholes on the image-processing entrance ramp to the data superhighway. (Now, there's a metaphor that's seen better days.)

I'll show you at least four different ways to change the color balance of an image, each easier than the last. You'll find you can make some perfectly wretched images look great—if you know what to do.

So What's Color Balance?

I've put most of the background material on color theory in *Chapter 12*, if you need it. Right now, you probably just want to know enough to correct your off-color originals or to use color creatively to produce new effects. So, we'll stick to the essentials, for now. Read through *Chapter 12* if you want to know more.

Color balance is the relationship between the three colors used to produce your image—most often red, green, and blue. You need to worry only about three different factors:

- *How much red, green, and blue are in your image.* If you have too much red, the image will appear too red. If you have too much green, it will look too green. Extra blue will make an image look as if it were created under full moon at midnight at the North Pole. Other color casts are produced by too much of two of the primary colors, when compared to the remaining hue. That is too much red and green produce a yellowish cast, red and blue tilt things toward magenta, and blue and green create a cyan bias. The color wheel shown in Figure 10.1 can help you remember the relationships of these colors. The same relationships also exist if you are using a color model with cyan, magenta, and yellow as your primary colors. (See *Chapter 12* for the gory details.)

- *The saturation of each color*—that is, how much of the hue is composed of the pure color itself and how much is diluted by a neutral color, such as white or black. Think of a can of red paint and white paint. Pure red paint is fully saturated. As you add white paint, the color becomes less saturated, until you reach various shades of pink. Color can also become desaturated by adding black paint, making it darker. Your image editor can help you adjust the saturation of a color by removing these neutral white or black components.

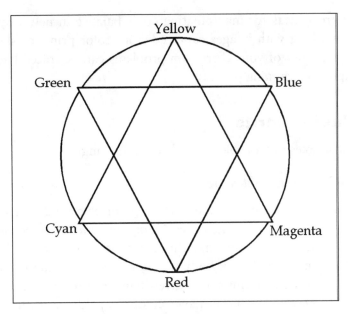

Figure 10.1 *This color wheel shows the relationships between the primary colors in RGB and CMYK color models.*

● *The brightness and contrast of the image.* Brightness and contrast refer to the relative lightness/darkness of each color channel and the number of different tones available. If, say, there are only 12 different red tones in an image, ranging from very light to very dark, with only a few tones in-between, then the red portion of the image can be said to have a high contrast. The brightness is determined by whether the available tones are clustered at the denser or lighter areas of the image. Pros use something called histograms to represent these relationships, but you don't need to bother with those for now.

What Causes Bad Color Balance?

Before I show you how to change color balance, it might be worthwhile to explain why color correction is even necessary. Then, you can avoid or minimize this step routinely and use it only for creative purposes (*Chapter 11* has some great ideas for manipulating color balance in new ways.) Since you'll be working with images captured from color prints or slides most often, the majority of your correction problems can be traced back to the photographic or scanning process.

The Chief Culprits

The major sources of bad color include the following:

Problem: *Wrong light source.*

Reason: All color films are standardized, or balanced, for a particular "color" of light, called *color temperature*. (Technoids will want to know that this figure is arrived at by heating a mythical "black body radiator" and recording the spectrum of light it emits at a given temperature in degrees Kelvin.) Daylight at noon has a color temperature in the 5500° to 6000° range. Indoor illumination is around 3400°. Hotter temperatures produce bluer images (think blue-white hot) while cooler temperatures produce redder images (think of a dull-red glowing ember). Because of human nature, though, bluer images are called cool and redder images are called warm.

If a photograph is exposed indoors under warm illumination using film balanced for cooler daylight, the image will appear much too reddish. If you were using a slide film, you get reddish slides. The photoprocessing lab can add some blue while making prints from "daylight balanced" color negatives exposed under this warm light, though, giving you well-balanced prints.

Some professional films are balanced for interior (tungsten) illumination. If one of these is exposed under daylight, it will appear too blue. Again, prints made from tungsten-balanced color negatives can be corrected at the lab.

Solution: You can often make corrections for this type of defect digitally with your image-editing software. However, to avoid the need entirely, use the correct film, or use a filter over the camera lens to compensate for the incorrect light source. You may not need to bother with color negative films, but will certainly want to do something in the case of slide films. Note: the light a filter removes must be compensated for by increasing the exposure in the camera.

Problem: *Fluorescent light source.*

Reason: The chief difference between tungsten and daylight sources is the proportion of red and blue light. Some types of fluorescent lights produce illumination that has a severe deficit in certain colors, such as some particular shades of red. If you looked at the spectrum or rainbow of colors encompassed by such a light source, it would have black bands in it, representing particular wavelengths of light. You can't compensate for this deficiency by adding all tones of red, either digitally or with a filter that is not designed specifically for that type of fluorescent light.

Solution: Your camera retailer can provide you with color filters recommended for particular kinds of fluorescent lamps. These filters are designed to add only the amounts and types of colors needed. Because it's difficult to correct for fluorescent lights digitally, you'll want to investigate this option if you shoot many pictures under fluorescents and are getting greenish results.

Problem: *Incorrect photofinishing.*

Reason: Equipment that makes prints from color negatives is highly automated and usually can differentiate between indoor and outdoor pictures or those that have a large amount of one color. Sometimes the sensors are fooled and you end up with off-color prints or those that are too light or dark. The processing of color slides won't usually have any effect on the color balance or density of the transparencies, unless something is way out of whack, so you'll usually be concerned only about the color balance of prints.

Solution: Change finishers if it happens often. Ask that your prints be reprinted. If you'd rather not bother, you can often make corrections digitally after you scan the prints.

Problem: *Mistreatment of original film.*

Reason: If you regularly store a camera in the hot glove compartment of your car or take a year or more to finish a roll of film, you can end up with color prints that are off-color—sometimes by quite a bit. If your prints have a nasty purple cast, or even some rainbow-hued flares in them, your negatives probably suffered this indignity.

Solution: Usually, film that has been "fogged" by heat or latent image-keeping effects cannot be corrected.

Problem: *Mixed light sources.*

Reason: You bounced your flash off a surface such as a colored wall or ceiling, and the pictures picked up the color of that surface. Or, you took an indoor picture with plenty of tungsten light, but the subject is near a window and is partially illuminated by daylight.

Solution: Don't do that. If some of your image is illuminated by the colored bounce flash or daylight streaming in through a window and other portions by another light source, you'll find it very difficult to make corrections. Investigate turning that picture into an "arty" shot.

Problem: *Faded colors.*

Reason: The dyes in color prints and slides are not stable and will change when exposed to strong light or heat for long periods (1–5 years) or with no further impetus even if kept in the dark for much longer periods (5–20 years and up).

Solution: In the case of color prints, you can sometimes make a new print from the original negative if (1) you can find the negative and (2) it was kept in a cool, dark place. Faded color prints and original slides can often be corrected digitally after scanning, because the color changes tend to take place faster in one color layer than another. You may be able to "add" missing colors by reducing the amount of the other colors in the photograph.

There are other reasons why you can end up with poorly balanced images, but this section has covered the ones you can do something about. Now, let's look at four different ways to color correct these images.

Color Correction Made Easy

I'll start out with several traditional ways to correct color in images and then move on to some newer, easier alternatives. You can select the method you're most comfortable with—hands-on, seat-of-the-pants correction or the simple, automated alternatives provided by some software packages.

WARNING

As you try to improve the color balance, brightness/contrast, and other attributes of photographs, keep in mind that none of the following methods can add detail or color that isn't there. All techniques work well with photographs that have, say, all the colors somewhere, but with too much of one hue or another. The extra color can be removed, leaving a well-balanced picture behind.

Or, you can beef up the other colors so that they are in balance once again. Your image editing-program does that by changing some pixels that are relatively close to the color you want to increase to that exact color.

Removing one color or changing some colors to another color doesn't add any color to your image. Either way, you're taking color out. If you have a photograph that is hopelessly and overpoweringly green, you're out of luck. When you remove all the green, there may be no color left behind. Or, you can add magenta until your subject's face turns blue (well, it won't happen that way), and all you'll end up with is a darker photo. You must start with a reasonable image; color correction is better suited for fine-tuning than major overhaul.

Using Color Balance Controls

The first way we'll color correct an image is using the color balance controls that virtually every image-editing program has. This method is oriented most toward brute force and may be a little complicated for the neophyte. Stick with me, though. Later in the chapter, I have two alternatives that are a breeze to master. This section lays down some principles you can use in *Chapter 11* to create wild color effects, even if you decide to perform normal color corrections by one of the other methods.

Depending on your particular software, you may have to hunt to find a set of sliders that can be used to adjust all colors for an entire image. For example, in PhotoStyler, you'll find the controls under the Image>Tune>Color Balance menu. In Fauve Matisse, there are actually three different color-balancing options in the Image>Tune menu: one each for RGB, CMYK, and HSL color systems. If you're using Photoshop, look under the Image menu, choose **Adjust** and then **Color Balance** (or just press **Control-Y** if you're in a hurry.)

No matter what program you're using, the dialog box will look more or less like Figure 10.2, with a few differences. (I used the Photoshop 2.5.1 dialog box, because that's the version of the program provided on the CD-ROM with this book; with Photoshop 3.0, the dialog box looks slightly different.) For example, Photoshop lets you set color balance separately for shadows, midtones, and highlights. What we're interested at this point are the color sliders.

These let you adjust the proportions of a particular color, from 0% to 100%. In the case of Photoshop, you can either add one color, or subtract its two *component colors* (the colors on either side of it on the color wheel in Figure 10.1). For example, moving the Cyan/Red slider to +20 (sliding it toward the red end) has the same effect as moving the Magenta/Green and Yellow/Red sliders both to the –20 position (toward the left).

Which should you choose? If you want to add pure red (or green or blue), you can move the relevant control to the right. If your needs lean a little more toward one of the component colors than the other, move those sliders to the left, instead. The following example below will show what I mean.

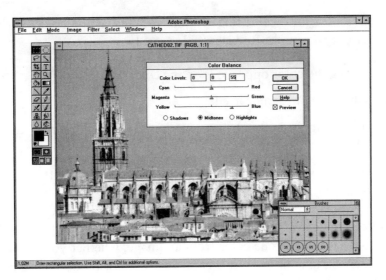

Figure 10.2 *Your image editor's color balance sliders may let you change only red, green, and blue values or may also include cyan, magenta, and yellow.*

Correcting One Color Only

Color insert Figure 7 shows an unaltered telephoto picture of a portion of the Toledo, Spain, skyline in the upper left. Unfortunately, the original print was over 20 years old and took on a strong reddish cast as it faded.

I could have removed this red tone by simply sliding the Cyan/Red control toward the Cyan, which is the opposite or complementary color of red (you'll see it's on the other side of the color wheel in Figure 10.1). Because Photoshop (and most other image-editing programs) lets you preview the results, it would have been just a matter of subtracting red (adding cyan) until the picture looked right. In this case, a value of −36 applied only to the middle tones of the photo (those other than the highlights or shadows) would have been about perfect. In most cases, that's all you'll need to do.

You can see that it is possible to remove red in one of two ways:

● Add cyan (thereby subtracting red)

● Add green and blue (thereby subtracting magenta and yellow)

I know it's a little confusing without looking at the color wheel, but the basic rules are simple. Reduce a color cast by

- adding the color opposite it on the color wheel,
- subtracting the color itself,
- subtracting equal amounts of the adjacent colors on the color wheel,
- adding equal amounts of the other two colors on its color wheel triangle.

If you keep the color wheel in mind, you won't find it difficult to know how to add or subtract one color from an image, whether you are working with red, green, blue or cyan, magenta, yellow color models. (You can find more information about color models in *Chapter 12.*)

Correcting for Several Colors

When color casts are not pure, it's not possible to make corrections just by using the first two methods. You'll need to use the other two methods, but instead of adding or subtracting equal amounts of two other colors, you can modify the amount of one color or the other to generate the exact amount of correction you need.

If, say, your image were too reddish but had a slight magenta cast to it also, you'd want to use the third method but subtract slightly more magenta than yellow. Although the sample photo in Color insert Figure 7 was too reddish, there was also a bit too much magenta.

Instead of adding cyan (subtracting red), I subtracted magenta and yellow (added green and blue), but a little more heavily on the green side (+36 green, but only +30 blue.) This adjustment subtracted more magenta than yellow, producing the exact colors I wanted, although still a bit on the light side. I reduced the brightness of the image to −63 and contrast to −31, and arrived at the middle photo in Color insert Figure 7.

The files I worked with are provided on the CD-ROM bundled with this book as **CATHED01.TIF–CATHED03.TIF** in the Chapter 10 subdirectory if you'd like to try these out for yourself. Depending on what image-editing software you are using and how your system is calibrated, your results may vary slightly, but I've pointed you in the right direction.

The biggest challenge here is deciding in exactly which direction you need to add/subtract color. Magenta may look a lot like red, and it's difficult to tell cyan from green. You may need to correct of both red and magenta or work with a slightly cyanish-green. Your photo retailer has color printing guide books published by Kodak and others that contain red, green, blue, cyan, magenta, and yellow viewing filters. Use them to view your image until you find the right combination of colors.

Adding Special F/X

Before we leave this section, I'd like to explain how I finished off this corrected photo with some special F/X, as shown in the lower left of Color insert Figure 7. You didn't think that just fixing the color would turn this old photo into something special, did you?

I'll explain how to perform this effect using Photoshop. The filter used, Lens Flare, is a Photoshop plug-in that may not work properly with other image-editing software that otherwise are compatible with these plug-ins. You can work with the file **CATHED02.TIF** on the CD-ROM and try out this effect using your own software if you like.

Just follow these steps or their equivalents.

1. Select the sky using the Magic Wand tool. Set the Tolerance level to 32 pixels, and turn on Anti-Aliasing, as shown in Figure 10.3. (Double click on the Magic Wand tool to bring up the dialog box.)

2. Double-click on the foreground color box and choose a dark blue from the color picker. Then double-click on the background color box and select a slightly lighter blue, as shown in Figure 10.4. (The foreground and background color boxes are the large overlapping boxes in the lower third of the tool palette.)

3. Click on the gradient tool (it's just below the magnifying glass). Then click at the top of the selected sky area and drag down toward the cathedral. Release the mouse button to produce a new, vivid gradient to replace the bland sky in the original photo. The gradient sky is too smooth to be realistic.

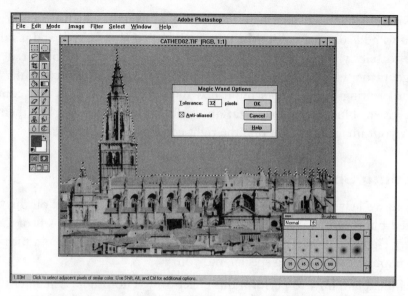

Figure 10.3 *Select the sky using the Magic Wand tool.*

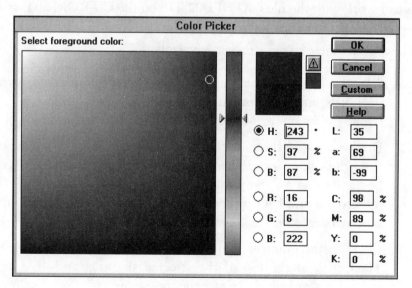

Figure 10.4 *Choose two blue shades from your image editor's color picker.*

Photoshop's Gradient Tool Options dialog box offers several often-misunderstood style choices. When you select **Clockwise Spectrum** or **Counterclockwise Spectrum**, your gradient will consist of the intervening hues between the foreground and background colors taken from the bright shades along the periphery of the color wheel. When you choose **Normal**, the gradient will consist of colors taken from the hues found in a straight line between the foreground and background colors. If you'll check out an actual color wheel, you'll see that these tones are less vivid. Choose **Clockwise Spectrum** or **Counterclockwise Spectrum** for a rich, fully saturated gradient, and **Normal** for a more "realistic" looking progression of tones.

4. From the Filter menu, choose **Noise** and then **Add Noise** and specify an amount of **12** and **Uniform** distribution. Realistic grain is added to the sky area.

   That's a good start, but we need something more. I decided to simulate a midafternoon sun peeking from behind the cathedral's tower, complete with lens flare.

5. Deselect the rightmost third of the Toledo sky. We don't want the lens flare to overwhelm this picture, so by reducing the selected area, we can limit the effect to the left portion of the picture. Select the Lasso tool, hold down the **Control** key, and remove the right portion of the sky from the selection.

6. Now, add the "sun." From the Filter menu, choose **Stylize** and **Lens Flare.** Click on the **105mm prime** button and move the cross hair (drag with the mouse) that determines the center of the flare effect to a position just to the right of the cathedral tower. The dialog box is shown in Figure 10.5.

7. Use the Lasso tool to reselect the sky area that you removed in Step 5. Hold down the **Shift** key while tracing the area to be added to the current selection. Then change the Foreground color to **White.** Finally, using the Airbrush tool (pressure set to 2%), paint a few light clouds to simulate a slight overcast.

The finished image will look like the one shown in Color insert Figure 7.

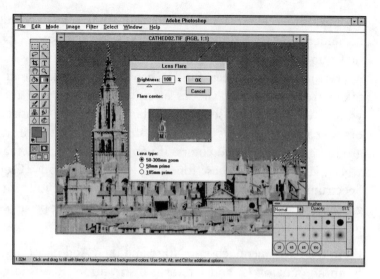

Figure 10.5 *Photoshop's Lens Flare dialog box.*

Using Hue/Saturation Controls

You can also color correct an image using the Hue/Saturation/Lightness or (Brightness) controls found in most image editors. The advantage of correcting color this way is that you can change the saturation of individual colors or of all the colors in an image, without modifying the hue or lightness/darkness of those colors. The Color Balance method changes only the relationships between the colors.

For this example, we'll use an image of a home that had only a minor color cast problem but that suffered from serious desaturation of its colors. The photo looked weak and lifeless. You can view the original in the upper left of Color insert Figure 8 or load the actual file **HOUSE01.TIF** from the Chapter 10 subdirectory on the CD-ROM.

The Hue/Saturation/Lightness dialog box of most image editors let you change the richness of the colors in an image without modifying the individual colors. You do this by applying Saturation changes to the main or master channel or layer of an image. If you need to beef up just one color (say, to make your reds more saturated), you can do that, too.

The Hue control allows changing the overall balance of the image (or one individual color layer, if you wish) by rotating the palette one direction or another around the periphery of the color wheel.

Adjusting Hue/Saturation/Brightness for All Colors

Because our sample photo has such poor saturation, we'll adjust all the colors first. Just follow the steps in the next section. You can load **HOUSE01.TIF** into your copy of Photoshop or perform the parallel steps using the image editor of your choice.

1. Access your Hue/Saturation/Brightness dialog box. With Photoshop, choose the Image menu and then select **Adjust** and **Hue/Saturation** (or just press **Control-V**). With other image editors you may have to switch from RGB mode to HSL or HSB mode.

2. Change the Saturation value until the picture gains, in Preview mode, the richness of color you are looking for. I used a setting of +50 for our sample photo.

3. The color is slightly off, too. Experiment with the Hue control to find a setting that corrects any imbalance. In this case, I entered a value of –20, which moved the color balance clockwise around the color wheel away from magenta and toward pure blue. Figure 10.6 shows the direction of the color change. Figure 10.7 shows the Hue/Saturation dialog box of Photoshop.

When you adjust hues for the *master channel* of an image, no colors are lost or removed: they are simply moved around the color wheel en masse. What's a channel? Each channel you work with is a layer containing only the values of a particular color: red, green, blue, cyan, magenta, yellow, or black. When you adjust the hue, saturation, or lightness of a particular channel, only that channel is affected, in contrast to the global changes you make on the combined or master channel, which includes all of them.

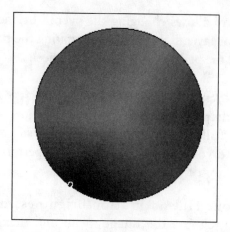

Figure 10.6 *Minus values move color balance in a clockwise direction around the color wheel.*

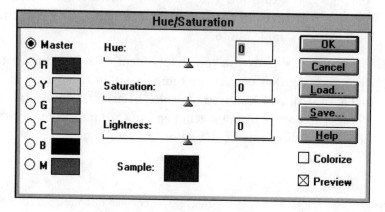

Figure 10.7 *Hue, saturation, and lightness values can be entered as positive or negative numbers.*

4. Adjust the brightness of the image by moving the Lightness (or Brightness, depending on your image editor) slider. This adjustment varies only the relative darkness or lightness of all the colors in the image. If you want to change the contrast at the same time, you should use your application's Brightness/Contrast control.

The richer colors of the altered image should be apparent in the second version of this photograph, shown in the lower right of Color insert Figure 8. The actual image file I ended up with is in the Chapter 10 subdirectory as **HOUSE02.TIF**.

Adjusting Hue/Saturation/Brightness for One Color Only

You may encounter images that can be improved by changing the hue, saturation, or brightness of one color only. Most image editors that can work with HSB or HSL color (see *Chapter 12* for a discussion of these color models) let you adjust individual values for each color channel (red, green, blue, cyan, magenta, and yellow).

You might have a holiday picture that needs to have its reds and greens enriched, but with muted blues. Perhaps the green grass and foliage in another color have picked up an undesirable color cast and you want to shift all the green values one way or another to improve the color. Or, you may want to darken or lighten just one color in an image (rather than all of them, which is done through the conventional Lighten/Darken controls).

Any of these changes are possible with the HSL dialog box. Just select the Color channel you want to work with and move the sliders to get the effects you want. In *Chapter 11* I'll provide some examples of images that have been modified in this way.

Using Color Ring-Arounds and Variations

Professional color labs charge a lot more for the same size print as, say, an amateur-oriented photofinisher. (Amateur finishers are professionals, too, of course, but they work for a customer base made up primarily of amateur, rather than professional photographers.) Instead of a dollar or two for a photofinisher's 8 × 10-inch print, you can pay $10.00 to $20.00 and up (way up) for the same size print from a professional lab. Why the difference?

Both amateur and professional labs can produce automated (or machine) prints, although the equipment may be very different. The professional lab also offers hand-made or custom prints, produced one at a time with an enlarger and painstaking manual techniques. The exact color balance of a custom print is often crucial, so a professional lab may produce five or six variations and let the client choose the preferred example. That's why custom prints are worth the extra money: you're paying not only for the hand work but also for the ability to choose from among several different prints. It's faster and more efficient for the lab to produce the variations all at once than to go back and make tiny corrections over and over until the exact version you want is produced.

The same logic holds true in the digital world. You can play with the color balance of an image for hours at a time, never quite achieving what you are looking for. There's no guarantee that, after a lot of work, you might decide that an earlier version really did look better, after all.

Image editors are jumping on the color ring-around or variations bandwagon. In this mode, the software itself generates several versions of an image, arranged in a circle or other array so that you can view a small copy of each one and compare them. Photoshop's Variations mode is especially useful, so I'll use it to illustrate a third way to color correct problem photos.

Working with Photoshop's Variations Option

For this exercise, I'll use a typical color portrait that has been goofed up big-time. It's been printed quite a bit too dark, with plenty of extra red. Yet, hiding underneath this disaster is a good photo. We can use Photoshop's Variations (or the equivalent in your image editor) to fix this image.

If you want to follow along, you can load **CATHY01.TIF** from the Chapter 10 subdirectory on the CD-ROM. Otherwise, experiment with a photo image of your own. The principles are exactly the same. Just follow these steps.

1. With Photoshop, generate a color ring-around by choosing the Image menu from the main menu bar and then selecting **Adjust** and **Variations** from the submenu. The Variations window, shown in Figure 10.8, and in Color insert Figure 9.

Figure 10.8 *Photoshop's Variations dialog box lets you adjust color cast and lightness/darkness of an image.*

There are several components in this window:

- In the upper left corner, you'll find thumbnail images of your original image paired with a preview with the changes you've made applied. As you apply corrections, the Current Pick thumbnail will change.

- Immediately underneath is another panel with the current pick surrounded by six different versions, each biased toward a different color: green, yellow, red, magenta, blue, and cyan. These versions show what your current pick would look like with that type of correction added. You can click on any of them to apply that correction to the current pick.

- To the right of this ring-around is a panel with three sample images: the current pick in the center with a lighter version above and a darker version below.

- In the upper right corner of this window is a group of controls that modifies how the other samples are displayed. I'll describe these controls shortly.

2. If the **Midtones** button is not depressed, click on it. Move the pointer in the Fine Coarse scale to the middle and check the **Show Clipping** button. The purpose of each of these controls is as follows:

● The radio buttons determine whether the correction options are applied to the shadows, midtones, or highlights of the image—or only to saturation characteristics. You may make (must make) adjustments for each of these separately.

● The Fine Coarse scale determines the increment used for each of the variations displayed in the two lower panels. If you select a finer increment, the differences between the current pick and each of the options will be much smaller. A coarser increment provides much grosser changes with each variation. You may need these options to correct an original that is badly off-color. Because fine increments are difficult to detect on-screen and coarse increments are often too drastic for tight control, I recommend keeping the pointer in the center of the scale.

● The Show Clipping box tells the program to show you in neon colors which areas will be converted to pure white or pure black if you apply a particular adjustment to highlight or shadow areas (midtones aren't clipped).

● You may load or save the adjustments you've made in a session so that you can apply them to the image at any later time. You can use this option to create a file of settings that can be used with several similarly balanced images, thereby correcting all of them efficiently.

3. Our image is too red, so the More Cyan thumbnail will look better. Click on it to apply that correction to the current pick. In fact, click twice, because the original image is very red.

4. Click on the Lighter thumbnail, because the image is also too dark.

5. Click on the **OK** button when you are finished. The file **CATHY02.TIF** in the Chapter 10 subdirectory on the CD-ROM contains the final version.

In this example, we worked only with the midtones. In most cases, the shadows, midtones, and highlights will need roughly the same amount of correction. In others, though, the shadows or highlights may have picked up a color cast of their own (say, reflected from an object off-camera). Variations lets you correct these separately if you need to.

More often, though, you'll use the Shadows, Midtones, and Highlights options to improve the appearance of images that have too-dark shadows or washed out highlights. Where any image editor's brightness/contrast control generally affects all the colors equally, this procedure lets you lighten shadows (bringing out more detail) or darken highlights (keeping them from becoming washed out) without affecting other portions of the image. The technique also lets you avoid nasty histograms and gamma curves.

Preserving Your Corrections

Once you make color corrections, don't lose all your hard work by converting an image from one mode to another without understanding the consequences. *Chapter 12* explains in more detail the differences between the RGB and CMYK color models, so I won't spoil the surprise. You should be aware of the following cautions:

- If you switch back and forth between RGB and CMYK, your colors can change. Colors that can be represented by the RGB model can't always be duplicated in the CMYK model (and vice versa). Anytime you switch between the two, you run the risk of losing some colors. It's especially deadly to change from one model to the other and then back to the original. Photoshop 3.0 added a preview mode that lets you view CMYK color schemes without actually changing the file's content, so that you can return to RGB with your colors intact. Otherwise, the results are similar to the phrase, "Out of sight, out of mind," translated into Russian and then back into English by a computer program. The English phrase that resulted was "Invisible, insane!"

- As a corollary, not all tones you can see on your screen (RGB colors) can be represented by printing inks (which use CMYK tones), so don't expect the printed version of your image to match exactly. You'll be closer if you work with the (slower) CMYK model, if your editing software supports it. Photoshop's color picker displays an exclamation point above the Current Color/Sample Color boxes when you've selected a hue that can't be printed. It offers a duller alternative color that does conform to the CMYK color model.

● If you change from either 24-bit models to Indexed Color (which boils all colors down to the 256 hues), you may get a good representation of your original, or a horrid one. This topic is worth the following separate section.

Converting from 24-Bit Color to 8-Bit Color

You'll find that 24-bit color image files tend to be large, because three full bytes are set aside to represent each and every pixel in your image. The files are squeezed down a little by compression schemes, such as the Lempel-Ziv Welch (LZW) method used for TIFF files. Other compression methods such as JPEG make 24-bit files even smaller by discarding some of the image information (at the cost of some image quality). However, don't think you can save some disk space by converting from 24-bit color to 8-bit, 256 colors, known as *indexed color*. The space gains are far outweighed by the information lost, particularly if you have a full, rich image with gradients and other tones that demand more than 256 different hues.

Where indexed color comes in is the vast world of users who simply don't have 24-bit color displays. When a PC user who has a 256-color display views one of your precious 24-bit images, the system must dither the image to simulate the additional hues. The results may be grainy, fuzzy, exhibit banding in the gradients, and not look anything like what you intended. Your carefully prepared desktop presentation can become a joke, without your even knowing about it.

Prevent problems by converting images to 256 colors yourself, so that you can preview them on your 16- or 24-bit display. After all, you might not need 24-bit color to represent a particular image. The 16.7 million colors possible refers only to the palette of colors your image can draw from. No image will need anywhere near that number of colors. After all, a 640 × 480-pixel image has only 307,200 different pixels. If each of them were a different color, you'd need only 307,200 different colors—a far cry from 16.7 million!

Indexed color is based on the notion that many color images can be represented by far fewer than 16.7 million hues. Indeed, many can be displayed with 100% accuracy using only 256 different colors, producing a file size that is somewhat smaller—and one that can be viewed on PC systems having only 256-color video. Other images may have more colors than 256 but still look good when similar colors are combined and represented by one of the 256 in an indexed color palette.

The key here is to create an optimized palette. What you don't want is an equal representation of all the colors in the spectrum. That might give you far too many blues but not enough greens to represent a given scene. Think of a portrait of a man wearing a brown suit and a solid green tie. You may need only 10–20 different greens to encompass all the subtle shades of green in the tie. Another 50 or so browns might be required for the suit. Only a few blues, yellows, or other hues would be needed. The bulk of your tones might fall into the pinks or browns that make up flesh tones. By carefully selecting the most frequently used 256 tones in an image, you can often accurately represent a 24-bit file using 8-bit color.

Image editors usually offer you a choice of methods for choosing the palette for converting an image to indexed color. Figure 10.9 shows Photoshop's Indexed Color dialog box.

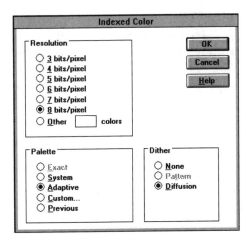

Figure 10.9 *Indexed colors can be calculated by a variety of methods.*

You need to specify three different parameters used to build a color look-up table (CLUT) that will be used to convert all the colors in your image to one of the colors in the CLUT (either an exact match, or the closest color).

Your software may not let you convert from CMYK to indexed color. Make sure that you are working in RGB mode before trying to convert colors.

- *Resolution.* The number of colors in your palette. If you're converting from a full-color 24-bit image, most often this will be the maximum—256 colors—selected by clicking the **8 bits/pixel** radio button. Your image editor will often calculates the resolution needed; if your image has 128 colors or fewer, it will use a 7-bit palette; 64 colors or fewer, a 6-bit palette, and so on. **Other:** represents an exact number of colors, fewer than 256. If your image has fewer than 256 colors, you can convert it precisely, retaining all the colors in the original.

- *Palette.* The crucial parameter. If your image already contains 256 colors or fewer, choose **Exact** to get a perfect rendition of the image. Choose **System** or **Uniform** (the **System** choice changes to **Uniform** if you select other than 8 bits/pixel resolution) to create a CLUT that is evenly distributed among all the RGB colors. You probably won't want to use this choice, except for images with an even distribution of color. Check the **Adaptive** button in most cases. The software will choose the most frequently used colors in the image. The **Custom** choice lets you load a previously saved CLUT (so that you can share color palettes between similar images, or apply one CLUT to a new image). **Previous** applies the last custom CLUT you used in this session (and is available only if you had used the **Custom** command earlier).

- *Dither.* The parameter that tells the software how to simulate colors that don't have a direct equivalent in the CLUT palette that is built. Choose **None**, and the software selects the closest color in the CLUT. **Pattern** can be used to create odd geometric arrangements of colors, and only if you chose the **System** palette option. You might like the special effects that result, but avoid this choice if you're looking for realistic color. Your best choice is usually **Diffusion**, which distributes the extra colors randomly and naturally.

Once you've converted an image to indexed color, you can still edit the hues, but you'll need to use some special techniques. Your image editor should have a provision to allow you to edit the colors in the color look-up table. In Photoshop, it's under the **Mode>Color Table** choice. You can select any color in the CLUT and substitute another color from the color picker.

The Next Step

This chapter took you through four different methods to correct the color balance and tonal appearance of full-color images. You learned how manual methods aren't really that difficult once you understand how colors are arranged in the color wheel. However, if you want the easiest, fastest color corrections possible, you'll want to use a color ring-around or variations method like the ones used by Photoshop and other image editors.

Now, let's see how easy it is to pervert the color correction features of your software to create some new and interesting images that might not have what you would define as standard colors. We'll do that in *Chapter 11*.

CHAPTER

11

Some Wild Special F/X with Color Correction

Now that you know how to adjust colors to make a photographic image look more realistic, I'll spend a little time doing the exact opposite: creating special F/X by manipulating the color controls of your image editor. This chapter will show you some ways to use the Color Balance and Hue/Saturation/Brightness tools discussed in *Chapter 10*. I also have a few new tricks in store for you.

I'll throw theory out the door for this chapter (there's plenty of that in *Chapter 12*) for one simple reason: When you're trying to achieve wild color effects, you don't really care about which colors add up to what (as you must when you're trying to make precise color corrections). The best thing you can do when exploring the outrageous is to forget what you know and just play with the color controls until you get something interesting.

In the next few sections, I'll show you some interesting effects (pictured in full color in the color plate section of this book) and explain how I got them. Don't worry why I added red, magenta, and yellow—just do it. Then take the leap to some experiments of your own. Remember that you can get back to square one just by clicking on **Undo** from the Edit menu or by loading the last version of your file.

Using Unbalanced Color

Good color balance does not always the best picture make. Look at the leftmost image in Color insert Figure 10. Or, you can load **PRFILE01.TIF** from the Chapter 11 folder in the CD-ROM. This profile study of a blonde model deliberately uses a red background and a reddish tinge in most of the highlights to counteract the "cool blonde" image we often see.

Can we carry the concept a bit further? The middle image in Color insert Figure 10 was produced using nothing more than the Color Balancing dialog box of an image editor. I took advantage of the application's ability to balance highlights, midtones, and shadows differently to change the colors wildly. I followed these steps, which you can duplicate with the tryout version of Photoshop included on the CD-ROM with this book. You can also perform the equivalent steps with your favorite image editor.

1. Load PRFILE01.TIF and select **Adjust** and **Color Balance** from the Image Menu.

2. Click on the **Highlights** button to make changes only to the lighter portions of the photograph.

3. Slide the Cyan slider all the way to the left and the Blue slider all the way to the right. This gives all the highlight areas (e.g., the lightest portions of the hair and face) a distinct violet tone.

4. Click on the **Midtones** button, so that you can make changes only to the middle tones of the images (those that aren't shadows or highlights).

5. Move the Red, Magenta, and Yellow sliders to their maximums. This really gooses up the reds in those areas.

6. Leave the shadow areas alone. Exit from this dialog box by clicking on **OK**.

Figure 11.1 shows the Color Balance dialog box. You can get a closer look at my results by loading **PRFILE02.TIF** into your image editor.

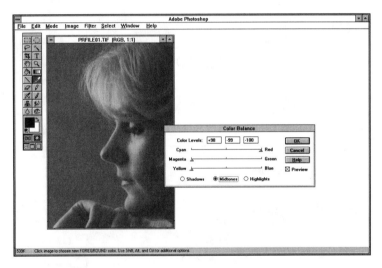

Figure 11.1   *The Color Balance dialog box allows making settings for each color independently.*

Using Hue/Saturation/Brightness

The third image in Color insert Figure 10 was produced using a different approach. I wanted to emphasize the red tones by providing a bright magenta background. To do that, I used the Hue/Saturation/Brightness controls. The effect you see was accomplished following these steps.

1. Load **PRFILE01.TIF** and select **Adjust** and **Hue/Saturation** from the Image menu.

2. Click on the **Red** channel radio button. Then, set Hue to −60 (Magenta) and Saturation to 85%. That setting produces a deep

purple background, bright red midtones, and yellowish highlights. Try it yourself with **PRFILE01.TIF**, if you can't visualize this.

3. Click on the **Yellow** channel radio button and set Saturation to 100% and lightness to +54. That boosts the reds to an almost luminous level.

The Hue/Saturation dialog box is shown in Figure 11.2, and you can glimpse the final result in the right-hand image of Color insert Figure 10, or the file **PRFILE03.TIF** on the CD-ROM.

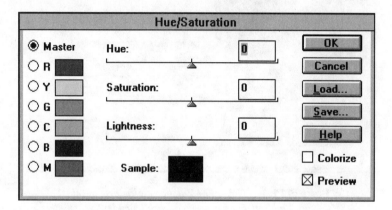

Figure 11.2 *The Hue/Saturation dialog box lets you set hue, saturation, or lightness without affecting the other parameters.*

As you've seen from the previous two exercises, the Color Balance dialog box is your best choice when you want to shift all the colors in an image in one direction or another. The Hue/Saturation/Brightness dialog box lets you change the colors, richness, and lightness/darkness of each color in an image independently.

Using Special Color Filters

In photography, color filters are pieces of glass or gelatin that allow certain types or colors of light to penetrate, while blocking others. In the digital world, filters are much more versatile: They can block virtually any kind of input, while admitting or modifying other streams of data.

Figure 1 Four intermediate views as summer turns to winter in this morph image created with Elastic Reality.

Figure 2 This hodgepodge of vacation snapshots can be combined into one outrageous image.

Figure 3   Compositing combined all the snapshots into this image.

Figure 4

Even this point-and-
shoot snapshot can be
recycled with some
judicious retouching—
off with the glasses
and on with the
new background.

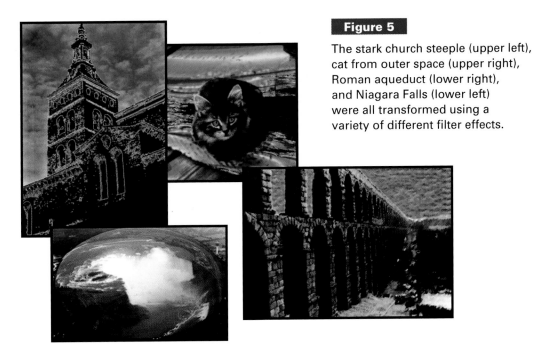

Figure 5

The stark church steeple (upper left),
cat from outer space (upper right),
Roman aqueduct (lower right),
and Niagara Falls (lower left)
were all transformed using a
variety of different filter effects.

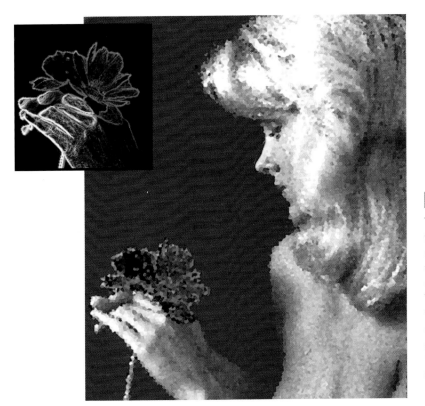

Figure 6

The plain red
flower in the
original image
was spiced up
using Photoshop's
Trace Contours
filter; then the
entire image was
given a painted
look with the
Crystalize filter.

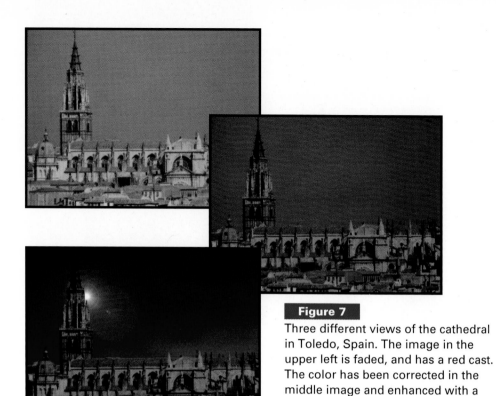

Figure 7

Three different views of the cathedral in Toledo, Spain. The image in the upper left is faded, and has a red cast. The color has been corrected in the middle image and enhanced with a sun-like flare in the bottom image.

Figure 8

Faded colors can be resurrected using the Hue/Saturation controls of most image editors. The photo in the upper left was transformed just by adding some color.

Figure 9 Photoshop and other image editors provide an easy way to correct color images by offering you variations to choose from.

Figure 10 The image on the left was predominantly red, so I emphasized the positive by adding various combinations of magenta, red, and yellow in the middle and right versions.

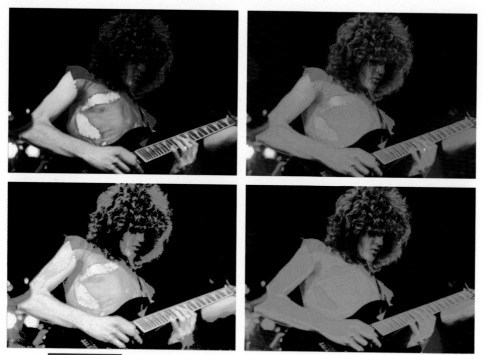

Figure 11 The original image of this would-be rock star (upper left) was okay, but I used an image editor's controls to produce the better images at top right and bottom.

Figure 12
The "King of the Blues," B.B. King is awesome in black and white, but subtle undertones of emotion are added by coloring this image a rich blue or red.

Figure 13

Swapping color channels
can produce outrageous
effects. In this picture, I
exchanged the red and
green channels, but kept
the castle in its original hues
for an other-worldly image.

Figure 14 The city walls of this Spanish city were drastically
in need of restoration, so I created a new castle with a
3D modeling program and dropped it into the photograph.

Figure 15   Pixar Typestry produced all these 3D type effects.

Figure 16

Filters can produce
exciting new images from
old ones in a few seconds.

Every image-editing program has its own set of filters, which produces sharpening, blurring, or other effects. While some filters are proprietary to the particular editing program, others are created in the form of Photoshop-compatible plug-ins, which can be accessed by any compliant application. Many third-party plug-ins are used to modify colors in an image.

Color insert Figure 11 shows four different versions of an image of an aspiring rock star. The picture in the upper left shows the unaltered version of the photo, exposed onto a high-speed color negative film using only stage illumination. This lighting happened to be a mixture of white front-light and a reddish backlight.

The upper right-hand picture is the same image, manipulated using the hue/saturation/brightness techniques described in the last section. I added a strong magenta cast, which livened things up a little, but I was looking for more. Chromassage can give you a virtually unending stream of variations on a single picture, although simple tools like jog wheels let you dial in the colors you want. The lower two pictures in Color insert Figure 11 show you the kinds of effects you can expect with this utility.

Colorizing Black-and-White Pictures

Your image editor's color controls can be used to add color to a black-and-white photo. For this exercise, I took a favorite photo of mine of B. B. King, and added color to it. The original was a black-and-white image taken with flash. (It was intended for newspaper publication, but the paper couldn't handle photos exposed under high-contrast stage lighting.) Still, I liked this mini-travesty and wished I had a color version.

I created two different versions, as shown in Color insert Figure 12. The original is shown in the upper left, along with blue and red versions. Either can be produced by following the same steps. You can follow along with the tryout version of Photoshop included on the CD-ROM or your own copy or an image editor of your choice (just substitute the appropriate commands from your version).

1. Load **BBKING01.TIF** from the Chapter 11 folder on the CD-ROM.

2. Change from Grayscale mode to RGB mode by using the Mode menu. Don't forget this step; you can't make color changes to a gray-scale image.

3. Select the Image menu and choose **Adjust** and **Hue/Saturation**.

4. Click in the Colorize box to assign every pixel in the image the same hue and saturation level. The brightness values are unchanged, so a dark gray pixel becomes a dark blue (or red or green or whatever) pixel in the colorized image.

5. Set Saturation to 100%. Ordinarily, a lower setting looks better when colorizing an image, but we want a vivid, dramatic effect for this image.

6. Adjust the Hue slider to create a single color scheme worthy of the King of the Blues. I produced the blue version to represent B. B. King's blues and rhythm-and-blues heritage. The red version reflects the fiery emotion of his playing and singing.

Figure 11.3 shows the Hue/Saturation dialog box in Colorize mode.

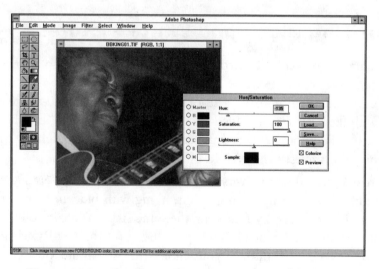

Figure 11.3 *The Hue/Saturation dialog box in Colorize mode allows adding hues to black-and-white photos.*

Make note of the Hue and Saturation values you used to produce your image. You can type them into the Photoshop color picker to duplicate the exact color value you'll need to retouch a colorized photo. Convert negative Hue values to a positive number by subtracting from 360°. That is, -148° converts to 212°. Once you've specified the photo's hue as your Foreground color, you can paint with any brush by setting the brush palette to **Color**. Figure 11.4 shows the two dialog boxes involved.

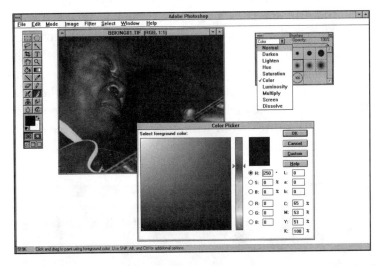

Figure 11.4 *You can edit colorized photos by setting the Foreground color to the same hue as the photo and choosing Color in the brush palette.*

Swapping Channels for Special Color Effects

Our next special F/X are produced by taking one of the three color channels and exchanging it for another in your image, producing a startling "false color" effect. Anybody can do that, however. Let's make the image really interesting by changing the colors on only part of the image. You can follow along using the Photoshop tryout version included on the

CD-ROM, your own copy of Photoshop, or another image editor. I'll to stick to F/X that can be done with just about any 24-bit editing program.

Just follow these steps.

1. Load the file **HCAST01.TIF** into your image editor. It's a picture of a castle on an ugly, but authentically brown hillside.

2. Isolate the castle by selecting it. A fast way is to use your image editor's Magic Wand to select only the sky area, using a pixel tolerance of about 30. That takes care of selecting around the tricky areas, such as the castle's ramparts. Then add the entire hillside to the selection (hold down the **Shift** key and drag with the mouse). You can easily draw around the hillside and the base of the castle. Once everything that is not part of the castle is selected, invert the selection (**Select>Inverse** with Photoshop) to select the castle itself. If your image editor lets you save masks or selections, you might want to do so, to avoid losing the castle selection. Figure 11.5 shows the selection.

Figure 11.5 *The castle has been selected.*

3. Choose **Copy** from the Edit menu to copy the image of the castle to the Clipboard.

4. Split the image into its component red, green, and blue channels. With Photoshop, the easiest way is to choose the **Window>Show Channels>Split Channels (Window>Palette>Show Channels>Split Channels** in Photoshop 3.0). The image will be split into separate red, green, and blue gray-scale images, as shown in Figure 11.6.

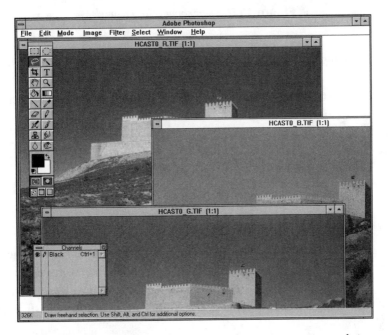

Figure 11.6 *The Split Channels option produces separate gray-scale images of the red, green, and blue color image channels.*

5. From the Channels menu, choose **Merge Channels**. Click on **OK** in the first dialog box that appears. The next dialog box, shown in Figure 11.7, asks you which of the available channels should be used to represent red, green, and blue, respectively.

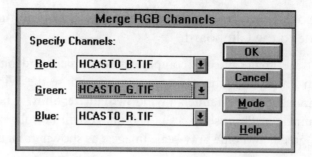

Figure 11.7 *Switching color channels.*

Let's switch the channels around using the three pull-down lists:

● To the red channel, assign the colors from the current blue channel.

● To the green channel, assign the colors from the current red channel.

● To the blue channel, assign the current green channel.

6. Click on **OK** when finished.

7. Choose **Paste** from the Edit menu to paste in a copy of the castle with its original color scheme. We have a normal-appearing castle perched on an unearthly green hill (it looks more like green cheese than grass!) and a purple sky straight out of a 1950s sci-fi film!

Your image should look like the right-hand image in Color insert Figure 13.

You can play with the individual channels while they are split, adding details that will later appear in one color only when you merge the red, green, and blue channels back together.

The Next Step

The special F/X with color correction tools that I demonstrated in this chapter are only a start. You can experiment with colors endlessly, producing new color schemes and effects. The best part about this sort of manipulation is that, because none of the resulting images are intended to be realistic, no one can say you've done something wrong. This is practically a goof-proof type of image play. Have fun.

In *Chapter 12*, I'll provide some background information about color that might explain why the effects and color corrections we covered in the previous two chapters work as they do.

CHAPTER

12

Background on Color F/X

Color will certainly be one of the most effective weapons in your PC F/X arsenal. Color grabs our eyes, leads our attention to specific areas of an image, and, through some unknown process, generates feelings that run the emotional color gamut from ardor to anger.

Strictly speaking, you don't have to understand how color works to use it to generate striking effects. If you worked through the previous chapters without reading this one first (after all, that is what I recommended), you found that you were able to create good images even if you didn't know a histogram from an antihistamine. It's possible to use trial-and-error experimentation to arrive at the results you want. But, just as you don't need a degree in electronics to operate a toaster, it's good to know a little something about electricity before you go poking around inside one with a fork.

This chapter provides a general introduction to the color theories you'll need to be familiar with to generate PC F/X successfully. I'll describe the most frequently used color models and explain the differences between the way color is displayed on your CRT monitor and the way it is output by your printer.

But first, let's look at the general topic of color and how it has come to be so important to PC users. For those of us who waited until we got our first color TVs in the late 1960s to discover that Huckleberry Hound was blue, all the ruckus borders on the amazing.

Introduction to Color

Human perception of color is a strange and wonderful thing. Most of us remember a little about how the eye sees from our high school science class: The retina of the eye contains tiny rods and cones that somehow react to light and provide information to the brain that we interpret as sight.

Color vision derives from the three different types of cone cells, that respond to different wavelengths of light. Our eyes are able to detect only a relatively narrow band of wavelengths, ranging from 400 nanometers at the short (violet) end of the visible spectrum to 700 nanometers at the long (red) end.

Artificial color systems, which include computer scanners, monitors, printers, and other peripherals, attempt to reproduce, or model, the colors that we see, using various sets of components of color. If the model is a good one, all the colors we can detect are defined by the parameters of the model. The colors within the definition of each model are termed its *color space*. Because nearly all color spaces use three different parameters, we can plot them as x, y, and z coordinates to produce a three-dimensional shape that represents the *color gamut* (color range) of the model.

The international standard for specifying color was defined in 1931 by the Commission Internationale L'Eclairage (CIE); it is a scientific color model that can be used to define all the colors that humans can see. However, PC color systems, which you use with one of three or four other color models, are more practical because they are based on the actual hardware systems used to reproduce the colors.

None of these systems can generate all the colors in the full range of human perception, but they are the models with which we must work. There are some efforts underway to define new models, but so far there is nothing that will completely take over the industry in the near future. Your best bet is to learn about all of them, because most image-editing and PC F/X programs will support any of the most-used color models.

Of the three most common models, the ones based on the hue-lightness-saturation (HLS) and hue-saturation-value (HSV) of colors are the most natural for us to visualize, because they deal with a continuous range of colors that may vary in brightness or richness. You used this type of model when you adjusted colors with the Hue/Saturation dialog boxes in *Chapters 10 and 11.*

Unfortunately, we must deal with two other models, called additive color and subtractive color, which are easier for computers to handle, because the individual components are nothing more than three basic colors of light. In earlier chapters, I referred to these two models as RGB and CMYK color, respectively. Now let's see why.

Additive color is commonly used in computer display monitors, while subtractive color is used for output devices such as printers. Because you need to understand how color works with these peripherals, I'll explain the additive and subtractive models first.

Additive Color

Color monitors produce color by aiming three electronic guns at sets of red, green, and blue *phosphors* (compounds that give off photons when struck by beams of electrons) coated on the screen of your CRT. The guns excite the phosphors in proportion to the amount of red, green, or blue light in a given pixel of the image. The phosphors glow, and our eyes add their illumination together, perceiving a color image. If none of the phosphors glows, we see a black pixel. If all three glow in equal proportions, we see a neutral color—gray or white—depending on the intensity.

Such a color system uses the additive color model—so called because the colors are added together. Additive color is explained in Figures 12.1 and 12.2. A huge selection of colors can be produced by varying the combinations of light. In addition to pure red, green, and blue, we can also produce cyan (green and blue together), magenta (red and blue), yellow (red and green), and all the colors in between. As with gray-scale data, the number of bits used to store color information determines the number of different tones that can be reproduced.

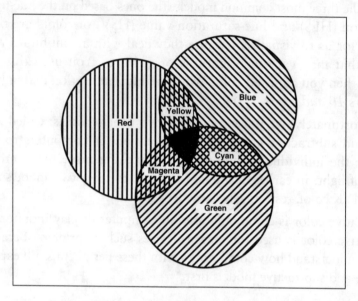

Figure 12.1 *Additive color can be represented by three circles of overlapping colored light.*

Figure 12.1 shows one way of thinking about additive color, in a two-dimensional color space. The largest circles represent beams of light in red, green, and blue. Where the beams overlap, they produce other colors. For example, red and green combine to produce yellow. Red and blue add up to magenta, and green and blue produce cyan. The center portion, in which all three colors overlap, is black.

However, this two-dimensional model doesn't account for the lightness or darkness of a color—the amount of white or black. That added dimension is dealt with in the model shown in Figure 12.2.

It shows red, green, and blue colors positioned at opposite corners of the cube, with their complementary colors arranged between them. White and black are located opposite one another, as well. Any shade that can be produced by adding red, green, and blue together can be represented by a position within the cube.

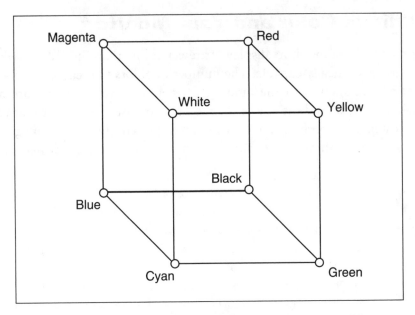

Figure 12.2   *In the three-dimensional additive color model,
the color space can be represented by a cube.*

No CRT device available today produces pure red, green, or blue light. Only lasers, which output at one single frequency of light, generate absolutely pure colors, and they aren't practical for display devices. We see images through the glow of phosphors, and the ability of phosphors to generate absolutely pure colors is limited. Color representations on a monitor differ from brand to brand and even from one monitor to another within the same brand.

Moreover, the characteristics of a given monitor change as the monitor ages and the phosphors wear out. Some phosphors, particularly blue ones, change in intensity at a different rate than others. So, identical signals rarely produce identical images on CRTs, regardless of how closely the monitors are matched in type, age, and other factors. We'll look at this topic a little more later on when I explain calibration.

Additive Color and Your Monitor

In practice, most monitors display far fewer colors than the total of which they are theoretically capable. The number of colors that can be displayed is largely a function of the amount of memory available to store and manipulate color and the size of the monitor you use. Remember that your PC must manage both the memory used to represent the current image and the temporary buffers used to store information not currently displayed.

Actually, the number of different colors a monitor can display at one time is limited to the number of individual pixels on the monitor. Recall the analogy in *Chapter 10*. At 640 × 480 resolution, your monitor has just 307,200 pixels, and if each and every pixel were a different color, if could display only 307,200 different colors at once—even if you have a 16.7 million-color video card. Don't confuse the millions-of-colors palette with the actual number of colors you may need to display a given file. It is likely to be much lower.

4-Bit Color

The smallest number of colors you'll find in any PC display (other than old monochrome or gray scale modes, of course) is 16, used by standard VGA displays, produced by what is sometimes called 4-bit color, because four bits (0000 to 1111 in binary) are used to store the color information. With a 640 × 480 PC display, 4-bit color requires just 154K of memory for the image and 154K for the buffer.

8-Bit Color

Upping the ante to 8 bits per pixel gives you 256 different colors at 640 × 480 pixel resolution and increases the memory requirement to 614K bytes. Today, the ability to display 256 colors is a bare minimum for most PCs sold. You can even do some color editing and special F/X at 256 colors, but your image will be *dithered*—the video card must mix pixels of the available colors to reproduce all the actual colors in the usual 24-bit image.

16-Bit Color

The term 16-bit color is somewhat of a misnomer, because some video cards use only 15 bits to produce 32,767 colors, while a few others use the full 16 bits and generate 65,535 colors. In either case, at this level, colors begin to look photorealistic, and you can usually do effective image editing. Most colors will look very close to the way they would appear in true color, even though some dithering may be necessary.

24-Bit Color

With 24-bit color, three bytes are used to represent each pixel—one byte each for red, green, and blue hues. That gives you 16.7 million colors, many more colors than the human eye can differentiate. Also called true color, this mode is the top level that most of us work with on a day-to-day basis.

Note that because the available video RAM determines how many colors you can display at a given resolution, when you increase resolution from 640 × 480 to 800 × 600 or 1024 × 768, one of two things must happen: 1) you get fewer colors from your available RAM or 2) you must add video RAM to your display card.

While 24-bit color cards have traditionally been expensive—models like SuperMatch's Thunder/24 can top $1500—newer models can give you 24-bit color for $100 or less (street price), albeit at 640 × 480 resolution only.

32-Bit Color and Beyond

You'll also hear the term 32-bit color, which may be something of a misnomer itself. You don't really get any more hues with 32-bit color; the extra 8 bits of information are used to store what is called alpha channel information, which can contain data about the transparency of a pixel or masking information. However, there is a movement toward the adoption of something called 48- and 64-bit color for high-end professional-level systems, which would provide more colors in addition to extra channels.

Subtractive Color

There is a second way of producing color that is familiar to computer users, and it, too, has a color model that represents the color gamut. When we represent colors in hardcopy form, the light source comes not from the image itself, as it does with a CRT image. Instead, hardcopies are viewed by light that strikes the paper or other substrate, is filtered by the image on the paper, and then is reflected back to our eyes.

This light starts out with equal quantities of red, green, and blue light and looks white to our eyes. The pigments the light passes through before bouncing off the substrate absorb part of this light, subtracting it from the spectrum. The light that remains reaches our eyes and is interpreted as color. Because various components of light are subtracted from white to produce color, this color model is known as the subtractive system.

The three primary subtractive colors are cyan, magenta, and yellow, and the model is usually known as the CMY model. When black is added (for reasons explained shortly), it becomes the CMYK model (black is represented by its terminal character *K*, rather than *B* to avoid confusion with the additive primary blue), which is used to produce color in most magazines.

In subtractive output devices, cyan, magenta, yellow, and sometimes black pigments are used to represent the full gamut of colors. It's obvious why additive colors won't work for hardcopies: It is possible to produce red, green, and blue pigments, of course, and we could print red, green, and blue colors that way (that's exactly what is done for spot color). However, there would be no way to produce any of the other colors with the additive primaries. Red pigment reflects only red light; green pigment reflects only green. When they overlap, the red pigment absorbs the green, and the green absorbs the red, so no light is reflected and we see black.

Cyan pigment, on the other hand, absorbs only red light (well, it is supposed to). It reflects both blue and green (theoretically), producing the blue-green shade we see as cyan. Yellow pigment absorbs only blue light, reflecting red and green, while magenta pigment absorbs only green, reflecting red and blue. When we overlap two of the subtractive primaries, some of at least one color still reflects. Magenta (red-blue) and yellow (red-green) together produce red, because the magenta pigment absorbs green and the yellow pigment absorbs blue. Their common color, red, is the only one remaining.

Of course each of the subtractive primaries can be present in various intensities or percentages, from 0 to 100%. The remainder is represented by white, which reflects all colors in equal amounts. The subtractive model is illustrated in Figures 12.3 and 12.4.

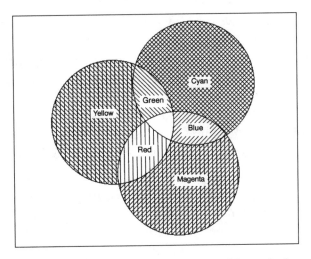

Figure 12.3   *The subtractive color model can also be represented in a two-dimensional way.*

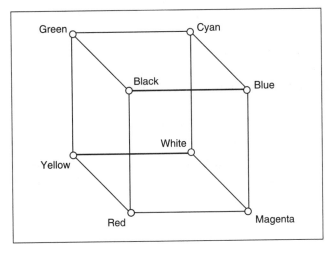

Figure 12.4   *A three-dimensional cube can also be used to represent the subtractive color model.*

In the preceding example, if the magenta pigment was only 50% present and the yellow represented at 100%, only half the green would be absorbed, while 100% of the blue would be soaked up. Our red would appear to be an intermediate color, orange. By varying the percentages of the subtractive primaries, we can produce a full range of colors.

Well, theoretically we could. Recall that RGB monitors aren't perfect because the color of the phosphors can vary. So, too, is it impossible to design pigments that reflect absolutely pure colors. Equal amounts of cyan, magenta, and yellow pigment should produce black. More often, what you'll get is a muddy brown. With many output systems, that's what you'll have to settle for. It's a complicated enough procedure to lay down sets of cyan, magenta, and yellow pigment in perfect register. Indeed, many daily newspapers that print color use this three-color system to this day.

However, better results can be obtained by adding black as a fourth color. Black can fill in areas that are supposed to be black and add detail to other areas of an image. While the fourth color does complicate the process a bit, the actual cost in applications like offset printing is minimal. Black ink is used to print text anyway, so there is no additional press run for black. Moreover, black ink is cheaper than critical process color inks, so it's possible to save money by using black instead of laying on three subtractive primaries extra thick.

The output systems you use to print hardcopies of color images use the subtractive color system in one way or another. Most of them are unable to print varying percentages of each of the primary colors. Offset presses, inkjet printers, color laser printers, and thermal wax transfer printers are examples of these. All these systems must simulate other colors by dithering, which is similar to the halftoning system discussed earlier. A few printers can vary the amount of pigment laid down over a broader range. Thermal dye sublimation printers are an example of this type. These printers can print a full range of tones, up to the 16.7 million colors possible with 24-bit systems.

Additive Versus Subtractive Color

When you view color images on your CRT during image editing, the colors in the image file are always converted to additive (RGB) colors for display—regardless of the color model used to represent the actual image. However—and this is important—the color model used for the actual file remains the same, unless you change modes and then save the file.

For example, if you load a file that has been saved using the CMYK color model, a program like Photoshop will let you work on it in CMYK mode, even though the colors must be converted to RGB for viewing with versions of Photoshop earlier than 3.0.

You may also convert from CMYK to RGB mode, and back again, but, because CMYK can represent some colors that are outside the RGB gamut—and vice versa—you can lose some hues each time. Stick with CMYK if that's the mode your file was created in, especially if you will be outputting to a printer or color separation system that expects to work with CMYK colors. In that way, you'll avoid creating RGB colors that cannot be reproduced by the CMYK output system.

Other Color Models

Other color models that have been developed, include hue-saturation-brightness, known as HSB or HSL (for hue-lightness-saturation). You'll find HSB or HSL supported by many software packages.

In this model, individual colors, called *hues*, are represented as they are in a rainbow, as a continuous spectrum, arranged in a hexagon like that shown in Figure 12.5. The full color space is represented as a double hexcone that extends upwards and downwards from the hexagon, as shown in Figure 12.6. The top of the axis drawn through the center of the cones represents pure white, while the bottom point represents black. Moving higher in the cone produces lighter colors; moving lower in the bottom cone produces darker colors. Saturation is represented by movement in a third direction, outward from the center axis. The center represents a desaturated color, the outer edges fully saturated hues.

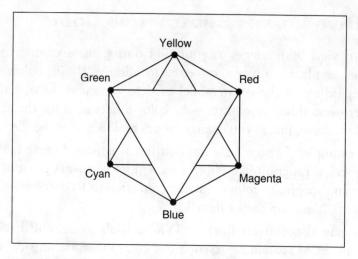

Figure 12.5 *The two hexcones represent all the colors in the HSB/HSL color model in three dimensions.*

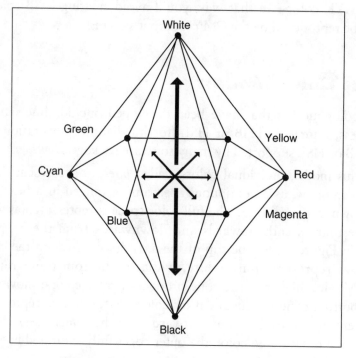

Figure 12.6 *The full color space, extending upwards and downwards from the hexagon.*

In Figure 12.3, the large overlapping circles represent pigments, which each reflect cyan, magenta, and yellow light, and absorb the other two. Where the three overlap in the center, all three colors are reflected, producing white. When cyan and yellow overlap, both colors are reflected (and magenta is absorbed), so we see the color green. Cyan and magenta absorb yellow and reflect a combination we see as blue. Similarly, magenta and yellow together absorb cyan and produce red.

The subtractive color model shown in Figure 12.4 looks a lot like the cube shown in Figure 12.2, only it has been rotated so that yellow, cyan, and magenta now occupy the *x*, *y* and *z* axes that represent red, green, and blue in the additive model. Any color can be indicated by a coordinate in this color space.

All colors can be represented by three parameters in this model. The hue is the particular position of a color in the color wheel. Hues are often represented by angles, beginning with red at 0 ° and progressing around in a counterclockwise direction to magenta at 60 °, blue at 120 °, and so forth. The saturation of the color is the degree to which that color is diluted with white. A hue with a great deal of white is muted; a red becomes a pink, for example. A hue with very little or no white is vivid and saturated. Brightness can be thought of as the degree to which a color is diluted with black. Add black to our desaturated red (pink), and you'll get a very dark pink. Various combinations of hue, saturation, and brightness can be used to produce just about any color we can see. Figure 12.5 may help you visualize how this color model works a little more clearly.

Individual hues can be found along the edges of the hexagon. Moving from that edge toward the center within the same plane indicates a color that is less saturated. The center of the hexagon represents zero saturation. The axis extending through the center of the hexcones represents lightness and darkness, with white at the top and black at the bottom of the line.

LAB Color

The LAB color model was developed by the CIE as a device-independent international standard. That is, LAB colors look exactly the same when output to different, but correctly calibrated monitors and printers. Some image-editing programs, including Photoshop, support this mode.

The LAB acronym comes from the three channels used to represent all colors in this model. One is used to refer to luminance (the L channel), while the A and B channels represent the colors from green to magenta and blue to yellow, respectively.

Because all the colors that can be represented in CMYK and RGB color models can be reproduced by LAB, you can convert either from or to LAB and then back again without altering any color values. That feature makes it a perfect mode to use to perform certain operations that can't be done with one of the alternative models. For example, because lightness attributes are assigned to a channel of their own, you can vary the luminance of a color independently of its hue or saturation. Consequently, a smooth gradient or blend in which the brightness of the tone is the key factor can be created easily.

The LAB color model also makes a good choice when transferring images from one system to another or for printing to color PostScript Level 2 devices, which also support this mode.

The Pantone Matching System

The Pantone Matching System is the check-standard trademark for color reproduction and color reproduction materials from Pantone, Inc. At least, that's the legal terminology that Pantone is quite zealous about insisting on from helpless journalists like myself. In simpler language, PMS is just another way of referring to colors. Instead of using a set of descriptive parameters to define every possible color, PMS takes a different approach. Pantone has identified 747 colors and defined the formulas needed to produce pigments of those colors. Each color is given a number. You use a printed matching guide—actually an ink swatch book, which is available at most graphic arts supply stores—to select the color. The samples are printed on both coated and uncoated paper. You can select a color and specify it by number. Your printer can then use the PMS formula to mix the proper ink. This is extremely useful when you want a specific spot color for, say, corporate trade dress or product packaging.

As useful as Pantone colors are for spot color, they can't be used to print full-color images; to reproduce 256 different colors, you would need

256 different inks and press runs. If you don't need an exact shade, it may be less expensive to let your printer use the three process colors to produce the spot color you want. That's because, using a specially mixed color requires cleaning the press and other additional make-ready steps.

You can also use the Pantone Matching System just as a way to specify colors. You can choose a Pantone color and then tell your printer to approximate it as closely as possible using the four-color process.

If the RGB, CMYK, and HSB color models produce continuous-color models, the Pantone model might be thought of as discrete points of particular color within the larger color space that humans can perceive. While the Pantone color selection is huge, it can't represent all possible colors, as the other models can.

There are other color systems used outside the United States that are supported by some image-editing programs, but you probably will never need to use them.

Capturing Color Images

Color scanners have been available for more than 40 years. The first ones I saw cost more than a million dollars when you included the computer equipment needed to drive them. Today, color scanners are affordable, and the difference in price between them and gray-scale scanners is evaporating. You may pay as little as $800 for a 24-bit color scanner for the PC today.

Color scanners are nothing more than a system for capturing the proper amount of each of the primary colors of light in a given image. These scanners use three different light sources—one each of red, green, and blue—to scan a color image. To do so, some make three passes over the image—once for each color. Others rotate their light sources, using red/green/blue light in succession to capture an image in a single pass.

The amount of light reflected by the artwork for each color varies according to the color of the pigments in the original. Cyan pigment, for example, absorbs red light and reflects blue and green. So, when a cyan area is illuminated by the red fluorescent light in a scanner, relatively little light is reflected. Most of the light produced by the blue and green fluorescents is reflected. Your scanner software records that area of the original as cyan. A similar process captures the other colors in your subject during the scan.

Color Calibration and Gamma Curves

PC color offers new capabilities but carries with it some added concerns. In most cases, you'll want your image to approximate the original closely. Neither color display systems nor color hardcopy output devices are consistent nor particularly accurate. The best you can do is calibrate your peripherals so that there is a relationship between the colors in the original, what you see, and what you get as output. The process is complicated by two facts. First, the response of any color system is rarely linear. And, to make things worse, it's difficult to describe a color in such a way that it means exactly the same thing to everyone.

Assume for a moment a 24-bit system with 256 different tones of each color. A value of 0 for a particular color should represent no color; a value of 255 should represent the maximum intensity of that color. On a linear scale, 64 would represent about 25% intensity, 128 would be 50%, and so on. Yet, in real applications, an intensity of 64 is not half that of 128. It is some other percentage. The relationship of the actual representation to the ideal is known as a gamma curve.

Scanners do happen to conform to the ideal rather closely, but CRTs and printers tend to vary. If you know the gamma curve of a particular device, however, you can correct it. For example, if you know that, with a certain device, a value of 64 produces an intensity that is only 90% of what it should be to be linear, you can boost that value by an appropriate amount whenever it occurs. This is done by building a gamma correction table that includes a value for each of the levels used in a system. The correction values can be automatically substituted by your software for the default values, theoretically producing a perfect, 45° gamma curve.

Now, all you need is a set of standards that can be used to determine what those correction values should be. A giant step in the right direction may be Eastman Kodak Company's PhotoYCC color interchange space specification and ColorSync software. The Kodak color management system is a set of tools and utilities that provides consistent color across devices and computer platforms. Kodak sells the system components to application/system software developers; CPU manufacturers; makers of displays, printers, and scanners; and end-users like you and me.

PhotoYCC takes into account the differences between different color models; the calibration of printers, displays, and scanners; and the impact of external conditions such as fluorescent lighting. It is designed to be device- and operating system-independent and will work in DOS, Windows, Macintosh, Sun, and UNIX 5.4 environments.

The system includes a developer's toolkit with a standard application programming interface (API) and a software color system processor. Users work within an environment that includes color management utilities and the color system processor. Device profiles measure and define the color behavior of a particular peripheral, while calibration tools enable them to perform up to the expectations of their profiles.

CRT screens are one of the devices that must be calibrated. Fortunately, as true color becomes more important, we're starting to see specific systems for doing such calibration. Color calibrators measure the output of your CRT at various color levels. Then, the system can adjust the levels of the electron beams in the monitor, if that is possible. Such systems require that each monitor have its own built-in sensors and calibration hardware. You can also use external hardware to make the measurements and then substitute new values for those in the gamma correction table used with that monitor. That's a cheaper solution, but it doesn't help when the colors produced by a monitor change because of age or user adjustments.

Radius, SuperMac Technologies, and other monitor manufacturers have introduced relatively low-cost CRT color calibrators that allow you to calibrate their equipment easily. These were initially available only for the Macintosh but have since become more widely offered.

Of course, getting true color on your screen is of little use unless the images you view bear some relation to your hardcopy output. Therefore, you must calibrate your system using the particular characteristics of your output device. Additional calibration steps are needed to match the colors produced by the printer with those seen on the screen. Printers have variations of their own, which are not limited to the exact hues of the pigments used. Dots may smear or enlarge as they are absorbed by the paper. Because printers use the CMYK model and CRTs use RGB, getting true color can be tricky, but, with enough care, satisfactory results can be had.

Some of the top software, such as Photoshop includes tools you can use to calibrate for your equipment.

The Next Step

You can apply what you learned in this chapter to make better color corrections of your images. We covered the major color models, image-capture hardware like scanners, and how your PC presents color.

In the next section, you'll learn about color separation, an important tool for turning your color images into files that can be printed by offset presses. Color separation isn't as difficult as it used to be, and you'll soon see why.

PART V

Special F/X

Some of the most stunning special F/X you can create involve three-dimensional or 3-D modeling. The idea is to create not a real-world object that you can touch but an image so realistic that it touches you in some way. Although you may end up with flat, 2-D images on a printed page, being able to create and manipulate those images in three dimensions adds—can we say it?—an extra dimension to your work.

This section will provide a close-up look at the capabilities of 3-D imaging packages you may want to explore further. One of them, Pixar Typestry, is available on the CD-ROM packaged with this book in a special tryout version. Although Pixar didn't have a demonstration version of Typestry for Windows available, the company prepared one especially for the readers of this book. Special thanks go out to this firm for going the extra mile in an effort to help you understand 3-D concepts.

Rendering Images in Three Dimensions

Most of this book has dealt with creating special F/X from existing images, such as photographs, through retouching, compositing, or manipulating color. You can also develop some outrageous images by building new images from scratch or by combining pictures you already have with elements you've generated on your own.

Of course, you can use the painting tools of Photoshop or Fractal Design Painter or the illustration tools of Canvas to develop new images with various degrees of realism, depending on your artistic skills. You must understand things like perspective or proportion, and how light works so that the shadows and shading are realistic. If you want accurate textures applied to your new objects, you'll need even more skill and experience.

Or you can use a 3-D drawing package such as Visual Reality or Strata Studio to take care of all those details for you automatically. These programs can do several things for you in your quest for the ultimate special F/X.

● 3-D drawing packages create new objects or scenes with photorealistic perspective, lighting, shading, and texture. You may be able to select the camera lens view, use multiple light sources, and otherwise develop the image exactly as if you were modeling it from clay or another malleable substance. You can then use a 2-D version of the image in your presentation, publication, or other project.

● 3-D drawing programs also allow you to change your point of view. Examine your image from any angle, including overhead, then take a 2-D picture.

● 3-D software allows you to move various objects in relation to others in the same scene. If you've drawn one too close to another, it's a simple matter to move them apart to get the effect you want. You can move an object farther back in a scene or closer to the foreground. That's something you could never do with a flat, 2-D drawing program. Best of all, the background, lighting, and other effects all change automatically to compensate.

In short, 3-D drawing software lets you create flexible, more realistic 2-D images of three-dimensional objects. You'll get a better idea of how to use this software through the examples in this chapter.

I'll show you what I mean with a simple demonstration. I'll create a basic 3-D object and then paste it into a photograph. Unless you happen to own a 3-D software package, you can't follow along exactly, so I'll use this quick example to explain some basic 3-D concepts and show how they are used. You'll be able to try out 3-D capabilities in *Chapter 14*, using Pixar Typestry.

What Is 3-D Rendering?

To reach the third dimension, it helps to start in the 2-D world. If you think about ancient Egyptian tomb drawings, you can understand just how flat two-dimensional representations can be. They have only height and width, with no depth at all. It's difficult to represent real-world objects in this way. The Egyptians frequently drew all human figures with their faces turned sideways in profile, because profiles were easier to sketch.

Moreover, in 2-D drawings every object exists in the same imaginary plane. You can't just draw something that is farther away in a smaller size: There's no way the viewer can tell if the half-size human, for example, is farther away or simply a smaller person. A 2-D drawing lacks the perspective that three dimensions give us.

When we view things in real life, we can perceive depth because we use two eyes to view the scene, each with a slightly different point of view. We know that when an object looks identical through either eye, it must be farther away, because the relative differences as seen through viewpoints only a few inches apart are small. When an object is very close to our eyes, those scant inches present the brain with significantly different views of the object, so that we know it is close. That's how depth perception works and why we see things in three dimensions.

A photograph or computer printout, on the other hand, is a flat representation of a scene. Everything in a photo is the exact distance away from our eyes. It's impossible to produce a true 3-D image unless we can give each eye a different view (as is done with 3-D pictures and holograms), but we can represent depth by including the visual cues that our brain has learned represent distance.

For example, objects appear to get smaller as the distance grows between them and our eyes. If we see two men in a photograph, and one appears one-sixth the height of the other, we assume that they are roughly the same size and that one is farther away. A single object that extends a great distance into a background, such as a stone wall, will recede or get smaller along its length.

Other visual cues help us discern 3-D information. A *visual horizon* or vanishing point exists at some point in an image, usually higher on the picture than the foreground. Objects that are farther away are both smaller and higher as they approach the horizon. The shading of the light falling on objects (shadows are shorter the farther away the object is) or even extremely subtle things (e.g, clear air produces a diffusing or "fog" effect that is visible over distant objects).

Artists understand all these things, but you and I don't. That's why it's so difficult to create realistic special F/X from images we create from scratch. The objects we create don't have the visual cues that say 3-D.

So, how do computers accomplish this? Some very, very smart people developed program routines that let your PC calculate the relationships between objects in a 3-D drawing. The software knows exactly how much smaller to make an object appear when it is moved farther away from the eye. The program can duplicate realistic shadows and reflections through a process called *ray tracing*, in which the path of the beam of light from the light source(s) illuminating an image are mathematically calculated, down to the amount of reflection and diffusion produced by various types of surfaces.

Sophisticated 3-D programs can add atmospheric fog, textures, and other visual cues. Moreover, they can produce a view of a set of objects from any viewpoint—actually recalculating all the values that make up the image for each viewpoint you choose. All this number crunching takes time, which is why 3-D drawing programs often generate rough versions of images, perhaps showing only the wireframe outline, until you're ready to produce the high-quality final image, which takes into account all the mathematical calculations, through a process called *rendering*.

Generating 3-D images may be more clear if we work through the steps I went through to produce the image you see in Color insert Figure 14. We'll start with a very simple example that touches on many of the concepts you'll need to understand.

Building Walls

I happen to like pictures of castles, and you'll find many examples of some of my photographs on the CD-ROM packaged with this book. We'll combine a picture of a real castle with a fake castle generated entirely with the computer, just to show you what you can do.

I used Visual Reality to build my 3-D castle. The program consists of several stand-alone components that work together. The first thing I did was load Visual Model, which is a modeling program that lets you create 3-D objects, in the same way that a drawing program like CorelDRAW allows you to build 2-D objects. Each object drawn retains a life of its own and a special kind of reality in the imaginary 3-D space we work within.

That is, you can separate the objects, rotate them in space, apply surface textures, and add lighting effects.

The first step was to build four flat walls from a rectangular shape that included crenellations—those slots the Medieval folks shot arrows through—at the top. Each wall formed a cookie-cutter-like shape, which was then extruded to create the wall itself. Imagine your Play-Doh Fun Factory for a moment. You (or your child,) placed a cookie-cutter-like sheet of plastic with an opening shaped like a circle, square, star, or other figure in the aperture of the Fun Factory. Then, when you pressed down on the handle, Play-Doh was extruded through the opening to produce a long piece of clay in that shape.

One way to create a 3-D object is to use a similar extrusion method. We first draw the cookie-cutter on one plane and then tell the drawing program to extrude it to produce a thicker shape using that outline. I extruded four such walls, assembled them in 3-D space to form an open box and added a cylindrical tower at one corner. I imported the castle shape into another Visual Reality module, Renderize Live, which was used to add texture and lighting effects. When the finished castle was rendered, it looked like Figure 13.1.

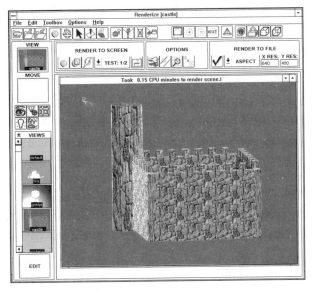

Figure 13.1 *Castle brought to 3-D life in Renderize Live.*

Finally, I exported the castle as a bitmap, which I selected and stored as a separate image, shown in Figure 13.2.

Figure 13.2   *Separate castle image as a bit map.*

I'll use this spanking new castle to replace the broken-down, old castle walls, shown in Figure 13.3 This particular fortification overlooks the semiremote town of Albarracín, near Teruel (just down the road a piece from Bug Tussel). They are actually the new part of the city walls, built in the 11th century. (Don't ask when the *old* walls were built.) We'll update them with some late-20th century construction.

I copied the castle shown in Figure 13.3, and pasted it into the photograph, resizing to fit. I even stretched the tower a bit to make it look fatter and more imposing. Then I copied the still-floating selection to the Clipboard, pasted it down, and flipped it horizontally to produce a mirror image. I placed that mirror image end to end with the first copy, producing the final image you see in Figure 13.4 and Color insert Figure 14. Finally, I used the Dodging tool to lighten the cliffs a little, so that we could see more detail in them. The overall effect is a combination of realism and surrealism, which is fairly appropriate for the country that spawned Salvador Dali.

If you're careful, you can make the shadows match in your original photograph and the 3D object you create. You can see the direction of the light is pretty close to the original scene on the right side of the castle, but not quite correct on the left side. You can use unusual lighting effects to add an other-worldly effect to your images.

Figure 13.3   *Eleventh century Spanish walls, long overdue for renovation.*

Figure 13.4   *One thousand-year-old walls and a brand-new castle give this picture a strange look.*

The imaginative folks at National Geographic Magazine got in a lot of trouble for moving the pyramids of Egypt in order to spruce up a cover, but, unless your intent is to commit fraud by misleading someone, or you work for a newsgathering organization, you should be able to make changes like this with impunity. Whatever makes your images look better or more exciting should be in your F/X toolbox.

So That's 3-D

After that exercise, you can more easily see the separate steps required to produce 3-D images:

- *Modeling.* Modeling is the creation and combination of the basic shapes, called *primitives*, such as cubes and spheres, along with objects that you design using lathing or extruding techniques, into complex 3-D components. Once you've built an object in 3-D space, you can rotate it to display it from any angle (or, if you prefer to think that way, move the camera around the object to change the viewpoint).

- *Rendering.* Once your object exists in space, you need to add surface attributes such as texture and lighting effects. Think of rendering as taking a snapshot of your object from a particular viewpoint, so that the texture you've applied will be displayed using the lighting effects you request.

3-D Modeling Tips

Now that you've gotten a taste of what 3-D software can do, I'll provide some tips to help you enter this arena on your own. There are two basic kinds of programs on the market. First, there are specialty programs intended for a certain kind of 3-D work, such as Pixar Typestry for type effects, or specialized 3-D modelers or rendering programs. You'll also find integrated packages like Visual Reality that are capable of doing the complete job, including building complex animated sequences. You should keep in mind several things when evaluating this kind of program.

● If you just want to create a few 3-D images to insert into your photos, most 3-D modelers may have a lot more horsepower than you need. That may not be objectionable if you can afford the $99 to $500 (and up) price tag for the package, because there's no requirement that you have to use all the features available. However, function-rich software may be difficult to learn and use, especially if you work with them only periodically. These programs are primarily used by people who work with them all day long and may not lend themselves to casual use.

● Among those extra features are sophisticated shading and modeling capabilities, including animation functions. Consequently, you might want to look at additional ways that you can use 3-D packages.

● 3-D modeling is slow. Don't even think about trying to run one of these programs on a slow 386-based machine, unless you have something to keep yourself occupied while rendering is underway.

● On a slow PC it's particularly important to use faster preview modes or quick-and-dirty rendering options to view the effects of your work. You may also be able to render only a small selection of an image to see how the shadows and textures work. Then, render the entire image when you're satisfied.

A Brief Look at Strata StudioPro

When you're ready to graduate from the 2-D special F/X I've been demonstrating in this book to full 3-D, virtual reality still images, and animations, you'll want to investigate Strata, Inc.'s Strata StudioPro, a DOS-based (non-Windows) high-end 3-D package. This software has sophisticated features that won't breathe hard when driven by professional illustrators and animators who charge more for a day than I make in a month. CAD users who want photorealistic images to bring their plans and prototypes to life will appreciate these products, too.

If you're serious about 3-D work, you'll end up with a package like these eventually. Because of the heavy number-crunching involved in 3-D rendering, Strata's products must be run on a PC with a math coprocessor and at least 4M of free RAM, but you're better off with at least a 486- or Pentium-based system with a lot more RAM.

Strata products have an extensible architecture, which makes it possible to integrate new shapes, textures, and even tools tightly into the program. StudioPro's tool palette includes a button bar for fast access to extension modeling tools. It also allows you to drag textures and shapes from a palette onto the scene à la Ray Dream Designer.

StudioPro's modelers let you carve out shapes with a lathe, squeeze them through an extruder, or sweep shapes through space to create complex objects. You may even sculpt a shape by pushing and pulling on surfaces, as you would modeling clay. There are skin and unskin modelers so that you can stretch a surface over a supporting skeleton or strip away the surface to reveal the interior.

Textures can be applied just to the surface or to the entire object (so that the same texture will show underneath if you cut away a piece.) A more complete set of shading options makes StudioPro a truly professional rendering tool. You're already familiar with ray tracing. Strata also includes Gouraud and Phong shading, a technique it's dubbed Raydiosity, and something new called Ray Painting.

Raydiosity can calculate special rendering effects, like the illumination of translucent objects and the bleeding of colors from one brightly lit object onto the surface of another. Photographers are familiar with the concept of light bouncing off a wall to provide softened fill light in the shadows. Raydiosity can duplicate that. However, it takes so long to process images using this effect that Strata recommends it as an experimental technique only and not for production animation work.

Ray Painting is a new effect that duplicates artistic techniques such as watercolor, oils, chalk, pencil on rag, or specific artists including van Gogh and Seurat.

StudioPro has powerful animation tools, too, but I won't discuss those in this chapter, which is dedicated just to 3-D still imaging.

The Next Step

This chapter introduced you to how 3-D objects can be created and added to your 2-D images for startling special F/X. In *Chapter 14*, we'll explore some of the things you can do with a more specialized 3-D program, Pixar Typestry.

Special 3-D F/X with Type

Up until this chapter, we concentrated on ways you can manipulate the components of photographic images. In *Chapter 13* you learned a little of how you can add new objects to photographs, using 3-D modeling software. In this chapter, we'll discover some new ways to add a special type of object to images: the alphanumeric characters we call type.

There are many reasons why you'll want to add type to your images. Primarily, you'll use type to communicate some message. You'll want to add a few words as a label for your image or as a headline for a layout intended as advertising or editorial material. Type can stand alone on the page or be incorporated into your photographic image. This chapter concentrates on 3-D type effects that are dropped into photos. In *Chapter 17* we'll look at other ways to create fancy text as slightly less dramatic 2-D objects.

The tool of choice for this chapter will be Pixar Typestry, since a tryout version of this software is available on the CD-ROM bundled with this book. As I noted in the introduction to this section, Pixar prepared the tryout version especially for this book; you'll be among the first people in the world to have access to Pixar Typestry's magic on a try-before-you buy basis.

You can work through the first exercise and duplicate the effects I describe. This tryout version is not save-disabled like some of the other demonstration software on the disc. What's the catch? A few key features of the application have been disabled—including the ability to enter new text. You may experiment to your heart's content creating different type styles and effects, but you'll end up with the single word, *Pixar*, for your efforts. I think you'll enjoy working with Pixar Typestry enough that you'll want to buy a fully functional copy for your own work.

Whose Idea Was This, Anyway?

When TrueType was added to Windows 3.1, choosing and using various styles of type became easier than ever for PC owners. Anyone with a few installed fonts and an image editor like Photoshop or PhotoStyler can easily drop titles and other text blocks into their images. However, those are flat, two-dimensional type effects. Creating lifelike, 3-D type is a job for a special application like Typestry. You'll find the basic 3-D concepts you picked up in *Chapter 13* useful as we explore the capabilities of 3-D type manipulation tools in this chapter. As always, I'll use some simple exercises as a way to dump you off the side of the canoe, so to speak, with some encouraging instructions on how to swim.

Creating A Simple 3-D Logo with Typestry

Pixar Typestry incorporates many of the 3-D modeling features you already understand. To create 3-D type, you need to follow just six easy steps:

● Create the text or shapes you want to model in three dimensions. Your basic object can be any word or phrase using any installed Adobe Type 1 or TrueType font in your system. (With the tryout version, you can select any font, but you must use the default text *Pixar*, as I noted.) You can also import Adobe Illustrator outline files to add new shapes to your text image. If you need a few special characters or a font that has some customized shapes, you may use a font-editing program like Fontographer or Fontmonger and save your manipulated character set as a new font. Typestry works with edited fonts just fine.

● Shape the text by resizing or skewing it.

● Position the text in 3-D space by rotating it along any combination of the x, y, and z axes. Pixar makes it easy to do this task. When you grip the text with the Rotation tool, a slab appears. It corresponds to the plane in which the type rests. You can tilt, rotate, or move this slab through the universe to get the exact orientation you want.

● Apply a surface texture to the text, from Typestry's large library of Looks. The tryout version comes with dozens of different Looks you can experiment with.

● Adjust your lighting effects. You can specify nine different lights from front or back and adjust their size, distance, color, and lighting quality.

● Render a final version of your type as a TIFF file you can use alone or import into a photograph with your image editor.

The first exercise we'll work through will incorporate these elements to one degree or another.

Creating Your Very Own Pixar Logo

Load the Pixar demo. An Untitled document is created for you, and you'll see a simple palette of tools with the letter *A* at the top, like that shown in Figure 14.1. If the toolbox does not appear, click on the Windows selection in the menu bar and choose **Show Toolbox** or **Window>Palette>Show Toolbox** in Photoshop 3.0.

Figure 14.1 *Pixar Typestry's Toolbox palette*

1. Click on the text icon to bring up the Add Text dialog box, shown in Figure 14.2. The text you'll be working with, the word *Pixar*, is already entered for you. Don't fret: you can have a lot of fun building variations on that single word using this tryout software. If your surname happens to be Pixar, or by some coincidence you live in a town by that name, you're in luck. If not, just continue with the exerciseby just following these steps.

   Choose a font from the drop-down font list in the dialog box. I selected **Arial**, which comes with Windows, because most readers will have that font installed. You can select another font if you don't mind that your work won't look exactly like the illustrations that follow.

2. Choose a bevel size. Your type is going to have thickness, because it is rendered in three dimensions, and the edge of the text can be beveled in several different ways. Determine how much of the edge will be chipped away by the bevel, using the slider control shown in Figure 14.2. Move it about a third of the way over toward the right to create a modest bevel effect.

3. Choose a bevel type. You can select from rounded, sharp-edged, or less pronounced beveling effects by checking off one of the radio buttons.

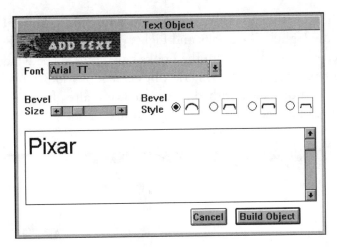

Figure 14.2 *Typestry's Add Text dialog box.*

4. When you've finished specifying the type font and bevel, click on the **Build Object** button to exit the dialog box and create your Pixar object.

Adding Texture

Pixar calls the textures that it uses *Looks,* and the term is actually much more accurate if you stop to think about it. The metallic texture you apply to an object isn't a uniform texture, after all, it's a type of surface that takes on other attributes depending on the lighting effects you select— satiny shadows in one part of the object and glaring spectral highlights in another portion. A texture is more of an appearance or look that you apply to the text rather than a homogenous surface.

There are several dozen Looks available with this tryout version, and Pixar offers an editor utility that lets you create your own Looks from scanned or self-generated images. The company also has an add-on CD-ROM with many new Looks you can use. We'll start simple with this exercise and use one of the striking Looks already included in the program. Just follow these steps.

1. Click on the Windows menu item and choose **Show Looks** and **Show Lights.** The Looks and Lights palettes, shown in Figure 14.3, appear. Let's work with the Looks palette first. The window within this palette shows a generic object (it looks like a teapot to this non-tea-drinker), with the current Look already applied, so that you can preview the texture of your text.

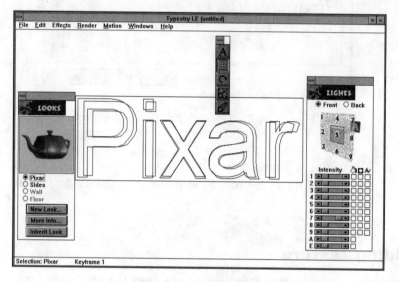

Figure 14.3   *The text object.*

2. Click on the **New Look** button to select a Look for our Pixar logo. Note that there are four buttons below the preview, **Pixar** (your text object), **Sides, Wall,** and **Floor.** Because we won't create any sides, wall, or floor in this exercise, the other choices are grayed out to indicate they aren't available at the moment. Below them are the **New Look, More Info,** and **Inherit Look** buttons.

The Select a Look dialog box appears next (see Figure 14.4). It consists of several components:

● A larger preview window showing the teapot with the currently selected Look applied.

● A standard Windows file selection window that opens onto the Looks subdirectory (or perhaps another subdirectory, depending on how your system is configured). Subsubdirectorys contain other subdirectories segregated by categories of Looks such as Stone, Wood, Metal, Pattern.

● A scrolling list of small Look previews, showing all the Looks you've "installed" into the dialog box. Your copy of Typestry may not have any Looks installed in this list the first time you open it.

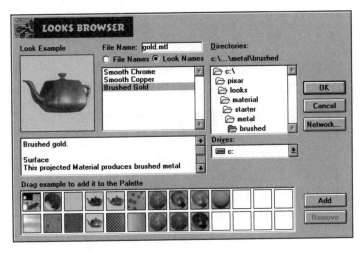

Figure 14.4 *The Select a Look dialog box is your gateway to multiple textures.*

You can choose a Look directly by navigating through the subdirectories to find the one you want, or you can add a Look to the scrolling list, either for comparison or to make it easier to retrieve that Look later on without resorting to the subdirectory-meandering routine again.

3. Choose several Looks from the subdirectories and click on **Add** to copy them to the scrolling list. Start with several brushed metal Looks, such as **Chrome, Copper,** or **Gold.** These Looks are all similar in effect, differing chiefly in their color. You may click on the **Get Info** button to read a description of a particular Look.

4. Select one of the Looks for your Pixar object. I choose **Brushed Gold**. Highlight the Look you want in the scrolling list, and click on **Select**. You'll be returned to the main window. Of course, your text object still looks the same, because you haven't rendered the image yet.

Rotating the Text in Three Dimensions

We have a few more steps to carry out before we can render our type. The first thing to do is to change the orientation of the text in 3-D space to give the effect we want. Just follow these steps to twist our logo through virtual reality.

1. Use the Move tool (second from the top in the toolbox) to move the Pixar logo around to center it in the window, if necessary.

2. Resize the logo, if you like, using the Resizing tool (third from the top).

3. Choose the Rotation tool and click on the logo. The cursor will turn into a grabbing hand, which you can use to rotate the logo's slab around as if you were using a 3-D trackball. Play with it a bit to get the feel for it; then attempt to orient the logo as shown in Figure 14.5.

Notice that with the slab activated, you'll be able to see planes representing the front and back surface of the logo, using a wire-frame mode that looks as if the logo were printed on a transparent sheet of ice. As long as the Rotation tool is active, the slab will blink on and off at intervals, so that you can see what your logo looks like in its new orientation.

4. Select the Extrusion tool, the last one in the toolbox stack. It changes the thickness of the slab the logo is embedded in. Use its arrow cursor to drag one of the slab's vertical lines to vary the thickness.

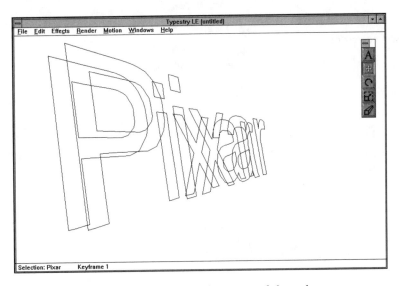

Figure 14.5   *The logo has been rotated through space.*

Changing the Lights

Lighting is a complex topic (we'll look at in more detail in the next exercise). If you want to play with the lights, feel free to do so. The Lights palette shows a set of nine lights for the front and nine for the back, with the position of each light in a plane parallel to the text object shown by a numbered panel in the dialog box. Switch from front to back lights by clicking on a radio button. You can vary the intensity of these lights individually by clicking on the darkness/lightness value next to each in the numbered rows (see Figure 14.5).

Rendering the Logo

You'll recall from *Chapter 13* that rendering is a process of calculating the appearance of the surfaces that can be seen from a given viewpoint, taking into account how the surface textures react to the light or lights falling on them. Unlike the full-fledged 3-D programs we already looked at, Typestry doesn't have multiple camera views to choose from: You change the perspective only by physically rotating the object in 3-D space or by switching from the fixed camera's normal lens view to some other, such as Fisheye or Zoom-Telephoto.

To render the image, just follow these steps.

1. Choose the image format you'll use to store the logo on disk. Click on the Render menu item in the menu bar and select **Image Format**. A dialog box like the one shown in Figure 14.6 will pop up. You can choose resolution, height, width, and file format from this dialog box, as well as EPS and several varieties of TIFF files. Choose **TIFF-RGB**.

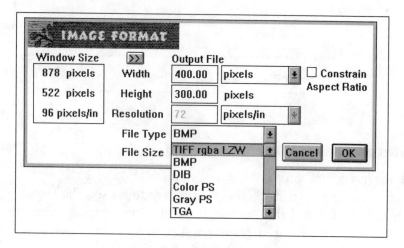

Figure 14.6 *Image Format dialog box.*

Now, start the rendering process. It's always a good idea to render to the screen and then save to disk if the results please you. To that end, Typestry offers four different rendering modes. **Quick 'n Dirty** creates a rough, low-resolution rendition suitable for judging effects and shadows, but not the texture of an object. This rendering may take only 1 or 2 minutes, or slightly longer, depending on the speed of your PC. **Reasonable** produces a higher-resolution rendering that can take four or five minutes to appear, but which will have enough quality that you can judge how a texture will look. **Excellent 'n Slow** generates a finished-quality image suitable for saving to disk but involves so much number crunching that you can wait 5–10 minutes (or much longer for complex individual frames—called key frames—to appear). The fourth option, **Custom** (available only in the commercial version of Typestry, not this tryout version), lets you define your own quality parameters. We'll look at that option a little more closely in the next exercise.

You can also select only a portion of your image and render only that (at any quality level you prefer). I'll explain how to use that option, too, in the next exercise.

2. Click on **Excellent 'n Slow** and watch your finished logo appear on the screen line by line. The finished logo is shown in Figure 14.8.

Render	Motion	Windows	Help	
Render to Screen			Quick 'n' Dirty	Ctrl+Q
Render to File...			Reasonable	Ctrl+R
			Excellent 'n' Slow	Ctrl+E
Image Format...	Ctrl+W			
Crop Marks				

Figure 14.7   *Choosing Render>Renter to Screen>Excellent 'n' Slow.*

Figure 14.8   *The finished rendering is ready to save to disk.*

3. Choose **File>Save** to store it on your hard disk in the file format you selected.

Moving On

I encourage you to play with the tryout version of Pixar Typestry as much as you like. You can experiment with various Looks and lighting effects, as well as add textured walls and floors to your 3-D space. All these features are fully functional in the demo, and you can even save your work to disk for posterity. Except for that pesky restriction on entering new text, you'll find Typestry one of the most entertaining programs on my CD-ROM.

The next exercise uses some of the features that we didn't explore in the first exercise. You can follow along if you like, even though I'm going to use the latest version of Pixar Typestry. Most of the commands and dialog boxes are similar, but I want to use this exercise to explore some of the new features in the full version of the program.

Using Pixar Typestry 2

The latest version of Typestry adds a few features not available in the demo model you've been working with. The most significant change is that Typestry 2 can import Adobe Illustrator 3.0 format files and include them in your 3-D effects. Before, you were strictly limited to using type elements from existing Type 1 or TrueType fonts or new font shapes you created with a font editor like Altsys' Fontographer for Windows. Other new features include:

- new options to build objects in tube shapes or on rubber sheets that can be distorted

- the ability to create custom bevels

- the facility to edit Looks using sophisticated parameters such as "metallness"

- fog and haze effects to add atmosphere

I'll demonstrate some of these new features in the next section. I'm going to create a whole bunch of interesting 3-D text effects based on my favorite country (excluding the United States), Spain, to show you how you might come up with variations on a single theme for a project of your own. You can recreate some of these using the tryout version of Typestry on the CD-ROM; others require the special features of Version 2.

Exploring Some Features

We can get a quick look at some impressive features quickly by running through a quick project. You don't have to follow along. I'll just list the steps I carried out so you can see exactly what was involved to produce the final image.

Adding Text

As always, the first step is to create some text that will be transformed with the other tools available. Although Typestry 2's toolbox looks a little different (it's lost its 3-D look), the same tools are available, but with added pull-out menus that appear when you click on the tool and hold down the mouse button. At the top of the toolbox is the Type tool. It can be used to select a position to enter text or, if you use the pull-out menu, to import an Illustrator 3 file. I elected to use one of my system's current fonts, Trajan, to spell out the word *Spain*. (The font choice is especially apt, since the Roman emperor Trajan was born near Seville, Spain about 53 A.D.)

Version 2 has three choices for building a new object: **Extrude**, **Rubber Sheet**, and **Tubes**. **Extrude** is the default mode we've already used, producing 3-D characters with beveled edges. **Rubber Sheet** places the characters on a flexible sheet that can be molded around objects or used in other ways. **Tubes** creates characters molded from tubes, and is great for neon effects. I chose plain old **Extrude** for my first project with Typestry 2.

Bevel Flexibility

When you choose **Extrude**, the Bevel Styles dialog box pops up automatically. You're given the choice of four different bevel types or you can create a custom bevel using the Bevel Editor. Bevels may be saved to disk for reuse at any time.

The right-hand column shows coloration variations you can apply to the bevels. The edges can be kept separate from the face of the type itself and assigned individual colors or Looks of their own. You can also adjust the depth of the bevel using the slider control at right. You get immediate feedback about the appearance you select from the "shadow" cast by the letter *A* icon in the dialog box.

Editing Looks

I applied a Look to the Spain text as always, but had the additional option of editing the Look using an editor. The parameters available vary depending on the particular Look. A ramp or color gradation may allow you to specify various colors and blending qualities. The texturized Look I chose includes parameters for surface color, size of the bumps, type of surface, and other factors. A scrolling Description box explains what each parameter means. You can save your modified Look to disk for reuse.

Adding Walls and Floor

The tryout version of Typestry included on the CD-ROM has the ability to add walls and floor to a 3-D space, and each of them may have its own Look. I didn't use those features in the first exercise in this chapter, but I plan to use them for this exercise. I selected the **Effects>Background>Walls and Floor** option and then then choose **Effects>Background>Wall Setup** to invoke the dialog box shown in Figure 14.9. It shows a bird's eye view of the project in progress, with the position of the camera, text, and wall located behind the text. You can move the endpoints of the wall to change the position and angle of the wall in relation to the text.

Be careful (or, in the words of the light-hearted Pixar manual: Danger! Will Robinson!), because you can move the wall so that it cuts through the text or is even in front of the text. Unless you make your wall transparent, any part of the text obscured by the wall will be invisible.

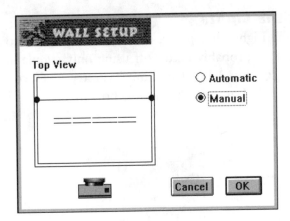

Figure 14.9 *The wall behind the text can be manually positioned.*

Setting up the floor is done in much the same way, using a side view of the 3-D space, as shown in Figure 14.10. Notice that I set the floor at an angle, just touching the bottom of the front of the text and submersing the back edge. You might actually want to sink part of your text in the floor if you use a watery, sandy, or other appropriate soft foreground Look.

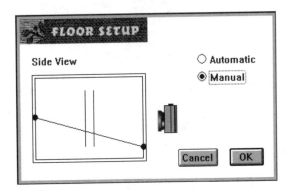

Figure 14.10 *The floor is set up using a side view of the 3-D space.*

When I finished setting up the walls and floor, I gave each of them a Look. I used the included Sky Look for the wall and the Tropical Lagoon Look for the floor. If I'm lucky, my finished image will have the text resting on a smooth ocean surface with sky at the horizon.

Adjusting the Lights

You can use the Lights dialog box to adjust the illumination that falls on your scene. You're probably better off using only simple lighting the first few times you try any 3-D effects, but Typestry gives you a remarkable degree of control. Look at the dialog box in Figure 14.11 for a few moments.

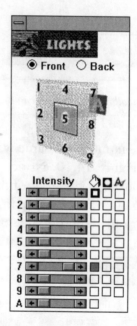

Figure 14.11 *Up to 18 different lights, plus ambient light and environmental light, can be set from this dialog box.*

Using this dialog box you can perform the following functions:

- Turn any of the 9 front or 9 back lights on or off, plus vary the intensity with the slider controls.

- Choose a color for the light by clicking on the box in the left-hand column after the slider controls.

- Elect to use a slide-projector effect to attenuate the light with a frisket or other shape, by clicking on the center box.

● Tell Typestry to allow the light to cast a shadow, by clicking on the right-hand box. Only in the digital world can you have a light that doesn't produce any shadows when it shines on an object!

● Control the ambient and environmental light sources, by clicking in the boxes to the right of the A and E sliders (which adjusts their intensity.)

Rendering a Preview

After the lights were set, I used the Rotate tool to move the text's slab a bit to provide a different perspective to the image. The only thing left to do is render the scene to the screen or to a disk file.

Because our image is more complex—including sky walls and shadows—it would be helpful to preview part of the image before taking the time to render the whole thing (which should take half an hour for this particular image). I selected just the letter *A* with the Crop tool and choose **Render>Slow 'n Excellent**. About 2 minutes later, I had the partial image shown in Figure 14.12. I could have made a few adjustments to the lights, or some other portion of the image if I wanted to, but everything looked good. I reselected the entire image with the Crop tool and started the rendering process all over again.

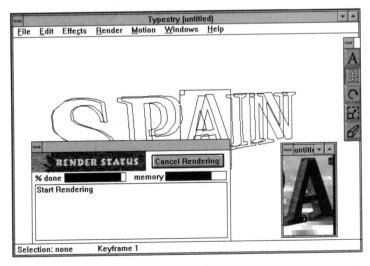

Figure 14.12   *You may preview a rendering by selecting a small portion of the image with the Crop tool and rendering only that section.*

It took exactly 36 minutes on my 486DX2/66 with 32M of RAM. You may need all the RAM you have available to render complex images, and more never hurts. The finished image is shown in Figure 14.13. It's a pretty dramatic scene, with type stretching off to the horizon over a broad expanse of glasslike ocean.

Figure 14.13 *The finished project has the text, walls, and floor all rendered in full color.*

Some Outrageous Variations

Let's take a quick tour of some outrageous variations on the Spain theme; three of them are shown in Color insert Figure 15. These pictures all turned out gorgeous, which is more of a tribute to the capabilities of Pixar Typestry than to me. Each of these projects gave me a chance to try out some other features of the program.

Creating Your Own Look

I actually used both Typestry and an image editor to generate the picture shown in Figure 14.14, which shows a 3-D image of the word *Spain*—but with a picture of the town of Toledo used as the Look! I dropped the whole thing into a corner-to-corner gradient (it's red-to-yellow in the original, which you can examine in the original file on the CD-ROM.)

Typestry 2 actually makes it easy to create your own Looks from scanned images or images you create yourself from scratch. Here's a quick description of how I accomplished this effect.

1. I created the variation of the scanned image I wanted to use as a Look in my image editor. Since Looks are 512 × 512-pixel images, I generated a new, blank image in that size, using RGB mode to allow full, 24-bit color. Then I loaded an image of Toledo, Spain, and sized, cut, and pasted a portion of that into the 512 × 512-pixel new image. I used the Sharpen filter to make it a little crisper and saved the image square as a TIFF file. Typestry can import TIFF files as Looks.

2. I created the text for the word *Spain* and then rotated and thickened it, using Typestry's standard toolbox, so I'd have a nice, thick, broad set of characters.

3. I selected the type and choose **New Look**. I found the Look I wanted under the name Pictures as Anything. This template lets you use your own images, not only for the actual appearance of the Look, but to control other factors such as shininess, transparency, or relief. That is, you can use a gray-scale image to attenuate, say, the shininess of an object: Where the gray-scale image is darker, the object will be more shiny; and where it is lighter, the object will be less shiny. That's a powerful capability. But, for this starter project, I just wanted to substitute my own scan for the surface applied to the Spain Text.

4. When you apply the Pictures as Anything template, it's somewhat generic, waiting for your input as to what picture(s) to use, and how to use them. In this simple mode, I just clicked on the **Edit Look** button and selected the **Color Picture-RGB** parameter, which brings up a dialog box you can use to select your own TIFF RGB picture.

5. As a last step before rendering, I clicked on **File>Preferences**, and made sure that Empty Space was specified as **Transparent**. Normally, if you render an image with no wall or floor, the space surrounding your type will be colored white. In other words, if you imported the image into another picture, you would get the type surrounded by a white rectangle, which is not good. When **Transparent** is checked under **File>Preferences**, that surrounding space has no color, so whatever background you paste the image into will show through.

6. After rendering, I saved the image as a TIFF file and loaded it into my image editor. Typestry can save an alpha channel that represents the area covered by the text. If your image editor supports alpha channels, like Photoshop, you can load it as a selection. That's what I did. Using **Load Selection**, I loaded the mask that represented the type and then inverted it, which quickly gave me a selection representing everything else in the picture.

7. Finally, I created a red-to-yellow gradient and applied it corner-to-corner to the background that had been selected. The finished image is shown in Figure 14.14.

Figure 14.14 *A view of Toledo was used as the texture for this text example, which was then dropped onto a red-to-yellow gradient in Photoshop.*

Shadowed 3-D Type

This next effect is really slick. Check out Color insert Figure 15 to see how well it turned out. I used a combination of techniques for this one, with both Typestry and an image editor. The Spain text appears to float over a background 2-D image of Toledo, with shadows cast on the image. You can duplicate this effect easily. Just follow these steps.

1. I created the text *Spain* word and did not rotate it this time. Instead, I just applied my Toledo Look, which I saved from the last project, and rendered it against a transparent background. I saved the whole thing as a TIFF file.

2. I loaded a picture of Toledo into my image editor and made it a little crisper with the Sharpen More filter.

3. I loaded the rendered Spain text TIFF file into the image editor and used **Load Selection** to select only the text.

4. I wanted my shadows to be fuzzy and diffused, so I chose **Select>Feather** and used a value of 12 to feather the edges of the text selection.

5. I copied the selection and pasted it into the Toledo image.

6. Using **Edit>Fill**, I filled the selection with the foreground color, black. Because the selection was feathered, it filled up with a fuzzy, shadowy effect, mimicking a shadow.

7. Switching back to the Spain text window, I used Load Selection again to reselect the text in a nonfeathered mode. I copied that text and then pasted it in the Toledo picture, offset slightly to allow the shadows to show through. The final image is shown in Figure 14.15 and Color insert Figure 15.

Figure 14.15 *Three-dimensional shadowed text created with Pixar Typestry and an image editor.*

Another Great Look

Although Typestry provides you with a selection of gradient ramps to use as Looks, it didn't have the exact one I wanted: a red-to-yellow-to-red again blend that resembled the horizontal color stripes of the Spanish national flag. (Many countries, unlike the United States, have two flags: a State flag, which is displayed on government buildings, and a National flag, which ordinary citizens may wave. In Spain's case, both have red-yellow-red horizontal stripes, but the State flag also has a coat of arms. Now you know.)

The special gradient was easy enough to create in an image editor. I opened a new document measuring 512 × 512 pixels, added a red-to-yellow gradient from the top edge to the middle of the image and another one from the bottom edge to the middle—ending up with yellow in the center each time. I saved that as an RGB TIFF file.

Then, I created the Spain text and used my new gradient as the Look applied to the floor of the image. I angled the floor to rise behind the text and gave the wall a brown color. I turned on shadow rendering for the single light source used and arrived at the final image shown in Figure 14.16 and Color insert Figure 15.

Figure 14.16 *The colors of the Spanish flag are used for the background in this image.*

Waving the Flag

The final image in this chapter uses the **Rubber Sheet** option instead of **Extrusion**. This capability is genuinely useful and can be used to create sophisticated effects. You can wrap the rubber sheet around a spherical surface, for example, or cause it to ripple in the wind like a flag. That's what I decided to do in the next exercise.

I used a boldfaced Helvetica font, and told Typestry to create it on a wavy rubber sheet, leaving a cut-out in the sheet for each character. (You can also apply the type to the sheet so that only the characters show.) I used Typestry's own Hot Look, which combines reds and yellows.

After rendering and saving the image to disk, I loaded it into my image editor and selected the text through the alpha channel by using **Load Selection**. Then, I applied a gradient of my own—going from yellow to red in the opposite direction from the gradient used for the flag. The results are shown in Figure 14.17 and in Color insert Figure 15.

Figure 14.17 *The Rubber Sheet option lets you produce flags and other effects.*

The Next Step

We'll look at some other type effects later in the book. Meanwhile, take some time to play with the tryout version of Typestry on the CD-ROM. You'll be amazed at the 3-D effects that you can create with very little work.

PART VI

Animations

This section is the only one in the book that deals with moving images. All the other chapters show you how to create still images from photographs, your own artwork, or, 3-D images rendered by programs like Pixar Typestry. Although we're treading dangerously close to multimedia (once you start moving your images, you'll be tempted to add sound or video), I still couldn't resist adding a few short chapters on how you can animate the two- and three-dimensional images you produce. Although high-end animation programs can be daunting and require a great deal of expertise to work with, I'd hate for you to miss out on the simple animations you can make without turning into another Walt Disney or Hanna-Barbera.

Best of all, the software you need is right on the CD-ROM bundled with this book. Work through a simple exercise or two with me, and you'll understand the principles of this exciting graphics area.

Producing Simple 2-D Animations

Whether you created simple flipbooks as a child or are making them today using yellow stick-on note pads, you probably toyed with animation at some time in your life. Now is your big chance to explore the concept.

In this chapter you'll learn how to quickly create your own cartoon, showing a flying saucer hovering across the ground and then pausing to zap an unoccupied building. The actual animation I produced, as well as files containing the individual frames, are all included on the CD-ROM, along with TakeOne, which generates the animations. What could be easier?

Well, there's one catch. TakeOne is the only 100%, fully-functional application I've been able to put on the disk. It's not save-disabled like some of the tryout software. It doesn't print its own logo across your work like one of the programs on the disk. The catch is that TakeOne is still a tryout version like the other software on the CD-ROM. If you have fun with it and want to continue using it, you should pay for it—which shouldn't break your wallet, since the suggested retail price of this program is an amazing $40.00!

A Slight Detour: Try Before You Buy Software

You guessed it: TakeOne is shareware. Only three things make this program different from the other tryout software on the CD-ROM:

- TakeOne is more limited in scope than the megapackages for animation that sell for hundreds of dollars.

- In view of that, it has a much lower cost—$40.00—than the other software.

- The vendor doesn't cripple features, using base incentives like inconvenience as a prod to get you to pay for the package.

I want you to promise me that if you have as much fun with TakeOne as I did, you'll pay for it by sending the U.S. representative of the German authors a check for $40.00 as soon as possible. By opening this book, you agree to abide by its licensing agreement, which stipulates this. Please initial here to indicate your concurrence: _____. Thanks! (Checks should be mailed to Pearl America, Inc., 4128 1/2 California Ave. SW, Seattle, WA 98116.)

I hope you try out the other shareware on the disk and register any of the fonts and applications you find useful. We now resume scheduled programming.

What's TakeOne?

Various 2-D animation programs for the PC and Macintoshes have been around for a long time. In fact, I included a version of Electronic Arts' Studio/1 program on a floppy disk bundled with a Macintosh book I wrote in 1992. TakeOne actually does some things that the commercial program won't do: Studio/1 was strictly limited to one-bit images. TakeOne can animate your 24-bit images if you have the hardware for it.

Even though TakeOne has limited image-editing capabilities built in, you may want to use it to animate individual drawings that you can modify into individual frames with another program, such as Photoshop, Fractal

Design Painter, or PixelPaint. Then it can animate the movies you produce on-screen.

To use this program, you need to follow just a few simple steps.

1. Create a basic image for your animation.

2. Save that image as a file and then modify it to produce intermediate images, with small changes between each frame. For example, if you want to animate an image of a ball flying through the air, move the ball a little bit in the direction of travel with each successive frame.

3. When you're finished generating all the frames, load each one into TakeOne and create your animation.

4. Play the animation or save it to disk for future use.

That's pretty easy. The next section will lead you through the creation of a simple cartoon. I put together the quick-and-dirty flying saucer sequence described previously. You can use the techniques I'm describing to do a much better job. I'll offer suggestions for improving on what I did.

Creating a Flying Saucer Sequence

It shouldn't take you more than 30 minutes to produce a super animation—or 5 minutes or less if you use my image files on the CD-ROM. If you want to skip the whole thing and jump right to the results, you can load **SAUCER.ANS** into TakeOne and just look at what I came up with. You may not be impressed, but at least my cartoon might spur you to prove how much better you can do.

To duplicate (or better) my project, just follow the steps in the next sections.

Create the First Frame

The initial step is to create the first frame of the animation. Here's how you can duplicate what I did:

1. Load your favorite image editor and create a new, blank document that measures 322 × 256 pixels. It may be gray-scale or 24-bit color, as you prefer. The more colors in your image, the slower your animation will run. I started out working in full color and then changed to 8-bit, 256-color mode after I finished the first frame.

2. Use 322 × 256 pixels to keep the size of the animation frame down to reasonable limits. The larger the image, the slower the animation, too, so this size makes a good compromise.

3. Create a foreground area by filling the bottom 40% of the image area with a green tone. Fill the rest of the image with blue. If you like, you can select either of these areas and add a little texture to them. The easiest way is to use your image editor's Add Noise filter.

4. Place a "flying saucer" in the sky, just a little above the horizon, by selecting a cigar-shaped area of sky with your editor's Oval selection tool.

5. Fill this selection with some color suitable for a flying saucer. I suggest metallic silver, clear, or, if you don't have either of those in your palette, the red I selected (it was the only color available under the We Paint Any Saucer for $69.95 deal).

6. Shade the underside of the saucer, using the Airbrush tool set at 32% pressure, and a dark gray paint. (This was not to simulate undercoating!) Then, use the Burn tool to darken the sides a bit.

7. If your image editor allows you to save masks or selections, save the saucer object selection. If not, you can still complete the exercise, but some of the later steps will be a little more difficult. Figure 15.1 shows our progress so far, just as we save the selection.

8. With the saucer area still selected, add to that selection and create a similar, but smaller oval underneath the saucer on the ground. Usually, you can create discontinuous selections by holding down the **Shift** key while you drag with the selection tool. The new selection will be added to the current selection.

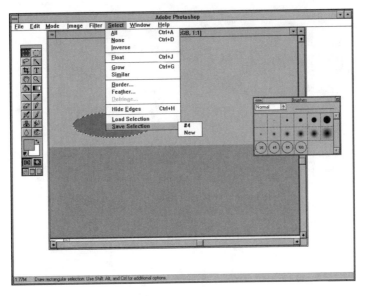

Figure 15.1 *Save the "saucer" selection before continuing.*

9. Now, feather the dual selection so the boundaries become fuzzy. (With Photoshop, use **Select>Feather**.) Specify a pixel boundary of 8.

10. Save the dual selection (both ovals) so that you have a single selection with both pieces and their feathered boundaries.

11. Deselect the saucer portion of the dual selection. Switch to the Lasso and draw around that part of the selection while holding down the **Command key**. Only the shadow portion on the ground is selected.

12. Fill the shadow with a fuzzy black tone. (In Photoshop, use **Edit>Fill**.) This is the same technique you will use several times in *Chapters 17* and *18*. I'll explain it in more detail there.

13. Reload your dual selection. (Use **Select>Load Selection** in Photoshop.) Both a saucer and its shadow are selected. This took only a couple minutes, plus you learned how to perform an operation on only part of a selection, without losing the selection (save it, operate, and then reload). Figure 15.2 shows the drawing so far.

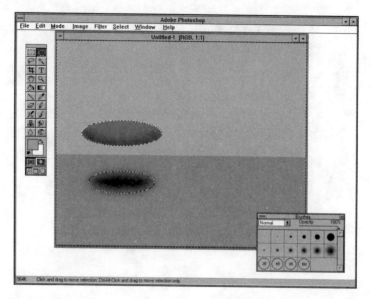

Figure 15.2 *Saucer and shadow are both selected, ready to move out.*

14. Place a sun in the sky by selecting a round area and filling it using Photoshop's Lens Flare filter.

15. Place a building at the right side of the frame, feather the building's selection, copy that, paste it in, and then fill it with black to create a shadow. I slanted the shadow a bit with **Image>Effects>Skew** and pasted it in a plausible spot in the picture. (The implausible things are the shadows—directly under the saucer but to the side of the building.) Figure 15.3 shows the final version of the first frame of our animation.

Although I enjoyed working in 24-bit color, that's a lot more color depth than this cartoon needs, and I certainly didn't want to slow down my animation. Consequently, I changed modes to Indexed color. (Use **Mode>Indexed Color** in Photoshop.) I saved the 256-color version to disk as Saucer1 in BMP (Windows Bitmap) format.

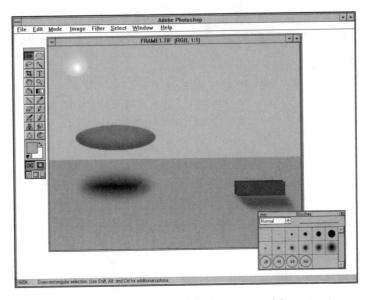

Figure 15.3 *Final version of the first frame of the animation.*

Generating Intermediate Frames

This next section will show you the quick-and-dirty method I used to generate intermediate frames. Later, I'll describe a method that gives you a little more flexibility. Just follow these steps.

1. Load the selection with both saucer and shadow and move the whole works a little bit to the right. Then save the new position of both as another mask or selection. You'll have a bit of a hole in your background where the selection used to be.

2. Fill in the hole with the appropriate colors. I used the eyedropper to grab the sky color and then painted around the hole. If you invert your current selection, you can ensure that the color you add will only go on the hole, and not the saucer or its shadow.

3. Save this intermediate frame using a numbered file name for convenience. Because the first frame was saved as Saucer1, the name Saucer2 for this next frame seemed clever to me.

4. Repeat steps 1–3, loading the new selection that you just saved. Assign a new number to each successive frame (Saucer3 would be a good bet.)

5. Keep repeating steps 1–3 five or six times until you've moved the saucer most of the way across the screen. The finer the movements, the smoother your animation will appear to be.

6. Once the saucer reaches its final position near the building, create some intermediate frames with a death-ray coming out. The first frame should have a little bit of ray coming out, the second a lot, and the third should show the entire ray. Since death-rays have been proven to move at the speed of light, you won't need more than three frames to animate it realistically. (Actually, you'd need just one frame, but who's counting?) Figure 15.4 shows the second frame, with the death-ray halfway to its target.

Figure 15.4 *This little red Interstellar Navy corvette isn't called the Sting-Ray for nothing.*

8. Show what the building looks like after it has exploded. You need two or three frames that say "kerblooie" in a subtle way. I just cloned the sun and painted more of it at the (former) site of the building over the course of three frames. Figure 15.5 pictures the mass destruction.

Figure 15.5   *Bye-bye building, as we animate it out of existence.*

Don't forget to save each frame as you make your changes. Otherwise, you'll have to go back to the previous frame and redo your work from there.

N O T E

9. As a final touch, make the saucer fly straight up when it is finished. Notice that the shadow gets smaller and smaller as the saucer goes higher. It's the attention to small details like these that put my animations in the same class as, say, Donald Bluth. Figure 15.6 shows what I'm talking about.

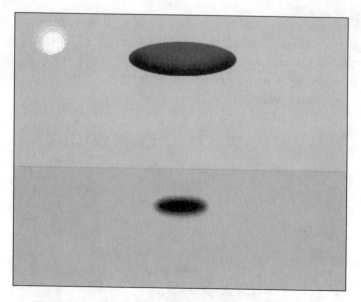

Figure 15.6 *As the saucer goes up, the shadow shrinks.*

I reduced the size of the shadow by selecting it and then selecting the Resize command. (In Photoshop that's **Image>Effects>Scale**; with other programs, you'll find it in a more logical menu.) I held down the **Shift** key to resize the image evenly. Then I filled in the holes with green paint to avoid one of those odd little circles they get in England whenever extraterrestrial beings put down in the middle of wheatfields.

Assembling the Animation

Now that we have all the intermediate frames, we can assemble our animation using the same image editor and AnimHelp. Just follow these steps.

1. Load TakeOne. You'll see the blank screen shown in Figure 15.7.

2. Pull down the File menu, choose **Load Frame**. Load the first frame, **SAUCER1.BMP**. It will be displayed in the animation sequence window at the right of the frame and in the close-up editing window at the left. You can change the magnification of the editing view by clicking on the **x2**, **x4**, or **x8** buttons in the ribbon above

the frames. Note the color palette and tools available if you wanted to modify the frame within TakeOne. Figure 15.8 shows the workspace so far.

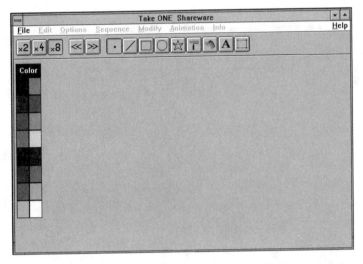

Figure 15.7   *TakeOne is ready to accept frames for your animation.*

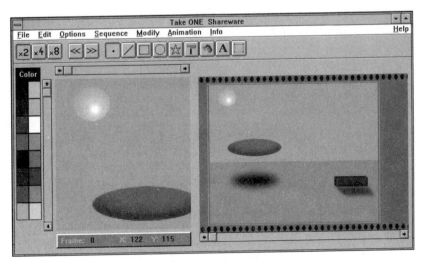

Figure 15.8   *TakeOne workspace with one animation frame loaded.*

3. Pull down the File menu, choose **Add Frame**, and load **SAUCER2.BMP**. Repeat this step until all the animation frames have been added. You'll end up with a film strip like that shown in Figure 15.9.

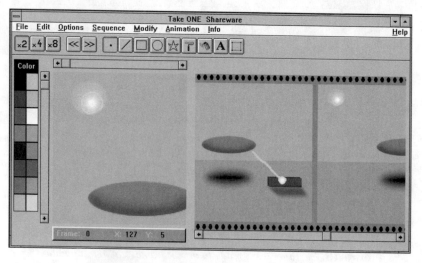

Figure 15.9 *Several frames have been loaded.*

4. Set the size of the animation window by choosing **Animation>Window** from the menu bar. Type in a title for the animation and set the Window Size for 400 × 300, as shown in Figure 15.10. Then Click on More... when finished.

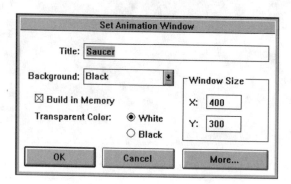

Figure 15.10 *Set Animation Window.*

5. Set the starting point for the animation at X:35 and Y:25 to center your frames in the window defined in the last dialog box. Move the Cycle Delay and Motion Delay sliders to the far left, as shown in Figure 15.11. Click on **OK** when you are finished.

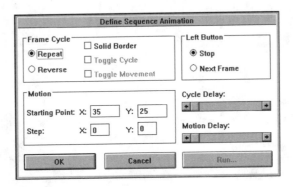

Figure 15.11   *Define Sequence Animation dialog box.*

6. Choose **Animation>Run** to watch your animation in action, using the menu shown in Figure 15.12. The animation will display over and over in a window like that shown in Figure 15.13.

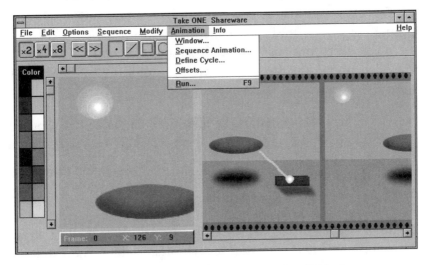

Figure 15.12   *Run the animation when finished.*

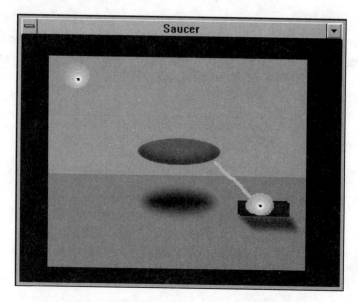

Figure 15.13 *The animation is displayed!*

Slower-and-Less-Dirty-Method

If you want to create some really sophisticated animations, you can still do it with TakeOne. You must follow procedures a little more closely aligned with those used by professional animators. That is, you must create your frames using layers: one for the background and one for each object that moves independently in the animation. You don't need an image editor with layers to do this. Just follow these guidelines.

1. Create three separate images, all exactly the same size. You might want to place them in a row on your screen for easy comparison.

2. Draw your background image in the first image. You can get fancier—or even use a photograph, since the background is going to remain separate throughout the process.

3. In the second image, draw the object that will be moving. It can be something you create from scratch or something you extract from a photo. Save the selection, because you'll be reusing the object over and over.

4. Select All of the background image and paste it into the third image you created.

5. Select the object that will be moving and paste it down in Frame 1on top of the background.

6. Save this as Frame1.

7. Create another blank image the same size. Copy the background and paste it down again. Then copy the object to be moved and insert it into Frame 2, only slightly repositioned, to account for its movement. Save Frame 2.

8. Repeat this step for the whole animation.

Because the background is separate, you don't need to worry about holes left when the object is moved. In fact, you can open three or four separate images, pasting each down in a new position in successive frames, thus animating whole swarms of objects—as many as you have the patience to track. In this case, TakeOne is as powerful as the image editor you use with it.

The Next Step

I hope you'll have fun creating your own animations with TakeOne. If you do, don't forget to send the author his $40.00. Let him know that putting that Save feature in the shareware version was worth it.

CHAPTER 16

3-D Animations

There's a funny story that has become apocryphal, even though it's only a few months old. You've probably seen the amazing 3-D animation on television that was run for several months on behalf of the vendor of the leading PC microprocessor chip, as a counter to all the hoopla surrounding the introduction of the Power Macintosh. It shows this powerful chip swooping through a virtual-reality landscape of system boards and components, lighting up each with the magic of its amazing processing ability. The amusing part, of course, is that, according to the story, the animated sequence was done on PC workstations. The state-of-the-art chip being showcased just couldn't cut it for this demanding professional application.

Does that mean we Windows users are out of luck? Luckily, that's not the case. Most of us have animation needs that can be easily handled by our run-of-the-mill hardware. Indeed, 3-D animation is one multi-zillion dollar professional graphic application that can actually be done using software and equipment readily available to folks like you and me. After all, vendors like Pixar produce professional animation software as well as the amateur versions you can buy, and much of the same code, algorithms, and rendering engines are used in both.

In the real world, professional animations aren't done using exactly the same type of equipment you and I use. The actual assembly of the animated sequence and heavy-duty rendering is more likely to be performed on megabuck systems designed exactly for that.

Even so, because you don't require the resolution demanded for professional animation, you might find it entirely practical—and a lot of fun—to create less ambitious moving images for your own presentations. It's gotten fairly easy in recent years to create and integrate movies into projects created by other programs.

In this chapter, I'll show you one application for animation: swirling, rotating type to use as an introduction to your next desktop presentation. We'll use Pixar Typestry for this exercise. This will be only a cursory look: Typestry is capable of quite sophisticated animations, complete with realistic motion blur and multiple moving objects.

I'll keep this chapter short, because this sort of special F/X really deserve a book of its own. I just want to show you enough of what is involved to help you decide if you want to explore 3-D animation more fully. Unlike 2-D animation, which can be set up and carried out with a minimum of fuss, 3-D work is not for the dilettante. You'd better be serious before you make the investment in time. Even so, some simple things can be done, if only for exploratory purposes.

Animation with Typestry: A Quick Overview

I'll run through the basic steps required to animate text in Typestry very quickly. It might help you to understand the explanations after you've looked at a few illustrations and understand how the process progresses.

1. Create some type that you want to animate. To simplify things, I generated only a single word *Pixar*, using a fat font, and did not add any background. I used the checkerboard Look. The basic wireframe version is shown in Figure 16.1.

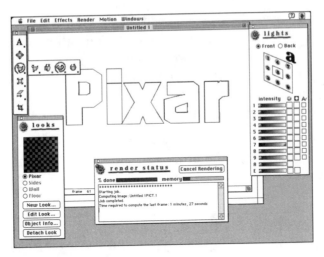

Figure 16.1 *The wireframe images can be rotated to preview the animation.*

2. Use the Rotate tool to manipulate these wireframe renditions so that you can try out your animation before it's rendered. One typical movement is to have the type revolve or spin around on one or more axes.

3. To see what at least one frame of your animation will look like, render the image to the screen using the **Reasonable** option. You'll end up with a preview like the one shown in Figure 16.2.

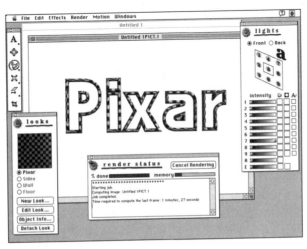

Figure 16.2 *One frame has been rendered.*

4. As you rotate the type, you can render individual images at intermediate points. If you want smooth animation, use small increments of movement between frames. (It's easy to calculate how much to move the type: if you want the type to make one complete revolution in one second, you'll need 30 frames, at 30 fps. Therefore, each individual movement should be about 12°.)

5. Prepare each rendering is a separate key frame. You can organize these frames into the order you want them presented using the Organize Keyframe dialog box, shown in Figure 16.3.

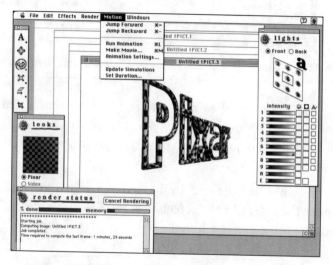

Figure 16.3 *The Organize Keyframe dialog box.*

6. Select the Motion menu, which offers a variety of functions for working on individual keyframes, advancing from one keyframe to the next, and, finally, running your animation. This menu is shown in Figure 16.4.

7. When you're ready to make your animation, select **Make Movie**. From the Make Movie dialog box, which is shown in Figure 16.5, you can generate your movie as a wireframe movie, playable on any PC with FLC video capabilities.

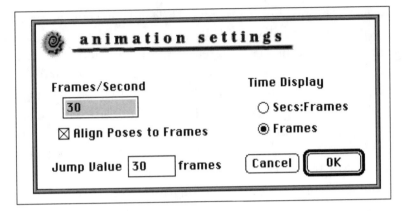

Figure 16.4 *The Motion Menu.*

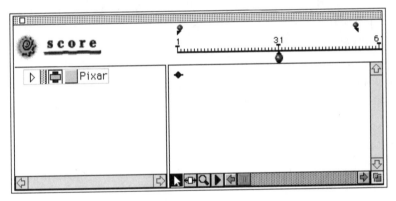

Figure 16.5 *When you're satisfied with the previews, it's time to make your movie.*

Pixar Animation: Version 2 Adds Capabilities

Let's look a little more closely at how Pixar Typestry 2's more sophisticated animation capabilities work. It uses something called a Score window is used to assemble animations.

The Score window has a short line with a small diamond resting in the middle of it. The line is the *animation timeline*, and the diamond is called the *pose nib*. The timeline represents the length of your animation (the time it will take to display all the frames you create at the frame rate you've selected), and the pose nib represents an individual selected object within a frame (its position in the frame, orientation, size, and slant; any one or any combination of all these can change during the animation).

In an animated sequence, each object in the scene will have its own pose for each frame, although the preceding example uses only one object, the word *Pixar*. To coordinate an animation, you need to position the time marker and pose nib for each object in each frame.

An object's path through an animation is defined by its position through time. Say you have an object move diagonally from the lower left-hand corner of the window to the upper right-hand corner in six individual frames. That motion defines a path. Typestry lets you define whether the path will be followed smoothly, or with acceleration and deceleration involved (e.g., an object usually slows down gradually, rather than suddenly coming to an abrupt halt).

Animations of this type are created by organizing all the objects in an image window, moving them in space and time, and creating a new frame for each new pose. When you're finished, you can create the finished animation. There are four options with Typestry.

- You can view a very simple version of the animation, with boxes replacing the actual objects, just to see how the movement looks in rough form.

- You can create an FLC wireframe version. This is still a simplified animation, but it does show the actual outline of the text and you can preview it in the final application that runs the animation.

- You can create a full-resolution version of the finished animation for use with your application.

- You can also generate individual files that can be imported into presentation software or other programs and used with that application's animation run-time software.

Typestry has some neat tricks to help you evaluate your animation. You can view the movie in "burn in" mode, which overlaps the images of the frames so that you can see the trail left by an object. The trail lets you examine the path of the animation more closely.

Typestry also can loop an animation over and over, in either forward or reverse mode, for concentrated study. If you are serious about multimedia production, 3-D animation can be very rewarding, although, as I warned, a bit complex for the beginner. There are many excellent software packages that can produce 3-D animations, from MacroMind Director through Spectra Studio Pro. You can spend a few hundred dollars to several thousand on software alone and, as I warned you earlier in the chapter, be prepared to either spend a lot of time waiting for renderings or upgrade your PC to megamemory levels. Consider adding an accelerator board, as well.

The Next Step

I'll wind up the how-to sections of this book with some interesting techniques in *Part VII*. You'll learn how to create dazzling lettering—even if you don't have the full version of Pixar Typestry—and to create images from scratch with your image editor or scanner.

PART VII

Other Cool Stuff

Creeping featuritis has long been a fact of life in the PC world. Software developers have been hard at work creating really cool capabilities in their products just for the sake of having some new feature to put a particular application one-up on a major competitor.

As a result, most of us use only 10% of the features available in any software package. Your favorite image editor has features that nobody bothered to tell you about or, worse, familiar features that can be applied in new and interesting ways. This section will provide you with a clutch of clever techniques you can use right now. You already have all the tools, and any extra files you might need are included on the CD-ROM packaged with the book. But, the real intent is not to provide you with a few more tricks to hide up your sleeve and then forget about. I'm hoping you'll be spurred by this section to go on and explore all the features of your software and to experiment to develop your own outrageous F/X. Some of the best ideas I came up with for this book were born while I was fooling around with a tool to see what would happen.

CHAPTER 17

Create Dazzling Lettering

Herewith is another chapter on using text that's guaranteed to be 100% free of typography and font technobabble. There will be no discussions here of kerning, leading, or tracking. No embarrassing details about intimate parts of a character, from stem to serif. Least of all, there will be no haughty evaluations of particular typefaces. If you want to immerse yourself in typography, go buy a typograph.

I've taken this approach because, when you're working with photographs and other bitmapped images, type is just another kind of graphic. After you paste some text down in your image, the editing software treats it exactly as if it were a bitmapped image of a kitten or anything else: just another pattern in the great sea of bits that make up a particular picture. If you haven't saved the text outline as a mask or selection, there's no way to separate it out without laboriously using the Lasso or another selection tool. You can't edit the text to change a typo, or vary the style without removing the type and replacing it with something else.

In truth, you might as well think of type as a special kind of clip art. Instead of importing type/clip art from individual files, you can create it as required using your image editor's Text tool, from the installed fonts

297

available on your PC. However, it's clip art that has special meaning, hidden within the words you use. In addition to the meanings of the words themselves, you can get additional communications mileage over the way the text is presented. That's what we'll explore in this chapter: more methods for applying special effects to type.

We already looked at 3-D type manipulations in *Chapter 14*. The techniques presented there required a special program, such as Pixar Typestry, to achieve. You can accomplish the tricks I'll show you in this chapter with just about any image editor.

You may have to use some skills you developed earlier to put some of these effects to work. I won't repeat some of the step-by-step instructions involving techniques that you already know. But, if you worked through this book, you should be able to duplicate most of the following effects.

Overlaying Text with Textures

This first section will show you how to fill text with an image or texture rather than just with a simple color or gradient. You'll need the **PAINTED.TIF**, **PENNIES.TIF**, and **QUARTERS.TIF** texture files from the CD-ROM. Then, just follow these steps.

1. Load the three textures into your image editor as separate windows. Size them so you can move from one to the other easily. We're going to play with the phrase "A Penny Saved…Is A Quarter Earned." (Yes, I realize that doesn't make sense, but it gives us an excuse to use both "money" textures.) Use your editor's type tool to create the first part of the phrase, "A Penny Saved," with a "fat" font such as the Arial Black that I used. Insert the type, sized at 30 to 40 points, into the Pennies texture as shown in Figure 17.1.

TIP

If you're using Photoshop and want to duplicate my efforts exactly, use 30-point type, but first double the size of PAINTED.TIF with **Image>Image Size…>Width: 200%**.

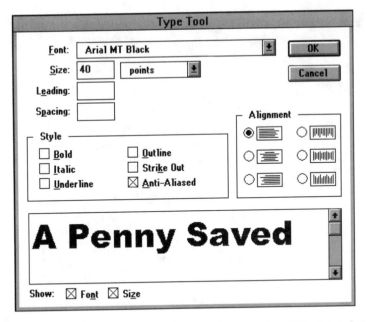

Figure 17.1 *Choose the font and type in the text using a 30–40 point size.*

The text is inserted into the image. Unfortunately, the text is filled with the current foreground color. What we really need is empty text or a selection shaped like the text, which we can use to grab portions of the image we want to use as a texture. There are several ways to accomplish this. One should work with your image editor.

3. Change your text to a selection. Try one of these ways (the first two both work in Photoshop).

● Eliminate the background color already in the text using your editor's paste controls. (In Photoshop, these are found in the Edit>Composite Controls dialog box.) Change Opacity to 1% (0% is not allowed), and the text changes into a transparent selection. This technique is shown in Figure 17.2.

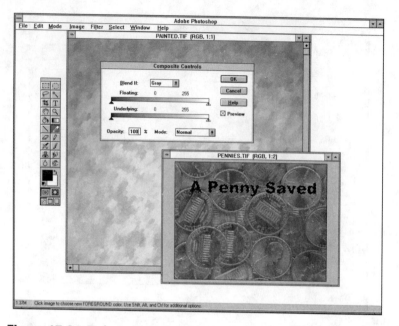

Figure 17.2 *Reducing the opacity to 1% produces a transparent selection.*

- Use **Cut** to remove the text from the image temporarily and **Select>All** to select the entire Pennies image. Then use your image editor's **Paste Behind** command to paste the text selection behind the pennies. (Use **Edit>Paste Behind** in Photoshop.) Then defloat the image so that the selection becomes part of the underlying pennies image. Because the text itself has been placed behind the pennies, you won't be able to view the background tone, but the selection itself will still appear on the surface.

- Some image editors have a built-in feature that lets you convert text to a selection.

4. Move the selection to an area of the Pennies texture image that includes lots of bright copper detail. Save the selection or mask at this point, because we'll be reusing it shortly. The selection I used is shown in Figure 17.3.

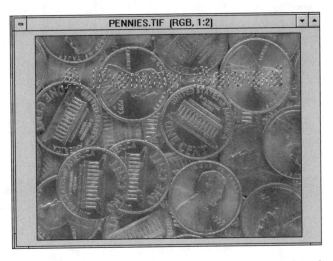

Figure 17.3 *The transparent selection allows the pennies underneath to show through.*

5. Feather the selection to fuzzy up its edges. (In Photoshop, use **Select>Feather** and then choose a Feather Radius of 8 pixels, as shown in Figure 17.4. In PixelPaint Pro 3, the same effect can be achieved with **Select>Modify>Feather.**)

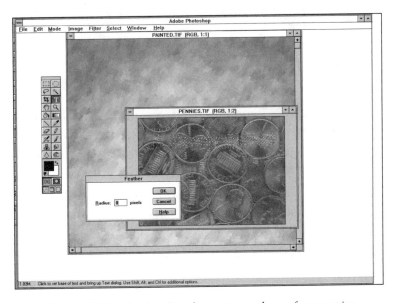

Figure 17.4 *Feather the selection to produce a fuzzy version that will produce a shadow image.*

6. Copy the selection, change to the window with the Painted Green texture, and paste it into the image, about a third of the way down. We'll use this first instance of the phrase as the shadow underneath, similarly to the effect we used in *Chapter 14*.

7. Fill the feathered selection with black, and then apply a Gaussian Blur to smudge it up even more. Your image should look like mine in Figure 17.5.

Figure 17.5 *Fill the diffused selection with black to generate a shadow.*

8. Go back to the Pennies image and load the original selection. Copy the penny-textured text, switch to the Painted texture once again, and paste the text into the window, a bit above the shadow, to give a floating effect.

9. Outline the text with a black line. (In Photoshop use **Edit>Stroke**.) Your image editor may have an Outline command or similar effect for drawing a line of pixels around the edge of a selection. The image so far is shown in Figure 17.6.

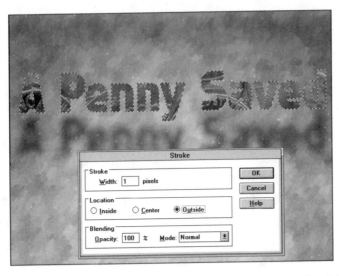

Figure 17.6   *Now sharpen up the outline by stroking it with a one-pixel wide black line.*

10. Repeat steps 2–9, but use the second part of the phrase, "Is A
Quarter Earned," and substitute the Quarters texture for the pennies. Your final image should look like the one shown in Figure
17.7.

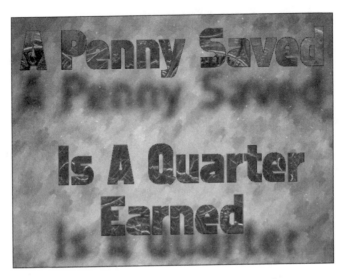

Figure 17.7   *The finished image shows that a penny saved is a quarter earned.*

The Shadow Knows

I've shown you one way to make shadows under text. Here's another way, which involves having the shadows fall in front of the text. I've used a plain background in this case, but you can use a texture or insert the text directly into an image. It's a little easier to see how the technique works when it's done against a white background. I used a font called Tancred. I was looking for a 1920s or 1930s look that would recall the golden age of radio. Choose a font of your own and then follow these steps.

1. Create the text, "The Shadow," in an empty document at an appropriate size.

2. Feather the selection as you did previously, but use a smaller pixel radius. I used a value of 3, as shown in Figure 17.8.

Figure 17.8 *Feather the selection to generate a fuzzy shadow (again!)*

3. Copy and paste the selection below the original text.

4. Apply a Gaussian Blur again. Then fill the selection with black, as shown in Figure 17.9.

The Shadow
The Shadow

Figure 17.9 *Paste the blurry shadow below the original type.*

5. Use your image editor's Rotate, Reverse, or Flip features to reverse the text vertically only, so that it becomes an upside-down mirror image of the original text. You now have a shadow, but it doesn't really look like it's been cast by the characters above (see Figure 17.10). You'll need to slant it first.

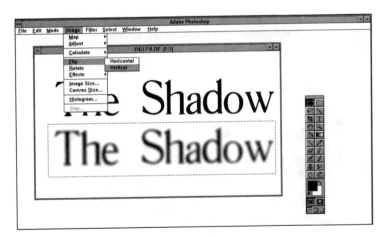

Figure 17.10 *Flip the shadow to create an upside-down mirror image.*

6. Skew the shadow to the right, as shown in Figure 17.11. Now it looks like it's been cast by a light behind and to the left of the text.

Figure 17.11 *Skew the shadow to produce a realistic effect.*

7. Move the shadow up and sew it to the "feet" of the text (remember Peter Pan?). You should end up with something like Figure 17.12.

Figure 17.12 *Attach the shadow to the foot of the text to produce this finished image.*

Tubular, Man!

This next effect is so ridiculously easy to achieve and so hard to screw up, you won't even need step-by-step illustrations. It's simply a method for creating 3-D, tubular-looking text with a minimum of fuss. You'll be amazed at the simple secret and angry at the world for keeping it from you so long.

How did I get the effect in Figure 17.13? It's nothing more than straight text, filled with a solid color and then gently painted with an image editor's Dodge and Burn (or Lighten/Darken) tools. Here's how to duplicate the effect.

Figure 17.13   *Just dodging and burning tools are needed to create this effect.*

1. Create your text using a favorite font. I used Helvetica, but the technique works just as well with fancier serif fonts.

2. Fill the text with a solid color or apply a texture using the first technique described in this chapter. Both types of text look pretty cool when tubularized.

3. Select your image editor's Burn tool, and use a fairly large brush size (40–90 pixels), depending on how large you make the text.

4. Now, just pass the Burn tool around all the edges of the text. It will darken the edges, fading out toward the center. If you burn too much, use **Undo** to remove the offending effect and start that portion again. I set the Exposure value around 80% to let me work slowly.

5. Now choose the Dodge tool and pass it over the centers of the strokes of the text. You'll end up with a nice, soft, rounded effect, with very little trouble. The exact amount of burning and dodging is not critical, so this is a fairly risk-free technique.

Backlighting Off the Backlot

Backlighting black characters against a black background (or some other dark tones) produces some dramatic text. The movie *Aliens* and other sci-fi flicks use techniques like this in their titles. Now you can do it, too. We'll reuse that shadow-casting trick we've already applied several times. See what fooling around with F/X can uncover? Just follow these steps.

1. Create your text in a document, save the selection for later use, then feather the selection, using a 4-pixel radius, as shown in Figure 17.14.

Figure 17.14 *Backlighting is easy—just reverse a feathered shadow!*

2. Fill the feathered selection with black. Select the entire picture, and reverse it (**Image>Map>Inverse** in Photoshop), producing a black background with fuzzy "white" shadow.

3. Load the original selection that included the text and fill it with black. You'll end up with a dramatic image like that shown in Figure 17.15.

Figure 17.15   *Aliens? No, just backlit black text on black.*

The Next Step

Explore the features of other programs you may use to find out how to do other type effects. For example, Fractal Design Painter can produce some neat duotone effects when you select **Invert Grain** in the Paper palette, coloring each version with a different set of tones. You'll find that Photoshop and other programs have built-in features that you can combine with type to produce truly sensational lettering.

Now, let's look at some other ways to use these tools to create images from scratch.

CHAPTER

18

Creating Images from Scratch

We're almost at the end of the trail in our quest for special F/X. I've explained all the cool, but easy techniques you can use for manipulating photos, compositing two or more images together, and creating special 3-D and 2-D effects with type.

This chapter will explore two more ways you can create images from scratch: using the painting tools of your image editor and capturing images with scanners. You'll find that both these tools are valuable. We'll start out with using painting techniques.

Painting by the Numbers

The reason why I like manipulating photographic images so much is that I'm a frustrated artist, but I don't have the motor skills to create works using traditional painting or drawing media. That's sad for those of us who have images in our heads that we just can't get down on paper (or CRT). For example, I recently was required to come up with a logo for my club's annual Es-Car-Go road rally, picturing our mascot snail driving a car (it's a very large snail and a small car). Wouldn't you know it, despite having 40,000 pieces of clip art on CD-ROM, there wasn't one decent picture of a snail driving a car? I tried drawing the snail freehand with an image editor. This was basically a process of drawing a line, looking at it, and if it didn't look like the line belonged on a snail, clicking on **Undo** and starting over. Gradually, by removing everything from my image that didn't look like a snail, I ended up with a fair image of one.

You may have the same problem, if you're lacking in traditional artistic skills. The real secret, though, is to use the tools and shapes already built into your software to create images that look professional, although they're not. That may mean you're limited to geometric shapes, but it doesn't mean you can't create something good. Figure 18.1 shows a painting I did that, in its original full-color, is pretty good. You can check out the original image on the CD-ROM if you want to see what I mean.

Figure 18.1   *Sci-fi image generated from scratch with an image-editing program.*

Let me run through the steps I used to create this image so that you can see how the tools in your image editor can be applied creatively to produce good images from scratch, even if you're not an artist.

Creating an Other-Worldly Image

I'm a big science fiction fan, so I decided to create a picture of an imaginary world. Here's what I did.

1. I selected the lower one-eighth of the image, filled it with a dark green to darker green gradation (stretching out to the horizon), and then used the Add Noise filter to generate random pixels repeatedly in the gradation. When I was done, it looked a lot like grass.

2. I selected an area along the horizon, using the Lasso to make it look like a mountain range. I filled that with brown and used Add Noise again to give it some texture.

3. Even a nonartist like me knows that things get blurry when they get farther away, so I used the Blur and Smudge tools to rough up the line where the grass and the mountain meet.

4. I filled the sky with a dark blue to medium blue gradation, applied diagonally from the upper left-hand corner of the screen.

5. I held down the **Alt** and **Shift** keys at the same time while dragging a circle to produce the huge, looming moon (maybe it's a planetoid about to strike?). I filled that with a gradation of its own to simulate shading.

6. Then I selected various-sized circles on the surface of the moon, and applied the Emboss filter to raise them above the surface. I made many of the "craters" overlap, as they really do on such satellites.

7. When the moon was finished, I used the Sphere filter to stretch the gradation and craters into a spherical shape. I then saved the moon's selection, cut the moon out of the picture, feathered the selection to produce a halo effect, filled that with white, and then pasted the moon back.

8. I positioned the Lens Flare filter at the outer edge of the moon to create a Sun peeking out from behind.

9. I wanted a second Sun in this system, but didn't want flare all over everything. So, I selected a circular area of the sky and applied the Lens Flare filter again inside that area.

10. Next, I selected an oval area above the grass, filled it with colors, and spherized the whole thing to produce a hovering flying saucer.

11. An oval area underneath was selected, feathered, and filled with a 60% black tone to generate a shadow for the saucer.

12. Finally, I selected an area under the saucer and filled it with yet another Lens Flare to simulate some sort of eerie ray effect.

I think this picture looks pretty neat, even if a real fumble-fingered non-artist produced it. It got me started, and I soon produced the picture shown in Figure 18.2, which uses exactly the same techniques to create a very different picture. The larger stars in the image are all tiny Lens Flares. This is a really cool filter.

Figure 18.2 *Another sci-fi image created from scratch.*

Creating Images with Scanners

The second way to build an image yourself is to capture it whole or in pieces using a scanner. All the exercises in this book used pre-existing images that I supplied to you on the CD-ROM, but many of them were captured using my own color scanner.

If you're serious about creating special F/X, consider getting a scanner of your own. There are several key uses for scanners, which were the most sought-after peripheral device until CD-ROMs came along (and after everybody has a CD-ROM drive, the interest in scanners will revive once again!). Among the ways you can use scanners to create special F/X:

- Capture images whole for retouching or manipulation.

- Grab parts of images that can then be isolated and dropped into your other files.

- Capture images of 3-D objects, simply by placing the object on the glass platen of a flat-bed scanner. That's how I got the images of the pennies and quarters used as textures in *Chapter 17*. A vendor loaned me a scanner for review, so I took the opportunity to scan in a few solid objects. I scanned in rocks, gravel, sand, money, anything.

- Scan in special text headlines or other type for autotracing or other manipulations in an illustration package or bit map editor.

Buying Your Own Scanner

This section provides a little information on scanner types and how they work, for those who might be interested in adding one to their F/X toolkit. There are five basic types of scanners: flatbed, sheetfed, overhead, hand-held, and video (although video scanners, or camcorders, have few serious uses for still image editing on the PC; they're better for capturing scenes for QuickTime movies). All five types have several elements in common and some unique aspects of their own.

Among the things they share are a light source and a sensor that receives light reflected by or transmitted through the subject being scanned. The sensor is actually a sensor array—many small individual sensors arranged in a line or matrix. Usually, the sensor is a silicon chip called a charge-coupled device (CCD).

Each element of the array captures information about a single pixel in the image. That information is based on how much light is transmitted or reflected by the original. If very little light reaches the sensor, the pixel is stored as a dark tone. If a great deal of light makes its way to the sensor, the pixel is represented by a light tone.

A scanner that has a linear array scans one line of pixels at a time. Then, the next line is scanned, until all the lines in an image are captured. The sensor can change its point of view from one line to another in a variety of ways.

On a flatbed scanner, you place the original face down on a piece of glass, much as you would on a photocopier. Then, a traveling bar passes under the glass, scanning each line in turn. The bar has a light source that illuminates the original and either the sensor itself or a mirror that reflects light to a fixed sensor at the end of the scanner. Figure 18.3 shows how this works.

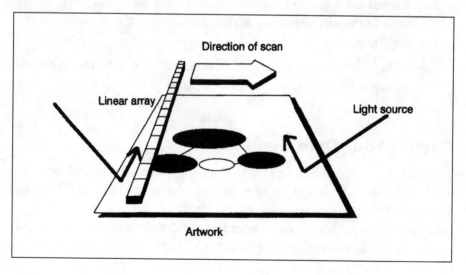

Figure 18.3 *The mechanics of how a scanner works.*

With flatbed and sheetfed gray-scale scanners, the light source is likely to be a full spectrum fluorescent light source. Color scanners use either three-colored fluorescent lights or a system of filters to change the color of a single light source. In a sheetfed scanner, the sensor and the light source remain fixed, and the original image is pulled past them using a roller transport system.

Hand-held scanners use your muscles to pull the scanning head past the material being scanned. In that respect, they resemble sheetfed models more than flatbed scanners, even though the artwork remains stationary. Like sheetfed scanners, hand-held models produce bad scans if transport is not smooth and at right angles to the edge of the page. The fact that it is the scanner rather than the paper that is the variable makes no difference.

Hand-held scanners lack both the space and the power needed for a fluorescent light source. Instead, a bank of light emitting diodes (LEDs) is used. Overhead scanners, seldom seen these days, place the sensor above the copyboard that holds the original, much like the arrangement found in a photographic copy camera. The sensor may be a linear array that is rotated to scan each line or that views a rotating mirror to achieve the same effect.

Some overhead scanners and all video scanners use a two-dimensional array of sensors to capture an entire original image at one time. This arrangement allows much faster scanning, of course, because the actual line-to-line scan portion of the process is done electronically. However, as you might expect, the sensors used in such scanners are either expensive or offer relatively low resolution because of the complexity of building a high-resolution, two-dimensional array.

Flatbed and sheetfed scanners must have an internal light source to illuminate the material being scanned. Color models use either three individual colored light sources—one for each of the primary colors—or a system of filters placed over the light or sensor.

The information that a scanner captures is converted from a continuous, or analog, value to a digital value before it is stored. The number of bits used to store scanned information is often referred to as pixel depth. You'll see references to 4-, 6-, 8-, and even 24-bit scans. All that means is that the analog information captured by the scanner is translated, or digitized, into the specified number of values. The more values available to represent a continuous-tone image, the more accurate the final image.

Scanner resolution is the amount of information per linear inch or square inch that can be captured or reproduced by a system. Many scanners will also interpolate the information they capture to produce image files that simulate higher resolutions. The scanning software looks at the values of the pixels that surround each picture element in an image. It is then able to make some reasonably intelligent guesses about the smaller elements that would make up that pixel if it had been scanned at a higher resolution. You're not getting any additional information; the data that are captured are simply divided up into smaller pieces. That can be useful when an image is enlarged later on; the image may appear less chunky.

I've used just about every scanner on the market, and two new good ones at the lower end that you might want to consider are the Canon IX-4015 and Sharp JX-325. At the high end—over $3500—there are new 30- and 36-bit color scanners, like the UMAX PowerLook, with some improved color accuracy and dynamic range.

The Canon's big advantage is its bundled Ofoto 2.0 scanning software. The image-processing software drives the tiny Canon scanner with uncanny accuracy to capture color-corrected, cropped, and straightened images with one mouse click on the **Autoscan** button. Even veteran users will find, to their chagrin, that this package is sometimes smarter than they are.

For example, Ofoto can automatically determine what type of original you placed in the scanner, adjust for its brightness and contrast, and then scan at a resolution and color balance ideal for your particular color or black-and-white printer. When it's done scanning, Ofoto can crop out the area outside the picture and straighten the image, if you placed the original on the scanner slightly askew. If there are *moiré patterns* (often produced when you scan previously halftoned images such as photographs in a magazine or book), Ofoto will zap those, too.

The Canon is fast, too, scanning a 3.5 × 5-inch 24-bit color photo with one pass in just 22 seconds. Other scanners, particularly those that capture images in three separate red/green/blue scans, can take two to three times as long. Ofoto's capability to work with the low-resolution prescan image is an incredible time-saver. Any scanning software will crop this initial image before making a final scan. Ofoto also lets you adjust the brightness and contrast, rotate the image, straighten it, or sharpen selected areas. There's no need to do the slower final-resolution scan until you've made these adjustments with the preliminary image.

Like most flatbed scanners, the Canon model handles only reflection copy. Many of the images I provided for you on the CD-ROM were originally color transparencies, which I scanned in using a Sharp JX-325 scanner with an optional transparency attachment.

The slide attachment, which replaces the stock scanner's top cover, is virtually a scanner in its own right. It has its own traveling CCD sensor, but works in tandem with the original table's trio of red/green/blue fluorescent lamps to scan by light projected through the transparency or negative originals.

Three film-scanning attachments for 35mm slides or 4 × 5 to 8 × 10-inch transparencies are available. The 300-dpi JX-32F3 attachment ($799) provides enough resolution to capture larger transparencies for less demanding desktop presentations and for position only (FPO) artwork placed in publications.

When configured for transparency scanning, the original lid is replaced by a thicker unit with its own glass face and a built-in sensor array that has been tuned for transparency scanning. Installation takes only a minute or two, and you can still use the scanner for capturing reflective art by sliding a white plastic cover board into a channel in the new lid. The transparency is placed on top of a translucent white sheet of diffuser plastic in a special holder. In that mode, light from the flatbed's three fluorescent lamps shines through the diffuser and transparency, and the image is captured by the sensor array in the lid attachment.

When scanning reflective copy (photographic prints, magazine tear sheets, artwork), the JX-325 operates exactly like conventional color scanners. The original is placed face down on a glass platen, and a traveling light source illuminates the subject for capture by a CCD array inside the flatbed. If you must scan many legal-sized documents, its 8.5 × 11-inch coverage may be annoyance.

Both the Canon and Sharp scanners occupy a niche that's wholly apart from that targeted by the UMAX PowerLook. Indeed, with desktop color scanners dipping below $1000, high-end models priced at $3500 and up are few and far between. UMAX Technologies' new PowerLook scanner proves there's still plenty of room for a high-speed, high-performance flatbed capable of capturing the most demanding reflective and transparency artwork.

This is a 30-bit (not 24-bit) color scanner with expanded sensitivity to fine gradations of color and tone. It features 600 × 1200 optical resolution (which can be interpolated by software up to 2400 × 2400 bits per inch) for grabbing the tiniest details. The built-in 2Mb output buffer feeds image data to your computer as fast as it can accept it. An optional transparency adapter can handle slides up to 8.3 × 10 inches. Those extra muscles qualify the UMAX PowerLook as one of the brawniest scanners you can put on your desktop.

At 20 pounds and with a 21 × 13-inch footprint, the PowerLook is roughly the same size as other scanners with a 10 × 14-inch scanning platen, although maximum scanning area is 8.3 × 11.7 inches for reflective artwork. Its tiny, IRQ-less SCSI interface installs in any 8-bit or 16-bit slot quickly, and, like most similar interfaces, it is unlikely to conflict with other peripherals in your system.

What differentiates this scanner is inside the unit's sealed case, assembled in a clean room to ensure dust-free optics. First, there's that 2M output buffer. The PowerLook was able to scan a test image in full color at 600 dpi in only 55 seconds, while another leading scanner—known for its speed—took 72 seconds to scan the same image at its maximum optical resolution of 400 dpi. When you're scanning multiple images over a long period of time—which is a likely scenario for a $3500 scanner—those seconds can add up to hours saved very rapidly.

This scanner uses a tri-color CCD that is capable of capturing the full RGB spectrum from the illumination produced by a single white lamp. Most other color desktop scanners use three different red, green, and blue lamps or a series of filters to capture color with a trio of scans in either one pass or three. UMAX's no-filter, one-pass design lends itself to faster, more accurate scanning.

Each of the three sets of sensors capture 10 bits of information per color channel, which allows more than a billion colors—compared to "only" 16.7 million colors for 24-bit scanners—and 1024 individual grays, instead of just 256 gray tones. The PowerLook also has a higher dynamic range—the ability to image a much broader spectrum of tones from very dark to very light. Given the limited range of colors that can be reproduced by computer monitors, color printers, and offset presses, are these expanded capabilities important?

That certainly proves to be the case both in theory and in practice. Reflective artwork, such as color photographs, has a relatively limited range of colors and brightness values, governed by things such as the whiteness of the paper, the color gamut of its dyes, and the deepest blacks that the paper can reproduce and still hold detail. But when color transparencies are involved, the picture suddenly becomes very different. Color slides can reproduce vast ranges of color and tones that you'll never see in prints and put heavy demands on scanners used to capture them.

PowerLook let me scan some very dark color slides that had stymied other desktop scanners I had tested. It reached deep into these transparencies and pulled out details that could be seen when the slide was held up to a strong light but that were invisible to other scanners. The UMAX unit was also very good at handling high-contrast originals that had details in both the shadows and highlights. Other scanners supplied the shadow detail, or the highlight detail, but not both. The $595 transparency adapter replaces the scanner's stock cover and contains a second light source; the flatbed's main sensor serves double-duty for reflective and transparency artwork.

The 30-bit color capabilities are nothing to sniff at either, even if you plan to save your work in a 24-bit format. Most 24-bit color scanners don't really give you 8 bits worth of color information per channel. A significant amount of information is always lost due to techie stuff like signal-to-noise ratios, so you may be lucky to end up with 7 bits per channel and a palette of little more than 2 million colors. By mimicking high-end drum scanners ($40,000 and up), that capture 10 or more bits per channel, the PowerLook is always able to interpolate the information it captures down to a true 24-bit palette.

Application support is through a TWAIN driver, which can be accessed from the File menu of any TWAIN-compliant program, such as Adobe Photoshop or Aldus PhotoStyler. The UMAX scanner can also be driven directly from a few non-TWAIN OCR programs, such as WordScan, TypeReader, and OmniPage/386.

The bundled MagicScan TWAIN driver tweaks every ounce of performance out of the scanner, automatically calibrating itself for individual images prior to each capture. I placed a group of 2 × 2-inch slides on the platen, did a gang preview, and watched as MagicScan adjusted its brightness, contrast, and color controls in real-time as I selected each one in turn for a final scan. Although I got excellent results from the scanner in its Auto mode, I could also modify gamma and other parameters from MagicScan using handy buttons. Other buttons let us perform blurring and sharpening and remove halftone screens from pictures printed in magazines.

At roughly $4000 for the UMAX PowerLook and its transparency adapter, most purchasers will be service bureaus and corporate in-house desktop publishing and printing operations looking for high performance and the ultimate in image quality. Individual graphics professionals who want better images and can't afford a drum scanner will also appreciate this unit. At a time when most scanner vendors are trying to slice margins and pack value into $1000–1500 color models, UMAX is proving that there's still room on the high road for innovative technology.

The Next Step

This chapter provided a little more background than I would have liked, but I had to do it as practice for the next section of this book, which unavoidably dips into color printing and output technologies. I needed to cover both in order to make this a complete look at creating and outputting special effects, but I saved the necessary technical stuff for the very end.

In the very last section of the book, you'll find detailed descriptions of the images and other things contained on the CD-ROM. I hope you'll use them to create your own special effects using the techniques you have already learned.

PART VIII

Output

Ever since the HP LaserJet brought laser printing to the PC realm in 1984, we've been able to effortlessly provide WYSIWYG output of anything we could see on the screen. More recently, color separation and calibration capabilities have given us the capability of producing output that could be printed accurately in full color on offset presses.

This two-chapter section discusses the latest output options you'll want to consider for your PC F/X.

Leading Color and Monochrome Printing Technologies

This chapter will concentrate on 300-dpi page printers and, to a lesser extent, higher-resolution output devices, because the vast majority of you will be using something that falls into one of these two categories. Most of you will have at least $1000 to spend for an entry-level printer, but will find it hard to justify spending more than about $7000. We'll examine each of the leading printing technologies and show you how they can be used for final output of our finished F/X images.

How Printers Handle Bitmapped Output

Most of the images you have worked with in this book have been bitmapped or have raster images. On first glance, printing a bitmapped image should be simplicity itself, because all PC printers (other than pen plotters) are devices that create a bitmap of each page before printing. If your printer produces 300-dpi output, all you need to do is create an image at the same resolution, and then map each pixel of your image to the equivalent printer spot, et voilà! Right? Wrong.

Black-and-white and most color printers don't have very many options when it comes to printing each dot on a page. With a monochrome printer, that dot can be a full, round, black dot (measuring a little less than 0.03×0.03-inch on a 300-dpi printer), or it can be left blank to produce the same size white space. Some printers use a technology called *resolution enhancement* which varies the size of the dot, but that still doesn't give us exactly what we want.

Think about it: With a gray-scale image, each pixel is not either black or white—it's some shade of gray, stored in digital form as a value between 0 and 255. Yet a printer won't give you 256 different gray dots (it doesn't have 256 different colors of toner); all it will do is print either a black dot or leave a white spot instead.

Most color printers aren't much better. They can print dots in yellow, cyan, magenta, or black. If the ink, toner, or dye is translucent and you print two dots in the same place, you can combine these colors to get red, green, and blue. Add in black and white, and that's only eight different hues, a far cry from the 16.7 million your PC can work with.

What happens is that we have to abandon our nice, sharp 0.03×0.03-inch dot and use these smaller dots to build larger ones that can simulate additional colors. For example, if you use 16 regular printer spots to build a cell that measures four dots on a side, you now have the option of either filling or not filling each of the dots in the cell with color. Although the cell is larger (so your effective resolution has dropped from 300-dpi to just 75 dpi), the human eye will still blur all the dots within it, combining their tones.

If 4 of the 16 dots have a black spot in it, we'll see that cell as if it were produced by combining white and black paint in a ratio of 1 to 4, producing what is called a 25% gray. Filling up half of the 16 dots generates a 50% gray. Because there are 16 different combinations of black/white dots in the cell, you'll be able to produce 16 different gray tones, plus pure white. If you collect enough of these coarser cells into an image, you end up with a halftoned or dithered picture, looking much like the photographs printed in newspapers or magazines.

Figure 19.1 shows a printer "cell" constructed of 16 printer dots, with 50% of its dots filled in, creating a 50% gray cell.

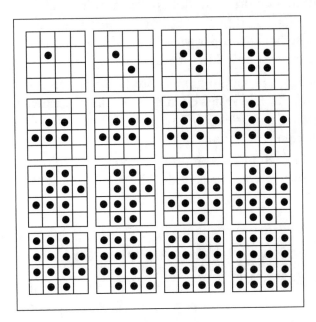

Figure 19.1 *A printer cell constructed of 16 printer dots can recreate 16 different levels of gray, plus white.*

An effective resolution of 75 cells per inch (using our 4 × 4 printer cells) provides resolution that is roughly comparable to what you see in a daily newspaper, but 16 gray tones are far too few to reproduce a black-and-white photograph. The human eye needs at least 64 grays to see a realistic image.

Obviously, an 8 × 8-dot printer cell cuts the effective resolution of a 300-dpi printer down to 37.5 lines per inch. We get enough grays, but not enough resolution—hardly a solution. For that reason, higher resolution monochrome printers have made serious inroads in the past few years. A 600-dpi printer offers a minimum of 64 grays and 75 lines per inch. Most of them use resolution enhancement to vary the size and position of the laser spot that images a dot, giving you higher resolutions and up to 256 grays.

Inkjet and thermal wax color printers use this same dithering technique, only with the ability to lay down multiple dots in the same place to create additional colors. The dots of each particular color are rotated slightly so they are not directly on top of each other. Because resolution enhancement techniques aren't widely available for inkjet and thermal wax printers, you may get only 256 different colors.

Thermal dye-sublimation printers produce black-and-white and color a little differently. They transfer exacting amounts of each color to a special printing surface, giving you 256 grays or 16.7 million colors at the printer's full resolution. That produces near-photographic quality.

I'll describe each of the competing printing technologies in the following section, starting with black-and-white-only printers. Then, I'll look at each of the three leading color technologies.

How Black-and-White Page Printers Work

The most commonly used output device for the kind of images in this book is one of several types of page printers, which you probably think of as a laser printer. However, not all printers of this type use lasers to write an image. The laser device found in the HP LaserJet and similar printers is nothing more than a very precise light source that is used to expose a pixel from the bit map of your page onto a photosensitive conductor, which may be a belt or a drum. Other, equally precise light sources can also be used. For example, some printers use LEDs to make the exposure, while others put a liquid crystal shutter to work to modulate the light that prints pixels onto the photoconductor. From that point on, the imaging process is more or less identical in all common page printers, involving several different components.

Controller

To print a page containing a scanned image, your computer downloads to your printer either a bit map of the page or PostScript instructions on how to build that bit map. This bit map is stored in memory until the full image is received.

The controller is sometimes called a *raster image processor* (RIP) because a bit map is a type of raster image. The controller has access to the full complement of memory in your printer, some of which can be dedicated to storing bitmapped images of various fonts, called *soft fonts* because they are created by software rather than hardware. Your application sends a code to the printer, activating a particular font. Then, when a particular ASCII code corresponding to an alphanumeric character is received, that letter, number, or symbol is printed using the selected font.

Image Writing

The actual writing can be done in one of two ways. The printer can expose the image area (the black lines of your scanned image or text), in which case it is called a *write black* printing engine. The printer can also expose the white areas on the page, skipping over those pixels that are to be printed black. Such devices are called *write white* engines.

Because the laser, LED, or liquid crystal shutter must scan each line on the page in all cases, it doesn't take any longer to write the white areas than to write black. However, each of these systems has its own advantages and disadvantages.

With write black systems, toner is attracted to those areas of the drum that have been illuminated by the writing light source. Such systems are better at defining very fine details, because the pixels and only the pixels of the image are written to the photoconductor. All other areas of the drum or belt are left untouched, so there is less chance that spurious pixels that can produce artifacts that reduce resolution. In write white systems, on the other hand, toner is attracted to those areas not illuminated by the writing light source. Because of the toning systems used, this usually results in much denser black areas.

Write black printers are often preferred by those who use their laser-printed pages as masters for offset printing, because ink used in lithography tends to soak into a page and spread (the degree depends on the type of paper stock). Masters that are not too dark tend to reproduce better on the press. If you plan to use your laser copy as the final output, you may prefer pages printed with a write white engine, because the black areas will be denser and more consistent. The manufacturers of individual printers can tell you what type of writing technique is used. Keep in mind that printers are getting better all the time and that the differences may not be important to you, particularly if you output copy for both offset reproduction and direct use.

Toning Engine

The rotating photoconductor belt or drum and the paper are supplied with an electrical charge from a set of charging coronas. The toner itself is also electrically charged, either through the addition of charging agents or because of its natural electrical characteristics.

Toner contains the (usually black) colored pigment itself and the somewhat larger carrier particles to which the pigment clings. The image areas on the drum are given one charge (positive or negative) while the surrounding areas have the opposite charge. Toner particles also have the opposite charge and are, therefore, attracted to the image areas and repelled by the nonimage areas. The toner is picked up by the drum, which rotates and transfers it to the paper, which is charged to attract the toner. The paper then passes through a set of heated fuser rollers that permanently fuse the toner to the paper.

Who uses them: Users include anyone who wants to produce text or rough black-and-white proofs of color or black-and-white images and who can justify some type of color printer.

Color Page Printers

Color page or laser-type printers work much the same as their black-and-white cousins. However, each image is run through the exposure, image writing, and toning steps four times, once each for cyan, magenta, yellow, and black portions of the image. Obviously, separate toning stations must be provided in the printer for each color. Once all four colors of toner are transferred to the electrically charged drum or belt, they are transferred to the paper and permanently heat fused to the paper.

Because of their complexity, color page printers are often considerably more expensive (at $11,000 and up) than any of the technologies described here. Even dye-sublimation printers, which have price tags that can climb into the $25,000 stratosphere, can be purchased for less.

Laser-type color printers typically don't provide quality that is as good as dye-sublimation printers for photographic output, but they do much better on fine lines and text. These printers are best suited for spot color—images with specific elements that must be represented in cyan, magenta, yellow, red, green, or blue.

At 2 pages per minute, or faster, laser-type color page printers are no speed demons, but are still much faster than color printers clocked in minutes per page rather than vice versa.

Who uses them: Users include those who have nonphotographic images and who want to include spot color in text documents.

Inkjet Printers

Inkjet printers offer good resolution—360 dpi and up—and the ability to produce color at reasonable prices ($800–$3000). They work exactly as you might think—by spraying a jet of ink onto a piece of paper, under precision computer control. Images are formed a dot at a time with a fine stream of ink, either water-based or solid (which is melted just before application) in disposable or refillable ink cartridges. Piezoelectric crystals in the ink containers vibrate as electric current flows through them, issuing carefully timed streams of ink from a tiny nozzle, generating a precisely positioned dot.

Liquid inks tend to soak into the paper. This spreading enlarges the size of the dots, so your 360-dpi printer may produce output that looks no better than 300 dpi when the page dries. Liquid inks can also smear when wet. You may need to use a special paper stock for optimal results with this kind of printer.

Neither problem crops up with solid inks, used in so-called *phase change* printers. These devices are less finicky about paper quality, because any tendency to absorb ink can be ignored. On the other hand, solid inks produce washed-out overheads when you print on transparency material, so your choice between these two technologies should include that factor, as well as the extra ink costs of phase change printers.

The first inkjet color printers used just three ink cartridges—cyan, magenta, and yellow—and simulated black by combining equal quantities of all three colors. There are several problems with that approach. So-called composite blacks tended to be brown and muddy rather than true black. In addition, black ink is a lot cheaper than colored ink, so it made little sense to use three times as much expensive ink to create black tones. Three-color printers are particularly wasteful when they generate black-and-white-only pages, such as pages of text. So, most color inkjet printers today use four cartridges, adding black.

Who uses them: Inkjet printers are ideal for users on a tight budget who still want to be able to produce color images. Solid-ink versions of these printers are especially prized by graphic artists and package designers who need rough proofs of output on special paper stocks.

Epson Stylus Color Inkjet Printer: A Closeup Look

UP CLOSE

As this book was being written, Epson America introduced a truly amazing product: a color inkjet printer with 720-dpi resolution that provides near-photographic output—yet costs as little as $600! It really blows the competition out of the water, so I wanted to take a closer look at this printer here. After all, if you're preparing PC F/X, wouldn't you love to have a color printer that provided photorealistic color images, razor-sharp text, high speed, and ease of use wrapped up neatly in a single low-cost box? The new Epson Stylus Color printer doesn't make you choose just one or two features from your dream list. This versatile inkjet device lets you have it all.

The 720 × 720-dpi Epson printer incorporates a more precise kind of inkjet print head to generate stunning color quality on special coated paper. Prints from full-color scanned photographs were better than you would ever expect to see on a sub-$1000 color printer. At standard viewing distances, you'll easily mistake output from the Stylus Color printer for conventional color photographs, thanks to a palette of up to 16.7 million colors and a clever selection of dithering routines optimized for different types of original images. My test prints had shadows rich in detail, with midtones and highlights drenched in saturated color.

The Stylus Color printer also output crisp text and was fast enough to please the most impatient PC user. The Windows printer driver is piloted using intuitive tabbed dialog boxes. That's an unbeatable combination of features for a printer with a suggested retail price of $699.

Though styled like a wide-carriage dot matrix behemoth with an 18.5×20.5-inch footprint, this printer is a lightweight that may throw you off balance when you lift it out of its box. Like all inkjet printers, the Epson Stylus Color has few moving parts inside and weighs in at less than 16 pounds.

Installation is a snap—literally—as you click the black and color ink supplies into place, slip a pair of flimsy plastic paper supports (one broke when I installed it) into their slots, and snap a serial or parallel cable into the appropriate plug. A second parallel or serial interface, or a network card can be added, allowing the Epson Stylus Color to "talk" to three different computers or to two computers and a network, in turn.

The Windows setup program (this is a Windows-only printer; DOS die-hards are out of luck) guides you through a simple calibration procedure the first time you use the printer. Vertical lines are printed at ideal and actual positions using all the available colors, and you choose the pairs that match up most precisely. Thereafter, the printer driver knows exactly where individual dots fall on the page—until it's time to recalibrate a few months down the road.

The Epson printer uses one permanent print head for black ink, and two permanent heads for cyan, magenta, and yellow inks. The piezoelectric disks in the Epson print heads vibrate when an electric current is supplied, using the mechanical motion to spit precisely sized and shaped droplets of quick drying ink onto paper. Epson claims that, compared to inkjet printers that use heat to fire the ink, their design produces faster delivery and allows quicker head movement, without splattering.

You don't need to be a lab technician to check out these claims: the photorealistic images I printed spoke for themselves. And, even with its maximum-quality "microweave" mode turned on and high-speed printing turned off, the Stylus Color blazed through a sample page that included color swatches, a 3 × 4-inch full-color image, and text in about 4.5 minutes at 720 dpi. Switching to 360-dpi output cut printing times roughly in half.

Some of the speed can be attributed to the driver, which works directly with Windows' GDI to translate image and text documents into a compact format in a hard disk file, which is then sent to the printer in the background after your application has been released for other tasks.

You can expect similar 3- to 7-minute printing times for average color images and documents; however, output shifted into slow-motion mode when I tried to print some 8 × 10-inch high-resolution (300-dpi) color images at the maximum settings. It took an hour or more to print such documents, although the gorgeous output was well worth the wait.

In rare cases, I had to wait as much as 30 minutes while the spooler created an intermediate file of as much as 100M, but most images required from 30 seconds to three minutes of hour-glass watching. A despooler dialog box displays progress information about the job being printed, and you can click on buttons within the box to cancel or pause printing or to reprint a page.

Epson recommends using only special coated paper (at around 12.5 cents a sheet) for 720-dpi mode to keep the tiny ink dots from spreading as they are absorbed into the paper stock. You can choose from transparency material, ordinary paper, or a coated stock for 360-dpi mode, in sizes from 8.5 × 11, 8.5 × 14, or A4 (210 × 297 mm). These options and others can be selected from the remarkably flexible printer driver, which lets you adjust brightness, contrast, and saturation and rebalance the red, green, or blue color channels.

Text quality was excellent, even when compared with the output of a LaserMaster printer rated at 800-dpi. Though the Stylus Color's black text output at 720-dpi was not quite as smooth, it was considerably "cleaner," with fewer artifacts and satellites—extra flecks of toner or ink—in the white area surrounding the characters.

Epson estimates that the black ink cartridge will last for about 840 pages of output (with 5% page coverage at 360-dpi), with the color cartridge good for about 20% fewer pages. If you print lots of dense, image-filled sheets at the higher 720-dpi resolution, expect to deplete your ink supply proportionately faster. Replacement color cartridges are around $35, with the black ink cartridges selling for half that.

The personal-sized input tray holds 100 sheets of paper, 50 transparency sheets, or 10 envelopes. There are four scalable and two bitmapped serif and sans-serif fonts built into the printer, along with bitmapped Courier, Prestige, and Script fonts, all selectable from the printer's front panel controls. Epson backs the printer with a two-year limited warranty. Extended warranties are available at extra cost.

The Epson Stylus Color printer is flexible enough to serve as your only printer for a broad range of word processing, desktop publishing, and presentation applications, yet it is priced low enough that you can justify adding one as a second printer used primarily for color and transparencies. In either case, you won't find any compromises in the quality of its output.

Thermal Wax Transfer Printers

Thermal wax printers aren't all as inexpensive as some inkjet models, but at $1500–$4000, they produce better 300-dpi quality at higher speeds. These printers no longer necessarily require special ultrasmooth paper, and many can now use ordinary cut-sheet paper.

Unlike inkjet printers, thermal wax models don't complete each line in all three (or four) colors before moving on to the next. Instead, each page is printed three or four times, depending on whether a three- or four-color process is being used. As you might guess, such printers must maintain rigid registration standards to ensure that the dots of each color are positioned properly in relation to those of other colors.

The print head is a component with thousands of tiny heating elements that turn on and off to melt dots of wax coated on a wide roll of plastic film. The roll contains alternating panels of cyan, magenta, and yellow (and often black), each the size of the full page. The print head applies all the dots for one color at a time as the page moves past. Then the roll advances to the next color (each panel is used only once), and those dots are printed. After three or four passes, the full-color page is finished.

Because a thermal wax printer always uses all three (or four) panels in a set, some capacity is wasted if your image requires only one or two of those colors or applies color only in a small area of a page. On the other hand, it costs no more to produce pages that have heavy color demands (such as overhead transparencies), so you may come out ahead of inkjet printers in cost (as well as image quality) if you do much work of that type. In addition, the capacity of each roll is precisely predictable: a roll capable of 100 images will produce 100 images, no more, no less.

Both inkjet and thermal wax printers take an all-or-nothing approach when it comes to laying down dots of color, so they suffer from the same tonal range constraints as monochrome page printers. However, the extra information offered by color images can make output from these devices look significantly sharper than that produced by a laser printer of the same resolution.

Who uses them: Thermal wax printers are popular among users who make many overhead transparencies or color handouts.

Thermal Sublimation Printers

The third type of color printer uses a thermal process to transfer dye to the printed page. The advantage of thermal dye-sublimation is that the heat used to transfer the dye can be varied continuously over a range of 0 to 255; therefore, different shades of a given color can be printed. The resolution lost through dithering isn't a factor, allowing these devices to reproduce photographic quality. If you want the best quality reproduction of your image F/X, a dye-sublimation printer is the only way to go.

Like thermal wax printers, dye-sublimation models use a continuous ribbon with alternating bands of color and a print head equipped with tiny heaters. However, these heaters aren't just switched on and off: Their temperature can be precisely controlled to transfer as much or as little dye as required to produce a particular color. The dye sublimates—turns from a solid into a gas, without becoming liquid—and then is absorbed by the polyester substrate of the receiver sheet. However, a special receiver paper with a substrate and coating that accepts the dye transfer is required for this type of printer. Media costs run to several dollars per page, compared to around 50 cents a page with inkjet or thermal wax printers.

Because they don't need dithering to reproduce colors, dye-sublimation printers can offer photographic quality without needing as high a linear resolution as other printers. The dots diffuse smoothly into the receiver sheet, producing smooth blending of colors. However, while you would never notice that a dye-sublimation printer uses just 163–200 dpi to generate dazzling full-color images, text printed in small sizes and finely detailed line art at that resolution definitely suffer from this diffusion. These printers are great for 24-bit images, but they are less stunning when your bitmaps are combined with text or lines. Some models provide antialiasing to reduce this effect, and most newer models have gone to 300-dpi output.

You might find such output useful for preparing special reports and other photo-intensive material in small quantities. However, thermal sublimation printers are expensive (both to buy and to operate) and slow (about three minutes a page).

Some of these color printers can accept PostScript output, either directly or through a software interface like Freedom of Press. At $7000 or less, they can be justified by desktop publishers who do a lot of color printing and want to proof their work and by those who need short-run color documents.

Because these printers are entirely practical for use as color-proofing devices, make sure you get and use a color matching system to calibrate your printer to the final output device.

Who uses them: Those who want the very best photographic image quality possible use thermal sublimation printers.

The Next Step

Chapter 12, which had a discussion on color concepts, might be a good section to review if you want more information on color printing. *Chapter 20*, which deals with color separation, can give you some ideas on how to use a color printer as a proofing or separating tool.

Other than that, we've finished our tour of the F/X battleground, and you're ready to apply what you know to more images of your own. I hope you'll go on and explore the CD-ROM. There's enough there to keep you busy for months to come.

Color Separating

This chapter will be your introduction to desktop color-separating concepts. It won't give you step-by-step instructions on how to make color separations. Rather, my goal is to explain the terminology and outline the key techniques to help you decide if you want to tackle this complex chore. After you read this chapter, you'll be better prepared for the tutorials and instructions you'll need to do a good job.

Color printing is expensive, and two-thirds of the cost is typically incurred at the printer. The $700 price of a set of color separations using traditional methods can be reduced to about $150 with desktop procedures. Yet, any saving you might realize by doing your own separations is apt to be a small part of the total budget for a given job, and the best quality is obtainable only with expensive, high-end equipment, anyway. While I've taken that stance in many books and articles over the years, I have since discovered that many of you are working hard to prove me wrong.

I blame my 15 years of writing about more traditional color separation techniques for my quickness to discount the possibility of doing it on the desktop. After all, during that span I've spoken to hundreds of color separators who use millions of dollars worth of equipment. For example, in the late 1970s one of my regular assignments was to visit top newspapers like the Boston Globe to report on the winners of an annual newspaper color reproduction contest. Some of the top professionals in the country told me their secrets for achieving prize-winning color.

Recently, I visited a leading color separator in Madrid, Spain, who had the latest color pagination equipment and a hard disk "farm" that filled a room larger than my office. His shop prepared all the color for Spain's leading automotive and motorcycle magazines.

Instead of globe-trotting, I should have spent a little more time with desktop publishers who have neither the funds nor the inclination to work with such high end equipment. You can judge for yourself whether you want to get involved with color separating in your own work.

In this chapter, I'll show you an easy way to generate color separations, discuss some of your options, and then, if that hasn't put you to sleep yet, provide a little of my famous tail-end background material on color separation, trapping, and other processes.

Not an Easy Job

None of the popular color-separating options is particularly appetizing for the beginner to intermediate readers of this book. You can use your image editor's color channels to split any image into CMYK channels and then save them separately as EPS file for output to a color PostScript device. Many desktop professionals also import all their color images into a page layout program with good color-separating capabilities, such as QuarkXpress, and then separate the entire page as one set of files. I don't recommend this route for beginners, but after you've gained some experience, you'll find that you can obtain excellent results from this method.

Your best bet may be to read some books on the topic and then, if you can afford it, experiment a little. Make sure you include the following details in your planning.

- Carefully calibrate your equipment. If you expect to do any serious color-correcting based on what you see on your monitor, you need to follow the directions that came with your image editor, monitor, scanner, and color printer/proofer to make sure that you have calibrated each of these as closely together as possible, given the limitations of each type of device. This may involve printing out a test-target, scanning it in, and then comparing the results with the original target. Some special programs can help you calibrate your monitor to your image-editing program through a similar visual comparison method. Some monitor manufacturers offer devices that can be used to calibrate their equipment. For repeatability, please, please properly calibrate your gear!

● Create a test image of your own with typical photos you'll be color separating and take the separations to a service bureau for a match print. Compare the results with the image on your screen and make adjustments until you can produce a match print that matches the image on your computer screen. Then make contact prints of the best set and use them as a comparison point with the color separations you make.

If the chapter so far hasn't discouraged you from making color separations, you may want to read on for the technical discussion that follows. You'll find some background information that will be useful as you delve into this topic more deeply.

Traditional Color-Separating Methods

In *Chapter 12,* my last "heavy" background chapter, you learned about the four standard process printing colors—the subtractive primaries cyan, magenta, yellow, and black. The printing press that will create the final output for your color-separating efforts uses these colors on separate printing plates to create full-color images. Printing can be accomplished either by running each sheet through the same press several times—each time with a new plate—or by a continuous run through a series of four presses arranged in a line.

With the latter setup, as with all offset printing, an arrangement of cylinders is used for each color being printed. The plate is fastened to one cylinder, which rotates to come in contact with a set of dampening rollers, which wet the plate so that the nonprinting area will repel ink. Then a set of inking rollers transfers ink to the printing area of the plate. The inked image is then transferred to a second cylinder, which has a rubber blanket wrapped around it to accept the ink. The paper passes between the blanket and a third cylinder, called the impression cylinder, to pick up the ink for the finished sheet. Some types of presses don't use impression cylinders but instead stack several printing units together so that both sides of the sheet can be printed at the same time. The blanket cylinder of one unit acts as the impression cylinder of the other, and vice versa.

The process by which the separations and plates are produced is known, quite logically, as the *prepress process*. The first step is to create four pieces of film that contain halftone images of the original in the proper proportions to print the cyan, magenta, yellow, and black colors. Originally, this was done using camera techniques. However, each separation halftone must be shot through a red, green, or blue filter to ensure that the tonal values are balanced for one of the primary colors.

Camera separations can be made using either direct or indirect screening methods. *Indirect screening* is a two-step method (actually, two sets of steps); continuous tone (non-halftoned) corrected separation negatives are made, and then the actual halftone screening is done from them. In *direct screening*, both the separations and the halftone screens are created in a single set of steps.

With either of these methods of color separating, color corrections are done with *masks*, which are low-density copies of the original produced with special filters. Portions of the image are held back in certain areas of individual separations, subtracting color as desired. That's a lot like the masking you've used in this book.

In both cases, you end up with four pieces of film. All the separations needed to print a given color are combined on a master page in a process called *stripping*. Originally, this was a tedious hand process that required a great deal of care, because all the elements had to be taped up in perfect register. Finally, the pieces of stripped film for the individual pages are used to make printing plates.

Electronic Separating

Color scanners and electronic page layout systems can eliminate hand stripping by separating an entire page at once. You scan your images, assemble them as they appear in the finished piece, and then use the color-separating features of your software to produce four files that can be sent to an imagesetter. The files include the registration marks the printer needs to align the films and plates perfectly for the printing step. Generally, these are Encapsulated PostScript files, like those produced by Laserseps, which are compatible with Linotronic and other imagesetters.

Color Proofing

One step that you will need to consider is the color proof. You learned a little about color printing systems in *Chapter 19*. Even using desktop pre-press systems to keep costs down, color printing remains expensive enough that it's a good idea to get a sample of what a page will look like before you run off a few thousand copies on an offset press. The press itself is usually not used for making the proof. When a printer's press is idle, the shop isn't making any money. So, you can't expect the printer to set up, print you a few copies for approval, and then sit there until you're ready to go.

Instead, another process is used to simulate a press proof. The goal is to get the colors of the proof to match the appearance of the press sheet. That's not always easy, however, because different pigments are used. Certainly, computer printers, even the $20,000 color models, won't do the job.

Most proofs are made using one of two popular proofing systems. One is 3M's Color Key, which consists of four acetate sheet overlays, each carrying one of the primary colors from your separation films. Laid over one another on a white sheet of paper, a $20 to $60 Color Key can give you a good idea of how successful your separation efforts have been. An advantage to Color Keys is that if your proof seems to have too much or too little of a certain color, you can reseparate that color and redo only that key.

DuPont's Chromalin system uses a single laminated sheet with all four colors to represent your color proof. While more accurate than Color

Keys, Chromalins are also more expensive and must be remade from scratch each time you change even one of your color separations.

Selection of Screen Angles

You may know that black-and-white halftone screens are angled at 45° to avoid conflict with strong vertical and horizontal lines in an image. However, you can't use the same angle for all four color separations, because the dots would overlap and obscure each other. Instead, a different screen angle is used for each—typically 75° for magenta, 105° for cyan, and 90° for yellow. If the correct angles are used, they create a rosette pattern.

The 45° angle is least obtrusive to the eye and is used for the strongest, most visible color—black. The magenta screen is angled at 75°, which is 30° from the black, and affords the least chance of moiré effects between them. The cyan screen is placed 30° from the magenta at 105°. Yellow is placed at 90°—only 15° from the cyan and magenta—because yellow is the least visible color and any moiré that results is likely to be insignificant.

Some Trapping Considerations

You must also take into account that when you print one color inside the boundaries of a second color, a white gap may appear between the colored areas if the positioning is not exact. Typically, this is avoided in color separating by making one of the images slightly larger so that it overlaps. You may be able to frame your image with a row of pixels in a transition color. This technique is almost universally and incorrectly called *trapping* in the desktop publishing world. (Printers call this process spreading and choking, and think of trapping only as the ability of ink to remain where it's put on the paper, or other layers of ink.) As long as you don't think of it as trapping, you are allowed to understand what is meant when your software uses the term improperly.

These (misnamed) traps are provided automatically by some software; the lines of one of the separations are thickened, causing the overlap. (You can see that just making the images larger won't work; "holes" must become smaller at the same time that outside borders grow larger.) If you want to know more about trapping in the DTP sense, Aldus has an excellent booklet, *Trapping with Aldus Products*, that explains the concept in easy-to-understand language.

Separating Photos

Color photos are difficult to separate, because you must deal with a range of color percentages rather than the fixed binary colors found in line art. Your separation program must take your scanned data, calculate percentages of colors, and transform them into a halftone pattern.

You can separate the photos you plan to use in your publication individually and then have them stripped in conventionally. Or, if you are feeling especially ambitious, you can separate an entire page, eliminating the stripping step. The latter technique provides greater control and even opens the possibility of creating files that can be used to make printing plates directly, eliminating the film step, too.

Color Correction

The discussions of color models that filled up *Chapter 12* were not included just to fill space. You can use your newfound knowledge of color to make color corrections as you scan and to help you make color separations from your scans.

Why do you need color correction? There are several reasons.

- To compensate for errors or deficiencies in the scanning process. Perhaps your scanner wasn't calibrated properly with the rest of your system. If not, you can correct slight color casts with your image-editing and color separation software.

- The original photograph was imperfect. Inaccurate color can be found in both prints and transparencies. Most desktop scanners handle only reflective artwork, although a few have transparency attachments.

- To correct a color cast in your original transparency. There are several possible causes for color casts. Daylight changes in color throughout the day, from slightly bluish at high noon to a more reddish tone in early morning and late afternoon. Transparency films accurately record those changes in color temperature. Daylight films exposed indoors and indoor-balanced films exposed outdoors without corrective filters will have reddish and bluish tones, respectively. You can sometimes correct for these casts, although in extreme cases nothing can be done to replace colors that are entirely missing from an original. Pumping blue into an extremely reddish photo produces neutral gray, rather than a properly balanced photo.

- To correct color negative films exposed under a variety of lighting conditions. Color negative films can be corrected successfully at the printing stage in most cases. If, however, a slight color cast remains on the print, it can be corrected in your image-editing software.

- To obtain a creative effect. You may want to change the colors in a subject simply to produce a rendering that will attract attention or make a creative statement.

- To correct for deficiencies in the printing process. You've already learned about dot gain as it applies to gray-scale reproduction. Dots can enlarge during the color printing process as well. If you know how your press will behave, you can compensate for it ahead of time.

- To compensate for poor trapping during printing. In this context, trapping refers to the ability of ink to adhere as well to another layer of ink as to bare paper. With poor trapping, some of the ink in some colors won't remain on the paper. You can correct for this ahead of time if you know about it—if not at the press, then by using techniques such as undercolor removal (explained in the next section) to reduce the amount of ink that must be overlapped to produce dark colors.

- To adjust for color-reproducing limitations of the equipment. A final problem in the printing process is the inability of any printer or press to reproduce the full range of tones found in an original photograph. As a result, the full tonal range that you can capture and manipulate with your scanner may be compressed on the final sheet. You can make corrections in your image before the printing plates are made to compress the colors in ways that are best suited for your particular subject.

Understanding color theory can help you make corrections more easily. If your image is dark blue, for example, you should know that you must remove magenta and yellow to produce a brighter blue. If a red is muddy, it contains too much yellow and cyan and not enough magenta, so you must reduce the yellow and cyan and boost magenta. If a yellow is too orange, you must subtract magenta. These techniques will become second nature to you after a while.

Undercolor Removal and Gray Component Replacement

Some folks find computers comforting because they produce clean and tidy output, with everything well-defined by the software and the limitations of the hardware. Unfortunately, real life is not nearly so neat and tidy. Equal amounts of cyan, magenta, and yellow ink never produce black. Instead, what you get is a muddy brown. As I noted earlier, that's why a fourth, black ink is added to correct for the impurities in the ink pigments.

As you might expect, this cure produces a new disease. Adding cyan, magenta, and yellow ink, each at their maximum density of 100%, and black ink on top of that, at some percentage from, say 10% to 100%, produces a nice thick black. It's so nice and thick that all that ink can easily clog the printing press, make it difficult to get the ink to stick to other layers of ink on the page (the proper use of the term trapping), and increase drying times. The image you invested all that time in may not look its best, either. It turns out that you can't use anywhere near 100% of all four inks (400% coverage); the true usable maximum is around 300%, depending on how absorptive your paper stock is.

Undercolor removal and gray component replacement are two related techniques that can be used to reduce the amount of ink we need to put down on the page to get the best results.

Undercolor removal is the removal of some of the cyan, magenta, and yellow from the neutral, dark shadow areas. This reduces the size of the halftone dots in each of these colors and reduces the amount of ink that prints in the shadows. Thus ink doesn't build up and pick off the sheets on the press (called poor trapping). The black printer can then carry more of the detail in the shadow areas, improving quality and reducing cost by replacing expensive colored ink with cheap black ink.

Gray component replacement is a related process in which some of or all the three process colors are replaced by black ink over the entire image, not just in the shadows. This technique is used to adjust the overall density of an image, including the color areas, while undercolor removal adjusts only the neutral density or gray areas. Also, GCR improves trapping (the real kind), as described above, and can help make colors look richer and more saturated.

While undercolor removal and gray component replacement are similar techniques, they produce different results. Even if your software can provide them for you automatically, you'll need to accumulate some experience to know when to use each. They are never used together.

The Next Step

This chapter has been strong stuff, but my publisher said I had to include a chapter on some of the technical aspects of color manipulation and output in order to meet their truth-in-advertising requirements. They didn't want to be responsible in case the gas tank exploded on your pick-up truck while you were attempting color separations at home. I saved this one for almost last. The final section of this book does nothing more than familiarize you with the CD-ROM we've been using throughout our journey together, just in case there are a few goodies on it that you've missed. Have fun exploring PC F/X!

PART IX

The Next Step

Well, the rest is up to you. As you further explore special F/X, you'll want to try out some new tools and images. This final section contains descriptions of the files, programs, and images on the CD-ROM packaged with this book, along with some suggestions for your own next step.

Using the CD-ROM

There was more than 300M worth of stuff on the magnetic media I used to compile the CD-ROM packaged with this book. The files may take up more or less space on the actual CD-ROM when it's produced after I finish writing this chapter; I don't understand enough about the file system and its overhead to predict exactly. However, there's a lot of stuff on there.

I'm particularly pleased that less than 16% of those files are shareware or tryout versions of software. It would have been easy to load up this CD-ROM with demos and irrelevant products that didn't really apply to your interests. Instead, I've pared down the software to less than 50M. The other 250M+ are all image files for you to work with, the working files I used in the exercises, and color versions of the figures in this book.

The CD-ROM's contents breaks down into the following categories:

- *Tryout software.* Working (but limited) versions of programs like Photoshop that you can use to practice the exercises in the book—or evaluate for later purchase of the software, if you like it.

- *Shareware.* Some excellent shareware and freeware applications and utilities that you'll want to try out.

Chapter files. Full-color (generally) versions of all the figures in the book, along with many intermediate TIFF files used in the projects. Each subdirectory is given the chapter number it corresponds with.

● *Fonts.* A selection of fonts ready to install using the Windows Fonts control panel.

● *Color plates.* Some 24-bit versions of the images used in the full-color section of this book.

● *TIFF images.* Separate subdirectories containing TIFF images you can work with, in Spain, Miscellaneous, Texture, Portrait, and Glamour categories. Most of these images are fairly high in resolution, having been scanned at 300 dpi. The files can range from 500K up to 5M in size. You may have trouble with some of the larger files if your PC doesn't have at least 8M of RAM.

In all cases, I don't recommend using any of the files directly from the CD-ROM. Image files, in particular, load very slowly from a CD-ROM drive, and with images up to 5M in size, you can wait quite awhile for one of those to feed into RAM. Instead, I recommend the following:

● For tryout software, copy the subdirectory containing the application you want to use to your hard drive. Many (but not all) won't run properly from the CD-ROM either because they must be installed to use or because they need to write files to the disk they're launched from. DOS treats the nonwritable CD-ROM as a write-protected disk. Each subdirectory containing a tryout program contains instructions for installing or using that program.

● For shareware or freeware, copy the subdirectory with the shareware or freeware application or utility to your hard drive. Some of these programs are still in self-extracting archives, or require **PKUNZIP.EXE**, so you must uncompress them before use. Instructions for each are in the subdirectory with the shareware program.

● For chapter files, consider copying that chapter subdirectory to your hard disk as you read through each chapter. The figure files and working files will be available to you as you work through the exercises.

- For TIFF images, leave these on the CD-ROM until you need one. If you have an image browser application, you can create thumbnail images to use as reference for finding the picture you want.

This next section will describe the individual files on the CD-ROM in a little more detail.

Using the Tryout Software

I've included many more applications on the CD-ROM than those I actually was able to use for specific exercises in the book. These are either demos or fully functioning versions with one or two features disabled (such as Save). The key subdirectories you'll find are:

- *Adobe Applications.* Here, you'll find Adobe Photoshop 2.5.1, Adobe Illustrator 5.0, Adobe Acrobat Reader (which lets you view "transportable" documents created with Adobe Acrobat), Adobe Dimensions (a 3-D tool), and Adobe Premiere (an animation program).

- *Aldus PhotoStyler.* This working demo is a version of the rival to Photoshop, which happens to be just about one of the most powerful image editors available.

- *Pixar Typestry.* We used Typestry extensively in the book, and here's a workable copy of the version 1.1.

- *Elastic Reality.* We used this demo version of the great morphing program earlier in this book.

Using the Shareware

The Shareware subdirectory contains a selection of the best shareware and freeware I could find. All the shareware and freeware relate directly to the topics covered in this book. As I noted in *Chapter 15*, if you like any of the programs that call for registration, you should send to the vendor the modest amount requested (often as little as $5–$10).

Using the Fonts

Load the Windows Control Panel and click on the Fonts icon. Choose **Add....** When the directory navigation dialog box pops up, locate your CD-ROM and the Fonts subdirectory. Click the Copy Fonts to Windows Directory box to install the fonts permanently.

Using the TIFF Images

The TIFF images can safely reside on the CD-ROM, but you'll want to copy to your hard disk those images that you are actively working with to speed up loading. If you make changes, you'll obviously have to save the images to the hard disk, since the nonwritable CD-ROM is "locked."

Any of the subdirectories containing photos may have a Specfx subdirectory beneath it. Each of these Specfx directories contains images that have been subjected to filters or other special effects described in this book. You can load and examine them to get ideas, but you probably can't edit them further, unless you want to add more special F/X on top of those already applied. Brief discussions of the images on the CD-ROM follow.

Spain Photos

These two-dozen plus pictures, located in the Spain subdirectory, were all taken during ten different trips to Spain between 1973–1993. (And if enough of you like this book so much that you tell your friends to buy a copy, I may get to go again!) I used some of them for exercises throughout the book where ever possible, because generic scenery, castles, cathedrals, etc., make fairly neutral subjects. Unlike the projects in which we used photographs of actual people, the results can be viewed without your friends and colleagues constantly asking, "Ah, so who's that?"

Many of these shots are of abandoned castles; the country just bristles with them. Over here, any one of these buildings would be turned into a tourist attraction instantly, probably with little cars you sit in and ride through the passages. However, on our trips between cities we would usually start looking for a likely castle around lunch time; then pass one or two before finding an interesting site to stop to eat a picnic. Invariably, we would have a lonely hilltop to ourselves (although one or two of these 500–800-year-old buildings showed signs of having been recently used as enclosures for sheep or goats).

That well-preserved crest on the side of the castle in **CASTLE03.TIF** was, believe it or not, out in the middle of nowhere. Other pictures show the Valley of the Fallen (Valle de los Caidos: **CAIDOS.TIF**), a memorial where the still-dead Generalissimo Francisco Franco is buried. **TOLEDO1.TIF** and **TOLEDO2.**TIF show a "View of Toledo" from the same hilltop where El Greco created his painting of the same name. MERI-DA01.TIF pictures some of the best Roman ruins outside Italy.

Miscellaneous Photos

In the Miscellaneous subdirectory you'll find a half-dozen odds-and-ends photos, including a couple photos of musicians, a cat, a 400-year-old door, and a family out for a walk. You'll also find a black-and-white photo scanned from a cracked, decrepit old image if you want to practice the highly salable skills of photorestoration. Many times you'll be given a damaged picture and asked to fix it up, even restoring facial features that aren't there. Just in case you needed a battle-scarred old photo, I included this one. It's about the only way I figured I could get my kindergarten class photo into this book. (I'm the sixth one from the left in the top row.)

Textures

I've included a group of background textures for you to use; four of them scanned (Marble, Leather, Pennies, and Quarters) and the rest created from scratch using Fractal Design Painter and other programs. You'll find a lot of use for these backgrounds and perhaps a few ideas for creating your own.

Portrait Photos

I've included some TIFF files of portraits for you to work with in the Cathy subdirectory. Some of them are gray-scale/black-and-white images (**CATHYBxx.TIF**), and the rest are 24-bit color (**CATHYCxx.TIF**). Many of these were taken for the model's portfolio shortly after she joined a Barbizon-affiliated modeling agency in Rochester, N.Y., while others are just casual portraits or snapshots.

They should give you a good chance to exercise the skills you picked up in *Chapters 4–12*. Some of these pictures are okay as-is (although there is always room for improvement), while others have various small defects, such as dust spots or bad shadows that you can practice correcting.

I suggest that you play with various filters available in your image editor or try to insert new backgrounds. If you have Fractal Design Painter or another program that mimics natural media, you can experiment with turning these photographic images into paintings.

Glamour Photos and Figure Studies

If you aren't tired of this model by now, you'll want to look within the Cathy subdirectory for another subdirectory labeled Glamour. This contains some gray-scale/black-and-white and a few color TIFF files with some tasteful, but interesting figure studies for you to work with. Most are posed against a plain black background (I used a vast black fake-velvet drape, which really soaks up the light), which can be readily selected with the Magic Wand and dropped out. You can then add the background of your choice.

These have all already been cropped a little (**CATHYG01.TIF**, for example, was cropped in tight to a head-and-shoulders shot), but you might experiment with different croppings. Sometimes it's possible to extract a whole new photograph from an existing one with a little judicious trimming here and there. For example, **CATHYG07.TIF**, always a favorite of mine, makes a striking, high-key image when cropped as shown in Figure 21.1.

Figure 21.1 *Tight cropping provides a whole new image.*

Special F/X

I took another group of images that I didn't include in their original format on the CD-ROM and processed them using the special effects filters available with Aldus Gallery Effects, Photoshop, PhotoStyler, Fauve Matisse, and Fractal Design Painter. These are located in the Glamour subdirectory, within a sub-subdirectory named Specf/x. As noted earlier, it would be difficult for you to do any further work with any of these (although you're welcome to try), but I wanted to provide some additional ideas for you to show what can be done.

Here's a brief description of the effects applied to some of the photos.

CATHYF1.TIF–CATHYF3.TIF. These are three black-and-white photos that have been modified with Gallery Effects' Watercolor and Dry Brush filters to give them the appearance of a painting.

CATHYF4.TIF. I applied the new Photoshop 3.0 Difference Clouds filter to this one.

CATHYF5.TIF.   This shot takes on a psychedelic appearance with multiple neon-bright color bands.

CATHYF6.TIF.   You can get some very interesting effects by using your image editor's Trace Outline, Trace Contours, or other modes to turn a continuous-tone picture into a line drawing. This one looked a bit like an etching on white paper, so I colorized it with red and pink tones to stir things up a little.

CATHYF7.TIF.   Believe it or not, that's not a new background created from scratch. The original photo was posed on a tree stump in a woodsy setting, with a backdrop of yellow and green leaves. The mood was very Fall-oriented, and I wanted something a little cooler and Springlike. I selected the entire background and then adjusted the Hue and Saturation controls to change the color scheme to a wilder, almost neon-fluorescent arrangement. Then I applied some brush-stroke texture to both the background and model to make the whole thing resemble some demented painter's vision.

CATHYF08.TIF.   This one was sepia-toned using the Adjust Hue controls, pixelated with a filter, and vignetted.

CATHYF09.TIF.   I salvaged a full-length figure study in which the model's hips appeared too wide simply by vignetting the upper half of her body to produce this portrait.

CATHYF10.TIF.   This one is another "faux" painting produced by adding brush-stroke texture.

CATHYF11.TIF.   This picture is actually the same as CATHYC07.TIF, but with the Chrome filter from Aldus Gallery effects applied. It turned an ordinary model into someone out of Terminator 2, but it's still an interesting effect. Chrome works best when the background is removed; otherwise, the background and subject all blend into one big glob of chrome.

I've included some other FX shots on the disk; you can see that even with just one model, you can achieve dozens of different effects given a little vision and the right tools.

The Next Step

That's everything you need to know to use the files on the CD-ROM. I hope you're able to surpass the images I prepared for this book—and I worked long and hard on them. This disc gives the tools and raw materials: your own imagination is the only thing I couldn't bundle in this package.

Where Do You Go from Here?

I aimed this book at a very special audience—those of you who were daunted by the impossibly complex "imaging" books that looked deeply into one software package—like Adobe Photoshop. I wanted to provide instructions that anyone with a fairly well-equipped PC, some decent software, and a little knowledge of how both worked could use. My goal wasn't to make you a graphics guru but just to show you how some fairly sophisticated special effects could be created using fairly simple techniques.

However, by this point you're probably ready for something more. If I've banished your fears (as I hope I did), you'll be eager to move on from the beginner or intermediate category to the lofty stratosphere of the advanced graphics worker. Some of you, though, may be happy just exploring further at the level I've taken you to already. In either case, I have some specific suggestions for you to follow.

● Work with the images I provided on the CD-ROM, or your own images, just experimenting to see what each tool in your image editor does. Some of the greatest special effects I've ever come up with were accidental, but looked they so good that I showed them around and said, "I meant to do that!"

- Consider buying an advanced imaging book and tackling just one or two chapters. With the background I've given you, I think you'll find that the concepts and techniques that looked so threatening before are much easier now.

- Practice, practice, practice. Even if you're not up to exploring new areas, try to use some of the techniques daily to keep your hand in. You'll find that selecting with the Lasso or using the Magic Wand in your image editor becomes a lot easier with a little practice. Editing Bézier points demands some experience to do successfully, if your image editor has outline-oriented tools.

- Think about upgrading your equipment and software. As you become more proficient at creating special F/X, you'll find that your PC or its software may actually limit what you can do, or at least slow you down enough to reduce your capacity to innovate. An extra 4M of RAM, or upgrading from 16-bit color to 24-bit color, or even just getting a larger hard disk can do wonders for your morale and creative juices. Investigate the "live/competitive" upgrade offers when you're ready to step up to a more powerful software suite. You've already seen that even a complex program like Photoshop or Pixar Typestry doesn't have to be difficult to use.

The Last Step

The last step is up to you. I've done all the instruction, urging, and pleading I can. Just go out and do it: Create your own special F/X that others will look at and exclaim, "Outrageous!"

Glossary

This mother-of-all-glossaries provides definitions of a high percentage of the specialized terms and jargon you'll encounter when using imaging software to produce PC F/X. You can use this word list to refresh your memory or find explanations of topics that aren't totally clear to you.

I did try to define many of these terms in the chapters in which they first appear. However, it's not practical to explain every term without bogging down the text with continual digressions. Beginners who find a few chapters a little confusing can use this glossary to get up to speed quickly. You'll also find many words that weren't used in the text at all but that are commonly used in image processing.

Achromatic color   A color with no saturation, such as a light gray.

Additive colors   The primary colors of light—red, green, and blue—which, when combined, produce white light.

Add-On   External program that adds functionality or new features to programs like Photoshop. Also called *plug-in*.

Airbrush   An atomizer used for spraying paint. Image-editing software usually has an airbrush-like tool, which can apply a fine spray of a given tone to a specified area. Fully controllable airbrushes allow you to adjust the size of the airbrush spray, its density or concentration, and the speed at which the spray flows.

Anamorphic   An image that has been enlarged or reduced more in one direction than another. The image looks squashed or stretched in a given dimension.

Antialiasing   A process that can be used to remove jaggies or stair-stepping in an image. It smooths out diagonal lines by placing dots of an in-between tone in appropriate places.

Applications program   Software, such as a word processing program, spreadsheet, or database manager, that performs useful work not directly related to the maintenance or operation of the computer. Photoshop and PageMaker are applications programs.

Applications program interface (API)   A common interface that allows software engineers to write programs that will operate with a broad range of computer configurations.

Archive   To store files that are no longer active. Programs like PKZIP combine and compress files into an archive file for more compact, easier storage.

ASCII

American Standard Code for Information Interchange (although the International Standard Organization has included this standard under one of its ISO descriptions). A standard code for representing the most common alphanumeric characters, codes such as linefeeds, punctuation marks, and symbols used in computer text. Strictly speaking, ASCII is a 7-bit code that defines only 127 characters. However, an extended ASCII code with an additional 128 characters is also in common use. Most programs let you enter these special characters into drawings by holding down the Alt key and typing the code number.

Aspect ratio

The relative proportion of the length and width of an image. For example, if you scan an original that measures 4 × 6 inches, it will have an aspect ratio of 4:6 or 2:3. To maintain the same proportions, you must place it in your desktop publishing document with dimensions that conform to the same ratio. That is, it could be sized at 2 × 3 inches, 1.5 × 2.25 inches, etc. CRT screens and printers also have aspect ratios.

Asynchronous

When used to refer to OLE or DDE, asynchronous means that the two programs that are communicating don't share information about when a task was completed. One of them might issue a command to be carried out by the other and then proceed to the next task, with no clear idea of when the first task was finished. Ideally, OLE-type communication should have the opposite attribute and function synchronously.

Attribute

Characteristics of a page, character, or object such as line width, fill, underlining, boldface, or font.

Automatic document feeder (ADF)

A device attached to a scanner that automatically feeds one page at a time, allowing the scanning of multiple pages.

Autotrace

A feature found in many object-oriented image-editing programs or stand-alone programs like CorelTRACE that allows you to trace a bitmapped image and convert it to an outline or vector format.

Background

The capability to run unattended while another program is executing. On the PC, background printing and telecommunications are most often used.

Back up

To make a copy of computer data as a safeguard against accidental loss. The copy that is made is called the backup.

Baseline

An imaginary line on which all the characters in a line rest.

BBS

Bulletin Board System. A computer system that has been set up to function as a clearing house for the exchange of information among other computer users via modem. Service bureaus often set up a BBS to allow transmitting PostScript files for output directly to the bureau.

Bézier curve

A cubic polynomial in mathematical terms or, simply, a way of representing a curve that allows great flexibility in manipulating the curve. Bézier curves are adjusted using endpoints and anchor points.

Bilevel

In scanning, a binary scan that stores only the information that tells whether a given pixel should be represented as black or white.

Binary	Base-two arithmetic, which uses only one and zeros to represent numbers. 0001 represents 1 decimal, 0010 represents 2 decimal, 0011 represents 3 decimal, and so on. In scanning, a black-and-white image.
Bit	A binary digit—either a one or a zero. Scanners typically use multiple bits to represent information about each pixel of an image. A 1-bit scan can store only black or white information about a pixel. A 2-bit scan can include four different gray levels or values—00, 01, 10, or 11. Other values include:

4 bits	16 gray levels/colors
5 bits	32 gray levels/colors
6 bits	64 gray levels/colors
7 bits	128 gray levels/colors
8 bits	256 gray levels/colors
15 bits	32,767 colors
16 bits	65,535 colors
24 bits	16.7 million colors

Bit map	A representation of an image in row and column format in which each individual pixel is represented by a number. A single bit or up to as many as 32 can be used with each increment representing a larger amount of gray or color information about the pixel.
Black	The color formed by the absence of reflected or transmitted light.

Black printer   The plate used for the black ink in the four-color printing process. It provides emphasis for neutral tones, detail in shadow areas of the image, and a deeper black than can be provided by combining cyan, magenta, and yellow alone. Black printers can take two forms. A skeleton black adds black ink only to the darker areas of an image. A full-range black printer adds some black ink to every part of the image.

Bleed   An image that continues to the edge of the page. It is often accomplished by extending the image past the edge and then trimming the page to the finished size.

Blend   To create a more realistic transition between image areas. Image-editing software will often allow you to merge overlapping sections of images to blend the boundary between them.

Blur   To soften part of an image, making it less distinct.

Boot   To start up a computer.

Brightness   The balance of light and dark shades in an image. See also *Luminance*.

Buffer   An area of computer memory set aside to store information meant for some sort of I/O, such as printing or writing to disk. The buffer allows the device supplying the information to feed it into memory faster, if necessary, than the device meant to accept it can handle it. A printer buffer, for example, allows an applications program to dump a document for printing quickly and then to go on to something else. The buffer can then feed the information to the printer at a slower rate. In scanning, buffers are often used to store images awaiting processing.

Bug	An error in a program that results in some unintended action.
Burn	In photography, to expose part of a print for a longer period, making it darker than it would be with a straight exposure. In lithography, to expose a printing plate.
Bus	A hardware interface used to connect a computer to peripherals or other computers. You'll often see references to the SCSI bus, which is used by PC computers.
Byte	Eight bits, which can represent any number from 0000000 to 11111111 binary (0 to 255 decimal).
Cache	A fast memory buffer used to store information read from disk or from slower RAM to allow the operating system to access it more quickly. Cache programs use various schemes to make sure that the most frequently accessed sectors, as well as the most recently accessed sectors, remain in the buffer as long as possible. A disk cache stores data that would otherwise be retrieved from a floppy disk, hard disk, optical disk, or CD-ROM, while a processor cache stores instructions and data that the microprocessor needs to work with. A processor cache can be built into the microprocessor or provided in the form of external memory on the motherboard.
CAD	Computer-Assisted Design. Also called Computer Aided Design and Computer Aided/Assisted Drafting/Design (CADD). A technique for creating engineering drawings and similar materials on a computer using line-oriented techniques.

Calibration

A process used to correct for the variation in output of a device like a printer or monitor when compared to the original image data you get from the scanner.

Camera ready

Artwork printed in hardcopy form that can be photographed to produce negatives or plates for printing.

Cast

A tinge of color in an image, particularly an undesired color.

CCD

Charge-Coupled Device. A type of solid-state sensor used in scanners and video capture devices. Compared to older imaging devices, including video tubes, CCDs are more sensitive and less prone to memory problems that can cause blurring of images.

CD-ROM

Compact Disk-Read Only Memory. An optical disk device that uses pits written on the disk by laser to convey bits of information. CD-ROMs are encoded with information during manufacture and cannot be written to by the user. They provide a means of distributing large databases on a compact medium.

Centerline tracing

A method of autotracing that "thins" out lines to leave only the centerline portion.

Center of rotation

A point within a shape or text block around which the object rotates when you drag a rotation handle with the Rotation tool. The center of rotation is marked by a circle with a plus sign in it and is by default found in the center of the object. You can drag it to a new location with the Rotation tool.

CGM

Computer Graphics Metafile. A standardized vector-image format that can be imported into many different types of programs such as Canvas or CorelDRAW.

Child directory

A directory created below a parent directory. C:\ is the root directory of drive C; C:\WP is a child directory of C:\, while C:\WP\LETTERS is a child directory of C:\WP. When running Windows, you'll see directories in the form of branching trees.

Chroma

Color or hue.

Chromalin

The DuPont trademark for a type of color proof used for representing how color halftones will appear on the printed page.

Chromatic color

A color with at least one hue available, with a visible level of color saturation.

Chrome

Photographer-talk for a color transparency, from film names like Kodachrome or Ektachrome.

Client

In a network, the computer you use to type commands is called the client, and the one that supplies the file or controls the peripheral you are accessing is referred to as the server. When referring to OLE, the client (also called the container) is the program receiving an embedded object from the server software. For example, when you edit a drawing that you have embedded in a Word for Windows 6.0 document, without leaving Word, the original drawing program acts as the server to the Word client.

Clip art

Artwork that is purchased or otherwise available for scanning or other uses in desktop publishing with few restrictions.

Clipboard

An area of random access memory (RAM) used by Windows to store temporarily a graphic or text that is copied or cut from an application. You can paste down the Clipboard's contents in the same application or move to another Windows application and paste the information there. Thus, the Clipboard can be used to exchange data between applications.

Clip

To compress a range of values into a single value, as when a group of highlight tones are compressed to white or a set of shadow tones are represented as black. See also Threshold.

Clone

In image editing, to copy pixels from one part of an image to another.

CMYK

The abbreviation for cyan, magenta, yellow, and black.

CMYK color model

A model that defines all possible colors in percentages of cyan, magenta, yellow, and black.

Color

See *Hue*.

Color correction

Changing the color balance of an image to produce a desired effect, usually a more accurate representation of the colors in an image. It is used to compensate for the deficiencies of process color inks, inaccuracies in a color separation, or an undesired color balance in the original image. Color correction is done using one of several available color models, including RGB and HSL .

Color key

A set of four acetate overlays, each with a halftone representing one of the colors of a color separation and tinted in that color. When combined, color keys can be used for proofing color separations.

Color separation	The process of reducing an image to its four separate color components—cyan, magenta, yellow, and black. These separations are combined using an individual plate for each color on a press. To create a color other than the three primaries, plus black, percentages of them are combined.
Color wheel	A circle representing the spectrum of visible colors.
Command	A word or phrase used to tell a computer what to do next.
Comp	A layout that combines type, graphics, and photographic material, also called a composite or comprehensive.
Complementary color	Generally, the opposite hue of a color on a color wheel, which is called the direct complement. For example, green is the direct complement of magenta. There are also two other types of complements the split complement (a color 30° away from the direct complementary color) and the triadic (a color 120° in either direction from the selected color).
Compression	Packing of a file or image in a more efficient form to improve storage efficiency. Compression and decompression take some time, so it takes longer to save and open compressed files.
Concatenate	To add together.
Connection point	A point on a shape, usually indicated by an, which can be used to glue connectors. Usually, connection points are located at handles and vertices of the shape, but you can create one anywhere in the shape using the program's Connector tool.

Connector

In drawing programs, connectors are shapes, usually one-dimensional, that can be used to link shapes. Some connectors are provided as master shapes on stencils, but you can also create your own connectors from lines or other shapes.

Contiguous

In reference to hard disks, contiguous sectors are those that are arranged consecutively on the disk. Your system software tries to allocate sectors to a file contiguously so that the disk drive can read as many sectors of a file as it can with a minimum of read/write head movement. However, as a hard disk fills, the unallocated sectors gradually become spread out and fragmented, forcing the operating system to choose more and more noncontiguous sectors. Fragmented files can be much slower to access.

Continuous tone

Images that contain tones from black to white with an infinite range of variations in between.

Contour tracing

An autotracing method that follows the outlines of a drawing.

Contrast

The range between the lightest and darkest tones in an image. A high-contrast image is one in which the shades fall at the extremes of the range between white and black. In a low-contrast image, the tones are closer together.

Control character

A nonprinting character used to send information to a device, such as the control characters used to communicate special formatting commands to a printer.

Control handle

A point, usually located at the corners or sides of the rectangle surrounding a shape, that can be dragged to reshape or resize an object.

Control point	A position on a line or arc segment, represented by a circle, that can be dragged to change the curvature of the segment.
Coordinates	A pair of numbers representing the x (horizontal) and y (vertical) position of a point in relation to the zero point of origin.
Copy dot	Photographic reproduction of a halftone image, in which the halftone dots of a previously screened image are carefully copied as if they were line art. The same technique can be used in scanning to capture a halftoned image. If the original dot sizes are maintained, the quality of the finished image can be good.
Crop	To trim an image or page by adjusting the side or boundaries.
Crop mark	A mark placed on a page that is larger than the finished page to show where the page should be trimmed to final size.
Current directory	The default directory that DOS or Windows assumes you mean unless you explicitly type some other directory name within a command.
Current directory	The directory a user is presently logged into.
Current drive	The disk drive a user is presently logged into.
Cursor	A symbol that indicates the point at which the next action the user takes—text entry, line drawing, deletion, etc.—will begin; the current screen display position.
Daisy-chain	To connect peripheral devices in series, as with the SCSI bus.

Darken
A feature found in many image-editing programs that allows gray values in selected areas to be changed, one value at a time, from the current value to a darker one. This is equivalent to the burning procedure used in conventional dark-rooms.

Data compression
A method of reducing the size of files, such as image files, by representing the sets of binary numbers in the file with a shorter string that conveys the same information. Many image-editing programs offer some sort of image compression as an optional mode when saving a file to disk.

Default
A preset option or value that is used unless you specify otherwise.

Descender
The portion of a lowercase letter that extends below the baseline. The letter *p* is an example of a character with a descender.

Diffusion
The random distribution of gray tones in an area of an image, often used to produce a mezzotint effect.

Digitize
To convert information, usually analog information such as that found in continuous tone images (or music), to a numeric format that can be accepted by a computer.

Directory
The list of file names stored on a disk, along with the size of the file, date and time it was created or last changed, and the type of file.

Dithering
A method of simulating gray tones by grouping the dots shown on your CRT display or produced by your printer into large clusters of varying size. The mind merges these clusters and the surrounding white background into different tones of gray.

Dodge
In photography, to block part of an image as it is exposed, lightening its tones.

Dot
A unit used to represent a portion of an image. A dot can correspond to one of the pixels used to capture or show an image on the screen or groups of pixels can be collected to produce larger printer dots of varying sizes to represent gray.

Dot etching
A technique in photographic halftoning in which the size of the halftone dots is changed to alter tone values.

Dot gain
The tendency of a printing dot to grow from the original size when halftoned to its final printed size on paper. This effect is most pronounced on offset presses using poor quality papers, which allow ink to absorb and spread.

Dots per inch
The resolution of an image, expressed in the number of pixels or printer dots in an inch. Abbreviated dpi.

Download
To receive a file from another device. For example, soft fonts are downloaded from your computer to your printer.

Drag-and-drop
A Windows feature that allows many functions to be carried out by grabbing an object with the mouse and dragging it to a new location. Drag-and-drop implies more than just moving an object. When you drag a file's icon from File Manager to a Program Manager window, a new icon is created to represent that file in the Program Group.

Drawing
A foreground and its associated background pages, including the shapes within them.

Drawing file   A file that can contain one or more drawings, as well as a stencil that contains all the master shapes used by its drawings.

Driver   A software interface used to allow an applications program to communicate with a piece of hardware, such as a scanner.

Drive specification   The letter used by DOS to identify a disk drive, from A to Z.

Drop cap   The first letter of a paragraph, set in a larger point size than the rest of the text. It may rise above the first line or extend below, in which case the drop cap is inset into the text block.

Dummy   A rough approximation of a publication, used to gauge layout.

Duotone   A printed image, usually a monochrome halftone, that uses two different colors of ink to produce a longer range of tones than would be possible with a single ink density and set of printer cells alone.

Dye sublimation   A printing technique in which solid inks are heated directly into a gas, which then diffuses into a polyester substrate to form an image. Because dye sublimation printers can reproduce 256 different hues for each color, they can print as many as 16.7 million different colors.

Dynamic Data Exchange (DDE)   A Windows 3 feature that allows applications to receive updates of information pasted in them from another program (such as a chart from one application pasted into a spreadsheet program), provided the linked programs are both active in memory.

Dynamic RAM

Type of memory that must be electrically refreshed many times each second to avoid loss of the contents. All computers use dynamic RAM to store programs, data, video information, and the operating system.

Eccentricity handle

A point that is dragged to change the angle and amount of an arc's eccentricity. Eccentricity handles are represented by circles at each end of a dotted line that appears when a control point of an elliptical arc is selected with the Pencil tool.

Emulsion

The light-sensitive coating on a piece of film, paper, or printing plate.

Emulsion side

The side of a piece of film that contains the image, usually with a matte, nonglossy finish. This side is placed in contact with the emulsion side of another piece of film (when making a duplicate) or the printing plate. That way, the image is sharper than it would be if it were diffused by the base material of the film. Image-processing workers need to understand this concept when producing images oriented properly (either right-reading or wrong-reading) for production.

Encapsulated PostScript

An outline-oriented image format that represents graphics and text in terms of descriptions of how to draw them. Desktop publishing programs like PageMaker, Quark Xpress, FrameMaker, and Corel Ventura can import these files, while vector-oriented draw programs can often modify them.

Endpoint

The beginning and ending points of a one-dimensional shape.

Export

To transfer text or images from a document to another format. Some applications provide a Save As option to save the entire file in the optional format, while others let you save a selected portion of the image or file in another file format.

Extrude

To create a 3-D effect by adding edges to an outline shape as if it were clay pushed through a Play-Doh Fun Factory.

Eye Dropper

An image-editing tool used to "pick up" color from one part of an image, so that it can be used to paint or draw in that color elsewhere.

Feather

To fade the edges of a selection to produce a less-noticeable transition.

File

A collection of information, usually data or a program, that has been given a name and allocated sectors by the operating system.

File format

A set way in which a particular application stores information on a disk. This standardization makes it possible for different applications to load each others' files because they know what to expect from a predictable file format. PCX and TIFF are both file formats found on the PC.

File name

The name given a file. It is limited under MS-DOS to just eight characters and a three-character extension.

File-oriented backup

Any backup system that stores information in files, just as they are stored on the disk. Such systems allow easier access to and restoration of a particular file.

Fill
A pattern or color used inside a closed shape, either white (the default) or some other color, with either solid or transparent attributes.

Filter
In scanning, image filters are used to process an image—to blur, sharpen, or otherwise change it. Programs like Adobe Photoshop have advanced filters that will spherize, change perspective, and add patterns to selected portions of the image.

Fixed disk
Another name for a hard disk drive, so-called because such disks are not commonly removed from the computer while in use.

Flat
A low-contrast image. Also, the assembled and registered negatives or positives used to expose a printing plate.

Font
A group of letters, numbers, and symbols in one size and typeface. Garamond and Helvetica are typefaces; 11-point Helvetica Bold is a font.

Format
To initialize or prepare a disk for use by writing certain information in magnetic form. Formatting divides the disk into tracks and sectors and sets up a directory structure, which are shown in Windows as folders and icons.

Four-color printing
Another term for process color, in which cyan, magenta, yellow, and black inks are used to reproduce all the hues of the spectrum.

FPO
For Position Only. Artwork deemed not good enough for reproduction but used to help gauge how a page layout looks.

Frame grabber
A device that captures a single field of a video scanner or camera.

Frequency
The number of lines per inch in a halftone screen.

Frisket
Another name for a mask, used to shield portions of an image from the effects of various tools applied to other areas of the image.

Galley
A typeset copy of a publication used for proofreading and estimating length.

Gamma
A numerical way of representing the contrast of an image, shown as the slope of a line showing tones from white to black.

Gamma correction
A method for changing the brightness, contrast, or color balance of an image by assigning new values to the gray or color tones of an image. Gamma correction can be either linear or nonlinear. Linear correction applies the same amount of change to all the tones. Nonlinear correction varies the changes tone by tone or in highlight, midtone, and shadow areas separately to produce a more accurate or improved appearance.

Gang scan
The process of scanning more than one picture at a time. It is used when images are of the same density and color balance range.

Gigabyte (G)
A billion bytes of information; a thousand megabytes. Only ten 8.5 × 11-inch full-color images scanned at 600 dpi would to fill up a gigabyte of disk space.

Gradient fill
A way of filling a shape with color that has a gradual transition from one tone to another.

Graduated fill
A pattern in which one shade or hue smoothly blends into another; also called a *gradient fill*.

Graphics tablet
A pad on which you draw with a pen-like device called a stylus, used as an alternative to a mouse.

Gray balance

The proportion of ink in each of the three process colors (cyan, magenta, and yellow) that will combine to produce a neutral gray color.

Gray component removal

A process in which portions of an image, which have all three process colors, have an equivalent amount of their color replaced by black to produce purer, more vivid colors.

Gray map

A graph that shows the relationship between the original brightness values of an image and the output values after image processing.

Gray scale

The spectrum of different gray values an image can have.

Grid lines

Dotted lines that can be turned on in a drawing window as an aid to precise positioning of shapes and text.

Group

A collection of other shapes or objects imported from other applications that can be moved or otherwise manipulated as a single group.

Gutter

The inner margin of a page, which must be included to allow for binding.

Halftoning

A method for representing the gray tones of an image by varying the size of the dots used to show the image.

Handles

Small squares that appear in the corners (and often at the sides) of a square used to define an area to be scanned or an object in an image-editing program. The user can grab the handles with the mouse cursor and resize the area or object.

Hardware

The physical components of a computer system, including the CRT, keyboard, microprocessor, memory, and peripherals.

High-level language   A language that allows representing machine-level operations by mnemonic keywords rather than 1s and 0s. BASIC, COBOL, Pascal, C, and FORTRAN are high-level languages.

Highlight   The brightest values in a continuous tone image.

Histogram   A barlike graph that shows the distribution of gray tones in an image.

HPGL   Hewlett-Packard Graphics Language. This language is used to define images to be printed with plotters.

HSB color model   A model that defines all possible colors by specifying a particular hue and then adding or subtracting percentages of black or white.

HSL color correction   A system of color correction based on the hue, saturation, and luminance of an image.

Hue   A pure color. In nature there is a continuous range of hues.

Icon   A small graphic that represents an object or function on the computer screen.

Image acquisition   Capturing a digitized version of a hardcopy or real-world image, as with a scanner or video camera.

Image editor   A program like Adobe Photoshop or Fractal Design Painter that is used to edit bit mapped images.

Imagesetter   A high-resolution PostScript printer that creates camera-ready pages on paper or film.

Import   To convert a file from another format, bringing it into another application for use.

Inkjet	A printing technology in which dots of ink are sprayed on paper.
Input	Incoming information. Input may be supplied to the computer by the user or to a program by either the user or a data file.
Instruction cache	A type of high-speed memory used to store the commands that the microprocessor used most recently. A cache "hit" can eliminate the need to access slower RAM or the hard disk, thus increasing the effective speed of the system.
Instructions	The basic set of capabilities of a microprocessor, allowing the chip to load information into a register, move it to another register, increment the data, add or subtract data from a register, and so forth.
Intelligent	Having sufficient programming built-in to carry out certain tasks independently. An intelligent disk drive can accept requests from the operating system, locate the data, and deliver it without detailed instructions on how to do the physical I/O.
Interactive	Allowing user input during run time.
Interpreter	A program that interprets and carries out each line of another program written in a high-level language like BASIC or COBOL. These languages can also be compiled so that the computer can carry out the commands directly. PostScript interpreters for printers perform the same function with the instructions found in PostScript files.

I/O
Input/Output. Used to describe the process whereby information flows to and from the microprocessor or computer through peripherals such as scanners, disk drives, modems, CRT screens, and printers.

Jaggies
Stair-stepping of lines that are not perfectly horizontal or vertical. Jaggies are produced when the pixels used to portray a slanted line aren't small enough to be invisible, because of the high contrast of the line and its surrounding pixels, e.g., at the edges of letters.

Justified
Text that is aligned at both the right and left margins.

K
Kilobyte. In computer terminology, 1K represents 1024 bytes, so that 16K represents 16,384; 64K equals 65,536; 512K corresponds to 524,288; and so on.

Kern
To adjust the amount of space between two adjacent letters.

Knockout
Area on a spot color overlay in which an overlapping color is deleted, so the background color shows through.

Landscape
The orientation of a page in which the longest dimension is horizontal, also called wide orientation.

Lasso
A tool used to select irregularly shaped areas in a bitmapped image.

Launch
To start a PC application.

Layers
Separation of a drawing or image into separate "transparent" overlays, which can be edited or manipulated separately, yet combined to provide a single drawing or image.

Leading
The amount of vertical spacing between lines of text from baseline to baseline.

Ligature
A combination of two characters squeezed together to form a composite character. Ligatures can confuse OCR programs that use pattern matching until the software has been trained to recognize each ligature combination.

Lighten
An image-editing function that is equivalent to the photographic darkroom technique of dodging. Gray tones in a specific area of an image are gradually changed to lighter values.

Line art
Usually, images that consist only of black and white lines.

Line screen
The resolution or frequency of a halftone screen, expressed in lines per inch. Typical line screens are 53 to 150 lines per inch.

Lines per inch
The yardstick used to measure halftone resolution, abbreviated lpi.

Lithography
Another name for offset printing, which is a reproduction process in which sheets or continuous webs of material are printed by impressing them with images from ink applied to a rubber blanket on a rotating cylinder from a metal or plastic plate attached to a another cylinder.

Logical
Any feature not physically present but defined anyway for convenience. The physical sectors on a hard disk are arranged contiguously. Logically, they may be arranged in alternating fashion through interleaving.

Luminance
The brightness or intensity of an image. Determined by the amount of gray in a hue, luminance reflects the lightness or darkness of a color. See also *Saturation*.

LZW compression   A method of compacting TIFF files using the Lempel-Zev Welch compression algorithm. It produces an average compression ratio of 2:1, but larger savings are produced with line art and continuous-tone images with large areas of similar tonal values.

Macro   A series of commands that can be triggered at the press of a key or two. Many applications programs let you create macros that can be recalled later, saving time.

Magic Wand   A tool that selects contiguous pixels that have the same brightness value or pixels of a selected range.

Map   To assign colors or grays in an image.

Marquee   The selection tool used to mark rectangular areas.

Mask   To cover part of an image so that it won't be affected by other operations.

Mass storage   Permanent storage of computer information, usually on magnetic disk but it can also include magnetic tape, optical disk, bubble memory, and other nonvolatile storage media.

Mechanical   Camera-ready copy with text and art already in position for photographing.

Memory buffer   An area of RAM used to store a file or an image between certain operations, such as printing, storing to disk, or displaying an image-editing program.

Mezzotint	An engraving that is produced by scraping a roughened surface to produce the effect of gray tones. Image-editing and -processing software can produce this effect with a process called error diffusion.
Microprocessor	The computer-on-a-chip that is the brains of a personal computer.
Midtones	Parts of an image with tones of an intermediate value, usually in the 25 to 75% range.
Millisecond	One-thousandth of a second.
Moiré	In scanning, an objectionable pattern caused by the interference of halftone screens—often produced when you rescan a halftone and a second screen is applied on top of the first.
Monochrome	Having a single color.
Monospaced	Text in which each character takes up exactly the same amount of space. Some OCR programs require specifying that text to be scanned is monospaced.
Motherboard	The main circuitboard of your PC.
Mount	To activate a floppy or hard disk for use. Disks must be mounted before you can open them.
Mouse	A pointing device used to indicate an area or point on the screen.
Multibit	Any scan that uses more than 1 bit to store information about a pixel.
Multisession CD	A Photo CD that has had images placed on it several times, as opposed to single-session CDs, which are written to once only.

Multitasking

The capability of a computer system to handle several different chores simultaneously. Because microcomputers have only one main processor, multitasking is usually done by slicing processor time into individual segments and allowing the programs to share the slices in rotation. DOS is not generally a multitasking operating system, although third-party enhancements can give it these capabilities.

Multiuser

The capability of a computer system to handle several different tasks performed by several different users simultaneously. UNIX is the best-known multitasking system among microcomputer users, although it is also available for larger systems.

Negative

A representation of an image in which the tones are reversed. That is, blacks are shown as white, and vice versa.

NTSC

National Television Standard Code. The standard for video in the United States.

Object graphics

Vector-oriented graphics, in which mathematical descriptions, rather than bit maps, are used to describe images.

Object Linking and Embedding (OLE)

A Windows 3 feature that allows inserting an object from one application into another in such a way that the two remain linked. Among OLE features is editing in place, which lets you modify an embedded object within the new application without loading the original program.

Offset printing

See *Lithography*.

OLE automation

The capability to create macros and other commands that can span individual applications.

Origin

The starting horizontal and vertical reference point for a scan.

Overlay	A sheet laid on top of another to specify spot colors for printing. In programming, a portion of a program that is called into memory as needed, overlaying the previous redundant section of the program. Overlays allow writing programs that are much bigger than those that could fit into memory all at once.
Page description language	A programming language that can be used to tell a printer how to handle a given page. PostScript is the most widely used page description language for printing and publishing.
Palette	A set of tones or colors available to produce an image. Also, a row of icons representing tools that can be used.
Pantone Matching System (PMS)	A registered trade name for a system of color matching. If you tell your printer the PMS number of the color you want, that color can be reproduced exactly by mixing printing inks to a preset formula.
Parallel	To move data several bits at a time, rather than one at a time. Usually, parallel operation involves sending all 8 bits of a byte along eight separate data paths at one time. This is faster than serial movement. Most scanners use parallel connections to move image information.
Parameter	A qualifier that defines more precisely what a program is to do.
Parent directory	The directory immediately above a child directory.
Paste	To copy text or a graphic from the Windows Clipboard into a Windows application. Paste Special embeds the information in the document and creates a link to the original application, so that the data can be updated from the original source.

Path

A series of continuous line or arc segments that make up a portion of a shape.

PCX

A standard graphics file format that can be used to store gray-scale and color images and that can be imported by many Windows programs.

Peripheral

Any hardware part of a computer system other than the microprocessor itself and its directly accessible memory. We usually think of peripherals as printers, modems, etc.

Photo CD

A special type of CD-ROM developed by Eastman Kodak Company that can store high-quality photographic images in a special space-saving format, along with music and other data. Photo CDs can be accessed by CD-ROM XA-compatible drives, using Kodak-supplied software or compatible programs such as Photoshop.

Phototypesetting

A process used to expose text and images onto materials that will later be used to produce printing plates. Phototypesetters generally have much higher resolutions than laser printers.

Physical

A feature that exists in reality.

PICT

A graphic image and file format used by the Macintosh and its Clipboard. PICT2 is an enhanced version, which can be used in both 8- and 24-bit formats. PICT graphics are sometimes exported to the PC world.

Pixel

A picture element of a screen image; one dot of the collection that makes up an image.

Plate

A thin, light-sensitive sheet, usually of metal or plastic, that is exposed and then processed to develop an image of the page. The plate is used during the printing press to transfer ink or dye to a surface, generally paper.

Plugging
A defect on the final printed page in which areas between dots become filled due to dot gain, producing an area of solid color. See also *Dot gain*.

Plug-In
A module that can be accessed from within a program like Photoshop to provide special functions. Many plug-ins are image-processing filters that offer special effects.

Point
Approximately 1/72 of an inch outside the Macintosh world, exactly 1/72 of an inch within it. Points are used by printers to measure things like type and other vertically oriented objects.

Pop-up menus
Context-sensitive menus that appear when you click with the right mouse button. For example, when you click with the right mouse button on a stencil, a menu pops up that lets you copy a shape or change the way the stencil's icons are displayed.

Properties
The attributes of text, a shape, or a page that determine its appearance or behavior.

Port
A channel of the computer used for input or output with a peripheral. The serial and parallel ports of the PC are the most widely used.

Portrait
The orientation of a page in which the longest dimension is vertical, also called tall orientation.

Position stat
A copy of a halftone that can be placed on a mechanical to illustrate where to position and crop the image.

Posterization
A photographic effect produced by reducing the number of gray tones in an image to a level at which the tones are shown as bands, as on a poster.

PostScript

Developed by Adobe Systems, PostScript is the most widely used page description language for PCs. It provides a way of telling the printer, typesetter, or imagesetter how to generate a given page.

Prepress

The stages of the reproduction process that precede printing, particularly those that generate halftones, color separations, and the printing plates themselves.

Preview scan

A preliminary scan that can be used to define the exact area for the final scan. A low-resolution image of the full page or scanning area is shown, and a frame of some type specifies the area to be included in the final scan.

Printer command language

As in Hewlett-Packard Printer Command language (HPCL), the instructions used to drive HP LaserJet printers and compatibles.

Process camera

A graphic arts camera used to make color separations, photograph original artwork to produce halftones and page negatives, and perform other photographic enlarging/reducing/duplicating tasks.

Process colors

Cyan, magenta, yellow, and black. The basic ink colors used to produce all the other colors in four-color printing.

Program

Code that instructs the computer how to perform a function.

Proof

A test copy of a printed sheet, which is used as a final check before a long duplication run begins.

Quantization

Another name for *Posterization*.

Raster image

An image defined as a set of pixels or dots in row and column format.

Raster image processor (RIP)	The hardware/software used to process text, graphics, and other page elements into a raster image for output on a printer.
Ray tracing	A method for producing realistic highlights, shadows, and reflections on a three-dimensional rendering by projecting the path of an imaginary beam of light from a particular location back to the viewpoint of the observing.
Read-Only	A file attribute that allows most DOS commands to read the information in the file but not to change it or overwrite it.
Read-Only Memory (ROM)	Memory that can be read by the system but not changed. It often contains system programs that help the computer carry out services.
Reflection copy	Original artwork that is viewed and scanned by light reflected from its surface rather than by light transmitted through it.
Register	To align images, usually different versions of the same page or sheet. Color separation negatives must be precisely registered to one another to ensure that colors overlap in the proper places.
Register marks	Small marks placed on a page to make it possible to align different versions of the page precisely.
Registers	The basic memory locations of a microprocessor, through which all information that is processed passes.
Rendering	To produce a realistic 3-D image from a drawing or other data.
Resolution	The number of pixels or dots per inch in an image, whether it is displayed on the screen or printed.

Retouch

To edit an image, usually to remove flaws or to create a new effect.

RGB color correction

A color correction system based on adjusting the levels of red, green, and blue in an image.

RGB color model

A way of defining all possible colors as percentages of red, green, and blue.

Right-reading image

An image, such as a film, used to produce a printing plate that reads correctly, left to right, when viewed as it will be placed down for exposure.

RIP

Raster Image Processor. A device found in printers that converts page images to a format that can be printed by the marking engine of the printer.

RISC

Reduced Instruction Set Computer. A computer system, like the new Power PCs that includes an optimized instruction set designed to complete each instruction in one clock cycle and that, therefore, operates faster. Such systems depend on the software for functions that formerly were handled by the microprocessor.

Rubber Stamp

A tool that copies or clones part of an image to another area.

Saturation

An attribute of a color that describes the degree to which a pure color is diluted with white or gray. A color with low-color saturation appears washed out. A highly saturated color is pure and vivid.

Scale

To change the size of a piece of artwork or the relationship between measurements on a drawing and the actual size represented. A map, for example, may use a scale of 1:1000, in which each inch on the map represents 1000 feet of the Earth's surface.

Scanner   A device that captures an image of a piece of artwork and converts it to a bitmapped image that the computer can handle.

Screen   The halftone dots used to convert a continuous-tone image to a black-and-white pattern that printers and printing presses can handle. Even expanses of tone can also be reproduced by using tint screens that consist of dots that are all the same size (measured in percentages, a 100% screen is completely black).

Screen angle   The alignment of rows of halftone dots, measured from the horizontal (which would be a 0° screen angle).

Script   A list of commands carried out by an application program.

SCSI   Small Computer Systems Interface. An intelligent interface, used for most scanners and for other devices, including hard disk drives.

SCSI ID   The number from 0 to 7 assigned to each device on the SCSI bus. You make this assignment by adjusting a jumper or DIP switch on your equipment or, sometimes, through software. No two devices can have the same ID number. The PC itself always has SCSI ID 7, and the boot disk is typically ID 0.

Secondary color   A color produced by mixing two primary colors. For example, mixing red and green primary colors of light produces the secondary color magenta. Mixing the yellow and cyan primary colors of pigment produces blue as a secondary color.

Sector   The smallest section of a track, containing 512 bytes of data.

Segment   An individual line or arc that makes up part of a shape.

Select
To mark various portions of an image or document so that you can work on them apart from the rest of the image or document.

Selection
The area that has been marked, usually surrounded by a marquee or an outline that is sometimes colorfully called "marching ants."

Selection handle
Square blocks that appear around a shape that has been selected with the pointer tool, used to resize the shape. Dragging the corners changes both height and width proportionately, while dragging top or side handles changes the size of the shape in that direction only.

Selection rectangle
A dotted line surrounding a shape, or objects imported into a program from other applications, indicating that it has been selected and is ready for manipulation.

Separation
See *Color separation.*

Separations
Film transparencies, each representing one of the primary colors (cyan, magenta, and yellow) plus black, used to produce individual printing plates.

Serial
Passing information 1 bit at a time in sequential order. Some scanners use serial connections.

Serif
Short strokes at the ends of letters thought to help lead the eye and make text easier to read. Sans serif type lacks these strokes. Serifs can sometimes touch in tightly spaced text, causing problems for OCR software.

Shade
A color with black added.

Shadows
The darkest part of an image, generally with values ranging from 75 to 100%.

Shareware　　Software that can be copied and distributed freely for evaluation purposes but that must be registered, usually for a small fee, if you decide to keep using it.

Sharpen　　To increase the apparent sharpness of an image by boosting the contrast between adjacent tones or colors.

SIMM　　Single in-line memory module. The small circuit boards used to add memory to PCs and other devices, such as laser printers. Today, SIMMs usually contain 1–16M of memory, but there are other sizes, including the 256K SIMMs used for VRAM.

Size　　To modify the dimensions of a shape by dragging one of its selection handles with the Pointer tool.

Smooth　　To blur the boundaries between tones of an image, often to reduce a rough or jagged appearance.

Smudge　　A tool that smears part of an image, mixing surrounding tones together.

Snap　　A feature that causes lines or objects to be attracted to a visible or invisible grid or special guidelines in an image or drawing.

Solarization　　In photography, an effect produced by exposing film to light partially through the developing process. Some of the tones are reversed, generating an interesting effect. In digital photography, the same effect is produced by combining some positive areas of the image with some negative areas.

Source code　　The program code generated by a programmer, which may not be directly executable by the computer. If not, it is translated by an interpreter, assembler, or compiler into machine language object code.

Spot

The dots that produce images on an imagesetter or other device.

Spot color

Individual colors used on a page. They are usually limited to one or two extra colors besides black to accent some part of a publication.

Spot color overlay

A sheet that shows one of the colors to be used in a publication for a given page. A separate overlay is prepared for each color, and all are combined to create the finished page.

Stacking order

The sequence in which shapes are arranged on a page in imaginary layers, using a front-to-back order.

Stamp

To create a copy of a master shape using the Rubber Stamp tool.

Static RAM (SRAM)

Memory that does not need to be refreshed and that, therefore, does not lose its contents when power to the computer is turned off. It is more expensive and typically faster than dynamic RAM (DRAM).

Strip

To assemble a finished page by taping or otherwise fastening pieces of film containing halftones, line art, and text together in a complete page negative or positive. The most common format is as a negative, because dirt and other artifacts show up as pinholes that can be easily spotted or opaqued out before the printing plates are made.

Subdirectory

A directory created within another directory, which stores its own separate files.

Substrate

A base substance that is coated with another. In printing, the substrate is generally paper or acetate, and the second substance is usually ink or dye.

Subtractive colors	The primary colors of pigments. When two subtractive colors are added, the result is a darker color that further subtracts from the light reflected by the substrate surface.
Surface properties	The transparency, texture, and reflective qualities of a 3-D surface.
System file	The file used to start up your PC and regulate the transfer of information among all the other components of the system software.
System level interface	An interface over which information is passed in logical form.
System software	Your PC's operating system, which includes the System file and Finder, as well as other components.
TARGA	Truevision Advanced Raster Graphics Adapter. A type of video board pioneered by Truevision, which produces files compatible with NTSC signals (an older technology that is still used in some applications).
Template	A framework that is used to provide the basic structure and layout for a publication.
Terminator	A device that absorbs signals at the end of a bus, preventing electronic "bounce-back." Your SCSI bus must have two terminators, one at the first and last devices. Some devices are internally terminated. Others require an add-on device.
Text file	Usually an ASCII file, which is often created by selecting **Save Text Only** from within an application.
Thermal wax transfer	A printing technology in which dots of wax from a ribbon are applied to paper when heated by thousands of tiny elements in a printhead.

Threshold   A predefined level used by the scanner to determine whether a pixel will be represented as black or white.

Thumbnail   A miniature copy of a page or image, which gives you some idea of what the original looks like without opening the original file or view the full-size image.

TIFF   Tagged Image File Format. A standard graphics file format that can be used to store gray-scale and color images.

Tile   To arrange windows side by side without overlapping. Windows and most of its applications include a **Window>Tile** or **Window>Arrange All** command to distribute multiple open windows in this manner.

Tint   A color with white added to it. In graphic arts it often refers to the percentage of one color added to another.

Toner   A pigmented substance used in page printers (and office copiers) to produce an image on a page.

Toolbar   A set of buttons, usually arranged in a single row, which contain commands, pull-down lists of choices, and stacks of tools that can be accessed quickly with the mouse.

Trapping   The capability of an ink to transfer as well onto another layer of ink as to the bare paper itself. In halftoning, poor trapping will result in tonal changes in the final image. In desktop publishing, trapping has an additional meaning: printing some images of one color slightly larger so that they overlap another color, avoiding unsightly white space if the two colors are printed slightly out of register. Printers call this technique spreading and choking.

Tree-structured   The hierarchical directory structure of a DOS disk that uses parent and child directories.

Triad   Three colors located approximately equidistant from one another on the color wheel. Red, green, and blue make up a triad; cyan, magenta, and yellow make up another. However, any three colors arranged similarly around the wheel can make up a triad.

Trim size   Final size of a printed publication.

True color   A system in which any pixel in the image can be any of the 16.8 million colors available in a 24-bit color mode. This is in contrast to systems that also access the full 16.8 million color gamut but limit a given image to a smaller palette of colors chosen from the larger range. For example, you may be able to use only 256 colors even though any of the millions available can be selected for that palette.

Undercolor removal   A technique that reduces the amount of cyan, magenta, and yellow in black and neutral shadows by replacing them with an equivalent amount of black. It can compensate for trapping problems in dark areas. See also *Gray component removal*.

Unfragmented   A hard disk that has most of its files stored in consecutive sectors rather than spread out over the disk. Such an arrangement allows more efficient reading of data, requiring less time to move the read/write head to gather the information.

Utility   A program that performs some useful system or maintenance function, as opposed to an applications program.

Vector image   An image defined as a series of straight line vectors. The beginning and ending points of each line are stored and later adjusted as the image is sized.

Vertex

A handle, represented by a diamond, marking the junction of two line segments, or the end of a line segment, which can be used to reshape (not just resize) the line.

Vignette

In prepress terminology, an image with a continuous gradation of tones.

Virtual disk

An electronic or RAM disk created in memory to mimic a real disk drive—only much faster. DOS 3.x and later versions are supplied with VDISK.SYS, a device driver that allows you to create multiple virtual disks in memory.

Windows

Microsoft's graphical user interface, which runs on 286 and higher microprocessors. Windows comes in several (generally) compatible varieties, including Windows for Workgroups and Windows NT. The latter two versions include networking capabilities.

Wireframe

A rendering technique that presents only the edges of a 3-D object, as if it were modeled from pieces of wire. This is much faster than modeling the entire object, including all surfaces.

WMF

Windows Metafile. A vector-based graphic file format for IBM PC-based computers.

WORM

Write Once, Read Many (or Mostly). Optical disk technology that allows writing to the disk by the user, although a given section cannot be erased and reused.

Wrong-reading image

An image that is backward relative to the original subject—that is, a mirror image.

X-height

The height of a lowercase letter, excluding ascenders and descenders.

Zoom

To enlarge part of an image so that it fills the screen, making it easier to work with that portion.

Index

What you will find on the CD-ROM

The CD-ROM's contents break down into the following categories:

- *Tryout Software:* Limited versions of programs like Photoshop and Elastic Reality that you can use to practice the exercises in the book—or evaluate for later purchase of the software if you like it.

- *Shareware:* A few excellent shareware and freeware applications and utilities you'll want to try out. The programs are hard-to-find, and are particularly apt for users of this book.

- *Chapter Files:* Full-color (generally) versions of all of the figures in the book along with many TIFF files used in the projects. Each subdirectory is given the chapter number it corresponds with.

- *Fonts:* There is a selection of Adobe Type 1 and TrueType shareware fonts you can install using Adobe Type Manager or the Windows Font Control Panel. You can then use them in your own project, or use them as you read through the book.

- *Color Plates:* 24-bit versions of the images used in the full-color section of this book.

- *TIFF images:* A large selection of TIFF images in Spain, Miscellaneous Texture, Portrait and Glamour categories you can work with. Most of these were scanned at 300 dpi and range in size from 500K to 5MB or more. You may have trouble with some of the larger files, if your PC isn't equipped with at least 8M of RAM.

In all cases, I don't recommend using any of the files directly from the CD-ROM. Image files, in particular, load very slowly from a CD-ROM drive, and with images up to 5M in size, you can wait quite a while for one of those to feed into RAM. Instead, I recommend the following:

- *Shareware:* Copy the software to your hard disk and follow the installation instructions included.

- *Chapter files:* As you read through each chapter, consider copying the chapter's subdirectory to your hard disk, so that the figure files and working files are readily available, as you work through the exercises.

- *TIFF images:* Leave these on the CD-ROM until you need them. Use an image browser application such as ImagePals or the Pixfolio shareware included on the CD-ROM to build a database of thumbnail images.

If you have trouble installing Elastic Reality, make sure you have copied all the files from the CD-ROM's \TRY-OUT\ELASTIC subdirectory to a directory on your hard disk. Then edit the file EREALITY.INF with NOTEPAD.EXE so the initial lines read like these:

```
[Source Media Descriptions]

"1", "Elastic Reality Demo Disk 1", "ir30.dl_", "."
"5", "TransJammer Demo Disk", "trnsjmmr.ex_", "."
"3", "Elastic Reality Demo Disk 3", "er.ex_", "."
"2", "Elastic Reality Demo Disk 2", "ntmsg.dl_", "."
"4", "Elastic Reality Demo Disk 4", "hiip.dl_", "."
```

You're simply changing the disk path descriptions at the end of each line to a period, which represents the current subdirectory on your hard disk where the demo setup software has been copied. Then run the SETUP.EXE program found in that subdirectory.

Enjoy!